Augsburg College
George Sverdrup Library
Minneapolis, Minnesota 55404

Navaho Neighbors

NAVAHO NEIGHBORS

Franc Johnson Newcomb

UNIVERSITY OF OKLAHOMA PRESS : NORMAN

By *Franc Johnson Newcomb*

Sandpaintings of the Navajo Shooting Chant (with Gladys A. Reichard)
(New York, 1937)
Navajo Omens and Taboos (Santa Fe, 1940)
A Study of Navajo Symbolism (with Stanley Fishler and
Mary C. Wheelwright) (Cambridge, 1956)
Hosteen Klah: Navaho Medicine Man and Sand Painter
(Norman, 1964)
Navaho Neighbors (Norman, 1966)

Library of Congress Catalog Card Number: 66-13432

Copyright 1966 by the University of Oklahoma Press, Publishing Division of the University. Composed and printed at Norman, Oklahoma, U.S.A., by the University of Oklahoma Press. First edition.

*Dedicated to My Daughters
Lynette and Priscilla*

Contents

1. Introduction — page 3
2. The First Year at the Blue Mesa Trading Post — 17
3. Changes and Visitors at the Trading Post — 35
4. Billy Yazzi — 42
5. War Over Water Rights — 53
6. Ahsonchee the Brave — 64
7. Reservation Dust Storm — 79
8. Laura Thapaha — 93
9. Election Day at the Trading Post — 108
10. Ruins and Rattlesnakes — 117
11. The Gift of a Child — 133
12. Silver for a Bride — 148
13. Hosteen Beaal, E S P — 161
14. Mountain Bear Hunt — 179
15. Coyote, Chindee-Man — 189
16. An Autumn Feast — 202
17. Reservation Gold — 215
    Epilogue — 229
    Index — 231

Illustrations

Franc Johnson Newcomb	facing page 22
Newcomb Trading Post at Blue Mesa	23
Newcomb Exhibit at Shiprock	38
Drying Corn	39
Three Wives of Hatot'cli-yazzi	54
Greyhair's Daughter Weaving	55
Women Getting Water	70
B'Dougal Nez (Long Mustache)	71
Water Supply for a Navaho Ceremony	86
Hogan Built of Squared Logs	87
Open-faced Shelter	102
Baking Bread	103
Navaho Farmers Build a Dam	118
Ahson Greyhair	119
Laura's Full Skirt	134
Grandfather Greyhair	135
Nathanie and Wife	150
Althbah	151
Jim Builds a New House	166
Lucy and "Little Chief"	167
Hosteen Beaal	182
A Navaho Grave	183
Hogan and Oven	198
Gathering for the Feast	199

Navaho Neighbors

1
Introduction

LITTLE DID I THINK, when I saw my first group of Navaho Indians standing near the Santa Fe depot in Gallup, New Mexico, that I would spend more than thirty years of my life among these people. It was a hot August day in 1912, and the train on which I had arrived departed in shimmering waves of heat as I approached the two boxcars which served as a depot for this small western city. A baggage cart carrying several boxes, my trunk, and my two suitcases clattered along the black brick walk beside me. I kept a watchful eye on the suitcases as one was carrying my contract with the Department of Interior, signed by the superintendent of Indian Education, stating that I was qualified to teach the primary grades of the Navaho boarding school at the Fort Defiance Indian Agency.

A log rail separated the brick walk from the parking lot where a number of dusty cars and their drivers were waiting for passengers. The baggage boy asked me where I wished to go, and when I said Fort Defiance, he pointed to a remodeled touring car at the end of the line. This cross-country stage was a high-wheeled, lightweight Ford, with two seats in front and a long rear compartment to carry the baggage. One of the seats was for the passengers and the front one was for the driver and her assistant, for the driver was an attractive young woman by the name of Christine Day—Mrs. Charles Day—known to her friends as Chris. Her assistant was a husky Navaho youth named Kee Tsosie who looked capable of handling the heavy trunks and suitcases Mrs. Day's vehicle was often called upon to transport. His greatest usefulness, however, was in digging the stage out of sand traps or off of high-centers as the trail between Gallup and the Agency boasted neither cement, gravel, nor bridges and its location shifted with every hard sandstorm or cloudburst that swept across the mountains.

When the stage finally backed away from the log railing, it carried five people and a medley assortment of trunks, boxes, mailbags, and suitcases. One of the passengers was a housewife from Fort Defiance who had come to Gallup for a day of shopping and was now on her way home. One was an inspector of Indian schools on his way to Fort Defiance to look things over, and the other was myself. As Kee Tsosie helped us to our seats in the stage, I noticed that the inspector stood back, and when his turn came, walked to the front step saying, "I will sit with the driver to have a better look at the landscape." Our seat seemed somewhat crowded when Kee took his place beside us, but once on the trail with its ups and downs, we were glad to be tightly packed.

The road or trail we followed curved along the sides of cedar-covered mountains, struggled up steep grades, and wandered across wide highland valleys, paying no attention whatever to direction. I was thoroughly disoriented, and if Gallup had come into sight around one of the curves, I would not have been at all surprised. In one valley there were dome-shaped rocks sixty or seventy feet high, which were known as the Haystacks because of their resemblance to dry, yellow-brown hay, and this valley was cut by three parallel arroyos approximately ten feet wide by twenty feet deep. To avoid a long detour the Day brothers (Charles and Sam) had placed six fourteen-inch planks across the gaps, pegging them securely into the hard adobe at each end. These planks, two laid across each gap, served as wheel-track bridges for the cars. When we came to these skeleton bridges, I could not believe that any car could pass over safely, but Christine never hesitated since it was all a part of her day's work.

The mountain scenery was magnificent, as the clear air enabled us to see in every direction when we reached any high position. Flocks of Navaho sheep were grazing in the valleys, small herds of ponies were feeding where the grass was still green, and in one

Introduction

swale a couple of Navaho children leading a pint-sized burro were herding a small flock of Angora goats. The space was so vast and the silence was so complete that all of these seemed to be miniatures painted on an endless screen. It looked like a high lonely land with little to recommend it as a place where families might earn a living, yet, as we progressed, we saw that there was scarcely a mile between little clusters of hogans with nearby corrals, which were the homes of Navaho Indians and pens for their goats, sheep, and ponies.

We passed the St. Michaels Mission School, stopping to unload their mailbags, and stopping again at the Good Shepherd Mission to leave several boxes as well as the mail. For another mile the road followed the side of a wide, shallow creek, beyond which lay cultivated fields of corn, oats, and alfalfa. The first notice we had of the nearness of Fort Defiance was the sight of a large flag of the United States flying proud and beautiful above the arm of rocks that barred our view in that direction. At a turn to the right the first buildings to meet our gaze were the hay barns and the long stables that sheltered the horses and milk cows belonging to the school. A second bend brought us in front of the two trading posts that furnished trade goods to the Navahos of this section of the Reservation. On the right of the highway was the long red wareroom and the equally long white store belonging to Lew and Clara Sabin, while almost exactly opposite were equally long and somewhat older structures built of large blocks of grey stone. Around these posts were several Navaho customers coming or going. One man wearing a bright purple sateen shirt, calico trousers, red deer-hide moccasins, and a wide-brimmed felt hat was tying his pony to the hitch-rail on our left. At our right a plump Navaho matron with two teen-aged daughters, all three dressed in enormously full skirts, bright velvet blouses, and gaily-patterned shawls, were loading their wagon with the flour, bacon, coffee, and other supplies they had purchased at the post. A young woman with her baby safely strapped to its cradleboard drew our attention as she swung it across her shoulders preparatory to mounting her horse. It was a gay and colorful pageant and I was thrilled with my first glimpse of Navaho people engaged in their normal pursuits.

The next building to come in view was a high-spired Catholic church where services were held by the monks from the St. Michaels Mission. The church and the two posts were not located on Navaho land but were on a strip that had been owned and sold to the present owners by the Santa Fe Railroad Company. A few yards further on, we passed through a wide gate and found ourselves traveling along the main street of the Fort Defiance Navaho Agency. Originally the fort had been built in a hollow square with the parade ground in the center. The buildings still faced the central athletic field but much of the parade ground had been cut into sections by streets with new structures on each side.

The first of these new structures was a large commissary for storing school and agency supplies. The second was a beautiful log cottage of Douglas fir that was the school kindergarten and beside which lay a small green playground with swings and slides for the tots. We passed the agency offices, several cottages that were the homes of the married employees, the low stone warehouse now used as a morgue, the icehouse, and finally stopped in front of a large, white two-story building, locally known as the Mess Hall. A wide flight of steps led up to a veranda that extended the width of the building and boasted several chairs and two swinging settees. Two doors opened into this house, one directly into the large sitting room at the right, while the other led into the hall that contained the stairway to the second floor. Behind the sitting room was a still larger dining room and then the pantry and a storeroom. On the other side of the hall was a library and writing room; behind this the kitchen was a cavern filled with cupboards, stoves, tables, food carts, pots, and pans. The second floor was a twelve-room dormitory for the unmarried women employees, and it was here I made my home during the two years I taught at Fort Defiance Indian School.

When September arrived, more than 400 Navaho children had

Introduction

been gathered from far and wide, to enroll as pupils in this government boarding school and five more teachers had been appointed by the Board of Indian Education. There was a kindergarten teacher whose tots played their games and sang their songs in the sunny red log schoolhouse. The next grades occupied the large red brick barracks that had housed the soldiers. The kindergarten children and my first graders were the only pupils who attended school all day. The children of the higher grades were in the classrooms half a day and then were assigned to work groups the other half. Some worked in the laundry, some in the bakery. The older girls made their own dresses in the sewing room, while the boys tended the stock, weeded the gardens, milked the cows, repaired furniture and were trained in other farm work and manual labor.

The Navaho first-grade pupils who came to my barracks classroom understood only a word or two of English and constantly whispered to each other in sibilant Navaho, giggling behind their hands as they did so. The first graders from ten to fourteen years of age would not admit to understanding one word of English and it was impossible to keep them interested in anything except music, sketching, and clay-modeling. They had been brought by government employees to the boarding school against their own choosing and were simply not going to learn anything more about the three *R's* than they were forced to. It posed quite a problem for a young teacher from the East and I spent many nighttime hours studying new methods of teaching. But it was not until I asked them, one and all, to teach me the Navaho language, that I made any headway. After that things went better and when they completed the year's work they could all read their primers, spell and write the words therein, and equal any white third grader in mathematics.

The teachers at the boarding school had little opportunity to become acquainted with the parents of the Navaho girls and boys who attended our classes as their homes were located many miles from the school. Sometimes we took horseback trips and paused to visit the hogans of one or two families, and twice we were invited to fall festivals. Occasionally the mother and father of one or two of my pupils would quietly enter the classroom, stand silently near the wall until directed to a seat, then carefully examine every detail that met their gaze. I was always impressed by their good manners, their quiet dignity, and their evident interest in the activities and purpose of the white method of learning.

Perhaps my attitude toward these Indians was different from that of most eastern girls of that time, as my home in Wisconsin had been near a Winnebago settlement and there were four Indian girls and two boys in my class at high school while Jerome Lookaround was the bandmaster. My father was an architect in the cities of Eau Claire and Wisconsin Rapids, which at that time were thriving lumber centers. With the first hard snow and freeze-up he went north on hunting trips through the unmapped forests and lake country of northern Michigan and southern Canada, taking with him as guide and camptenders, our Winnebago friends, John Whitedeer and his wife. The game he hunted was elk, deer, and sometimes moose, the hides of which would be left at some northern settlement of Foxes or Menominee Indians to be tanned and made into mittens, moccasins, fringed jacket, or purses, which he would pick up on his next trip. When the hunting party returned to our home in Eau Claire, the Whitedeer family would put up a couple of tents in our back yard, retrieve their three children from the relatives who had cared for them and live there until the money they had earned was spent for winter supplies. Then they would join their tribe in winter quarters. So I had played with Indian children during my earliest playdays and thought of them simply as people who spoke a different language.

During the two years I was employed at the Navaho School, Arthur Newcomb was managing the stone trading post that belonged to the Manning brothers. We were making plans to be married, and as we both were interested in the Navaho people, we decided to have a trading post of our own if we could find one for sale. In the fall of 1913, Arthur Newcomb bought a half-interest in the trading post at Blue Mesa, New Mexico. This post was located on the northern section of the Navaho Reservation near an arroyo

Introduction

called "Captain Tom's Wash" and not far from the great rock spire known as Ship Rock Peak. We were married in June of 1914, and we wasted no time on a honeymoon but went directly to the Blue Mesa Trading Post, where Arthur had already established a comfortable trade with the Navahos of that section.

My contacts here were quite different from those at the school, for the Navahos with whom we traded were almost entirely adults ranging from those in their teens to great-grandparents, all actively engaged in the problem of earning a living. Sometimes this was at the lowest level of human subsistence, such as twelve kernels of parched corn per day and sometimes there was plenty of corn and mutton for all, with even bones for the dogs.

During the greater part of the year, all children of school age were at boarding school where food and clothing were provided by the government. This was of great benefit to many Navaho families who were obliged to live on very short rations during the winter months, especially so when the summer had been hot and dry.

I had read that the Navaho form of life was a matriarchy, but did not realize what this meant until I lived among them. In our own way of life the father is usually considered the head of the family, the owner of the property, and the business manager. Certainly this system never came from the Navaho Indians where women have always held equal rights and, in some instances, have enjoyed superior authority and importance. To relate one instance which shows the status of women in the Navaho tribe: if a man is murdered, the murderer or his clan must pay the dead man's family five to seven horses and as many sheep; for the murder of a woman the price exacted is ten or twelve horses and just the same number of sheep. The net result of this law is the prevention of murders, for not many Navaho families or clans can afford to lose their stock.

Navaho children take the mother's clan and belong to her. Therefore she is responsible for their care and support and often becomes the breadwinner of the family. Her flock of sheep and patches of farm land generally come to her by inheritance or have been given to her by relatives, while the family hogan, loom, and the cooking pots and pans are always considered her property. Of course there are exceptions to this rule as would be the case of an elderly Navaho with a great many sheep and ponies who married a young woman whose dowry was small. In this case he would build her a new hogan but her holdings would be just the articles she brought with her.

Property rights in the Navaho tribe, are very clearly defined and strictly observed. Therefore few controversies about legal ownership or inheritance rights are brought before the Council. However, I remember one case which caused a bitter rift in an important clan. It happened that the mother and the father of four children were killed at a railroad crossing. They were quite prosperous and owned a good-sized flock of sheep, several ponies, and some corn acres which now belonged to the children. The mother had three sisters, each of whom claimed that the children belonged to her, as they were all of school age and would be of little expense to their foster parents while the property gain would be great. The Navaho Council failed to settle the argument and finally the government agent decided in favor of the older sister, but the other two never forgave her for not dividing the property with them.

Family disagreements, divorces, nonsupport, and desertion were nearly always settled by the clan without outside interference. Sometimes when a man and his wife quarreled, he would make a bundle of his belongings, tie it to the back of his saddle, and ride away, but again he might claim the sheep and the ponies, leaving his wife the hogan and the farm. When Tall Man decided to leave his wife and went to the Chaco Valley to live with a wealthy widow, he took half of all their sheep and the goats, several ponies, and the farm wagon, all of which he considered his property. His wife made no objection to losing the sheep, goats, and horses, but the loss of the wagon was a sad blow, as it left her without means of harvesting her corn, or taking her wool to market. One morning, as I was working in the front yard, I saw something queer taking place at the hitch-rail. Tall Man's team and wagon had been hitched there for some time as he was busy at the blacksmith shop. This was an opportunity for which his first wife had been waiting. She had

Introduction

brought two of her own horses, and now she quickly unharnessed his team, and took it to the other end of the rail, then harnessed her team to the wagon and calmly drove away. She came to the store in the wagon several times so I knew he had never reclaimed it, and in fact, the whole valley thought it a great joke on Tall Man and considered possession ten points of legal ownership. He was not greatly inconvenienced as his second wife owned an even better wagon.

The equanimity and matter-of-factness with which many Navaho divorces took place was always a surprise to me. A man had only to say he was leaving, gather his possessions, and ride away to be legally divorced and free from any further family responsibility. A woman who tired of an older husband could set his things a certain distance outside the hogan door to obtain a legal divorce. This sounds so easy that one might suppose the divorce rate would be high among the Navahos, but this was not the case. In fact it was so infrequent that one divorce in the valley would be the topic of fireside discussion for several months. Among the younger couples it was the children that held them together, but among the older people it was more apt to be the farms and the flocks.

In one case the man, Hosteen Tsas (Wide Man), was fat and lazy while his small, energetic wife worked hard to support the family. She was a good weaver and her rugs brought high prices at the trading post, but it was not easy to care for the small flock of sheep she needed to get wool for weaving, then to shear, card, spin, and weave while her man sat around at the trading post or at neighborhood "sings." She finally decided not to support him so she placed all of his possessions at a distance from the hogan door. When he came riding home that evening he found them there but refused to accept her ultimatum and would not be dealt with in this manner. He enjoyed his idleness and the good living his wife could provide, so he picked up his bedroll and all of the other things and marched them back into the hogan. His wife said nothing and things continued much as before. Then one day he rode away to attend a "sing" that would last three days and nights, and this gave his wife a chance to carry out a plan she had held in mind for some time. Going to the school's carpenter shop, she bought two heavy ten-inch planks as long as her door was tall. Then buying some large nails, she took her purchases home and nailed the planks into the doorway so there was an opening of only about twenty inches, which was wide enough for her to enter. Then she again placed her husband's belongings at the legal distance outside the door and sat down to await his return. When he finally rode up to the hogan, he looked at the bundles and then at the narrow opening and knew he was much too wide to enter. Slowly he packed the bundles on his horse and rode away to the home of his sister. His wife never took the planks away from the door, as to do so might encourage his return.

It was this independence of decision and of action that made each Navaho a distinct individual in spite of rigid tribal laws, limited occupations, and similar living conditions. There were many ways in which their individuality was expressed. The one we noticed first was that no Navaho rugs were ever woven with the same pattern, and when we asked for a design to be repeated in the next rug, we were met with refusal. Each silversmith engraved his jewelry with original designs, which no one else ever sought to copy, while no two velvet blouses or full squaw skirts were ever trimmed alike.

As the years passed and we became better acquainted with our Navaho neighbors, they told us many tales of the events that had happened during the lives of their ancestors, which subsequently influenced their own lives. Many of these stories began with the "Navaho Wars" and the "Long Walk" into captivity at Fort Sumner. There were still a few elders who would relate the details of this march and tell of the hunger and suffering the Navaho people had endured while forced to live in this unfriendly land.

During the four years after 1864 in which the Navahos were held captive at Fort Sumner, hundreds had escaped to attempt the perilous homeward journey through Pueblo country, where to be caught would mean years of slavery. When in April of 1868 a

Introduction

council of Navaho elders traveled to Washington to ask the President's permission to return to their former homes, the Navaho spokesman said, "Let us return to the land of our ancestor and we will ask nothing more from your government forever." This independence was not to be ignored and they were granted a part of the large reservation they had designated. Besides the land grant which covered parts of New Mexico, Arizona, and Colorado, the treaty contained a clause promising educational facilities and medical care. These last promises meant little to the half-starved Indians who had been subsisting on meager government rations when their crops had failed, or had been destroyed by grasshoppers and army worms year after year. As far as schools were concerned, so many children had died or been stolen that the few remaining would be needed at home, and as for doctors, they had their own medicine men.

The tribe not only survived but increased greatly in numbers and many families became wealthy sheep owners without seeking assistance from Washington or from any other white agency. During their years of captivity they had been in contact with people of various nationalities, including the Pueblos, the Mexican ranchers, the Apaches, and the Americans at Fort Sumner. They had learned how these people lived and had examined different types of houses and public buildings but on their return they made no changes in their hogans or in their manner of life. Their ancient customs seemed best fitted to the deserts, mesas, and mountains of their homeland, and this simple way of life required little that could not be obtained from native sources.

. Their dome-shaped, thick-walled houses were cool in summer and warm in the winter. The circular walls and low-domed ceilings radiated the heat evenly so that only a small fire was needed even in the coldest weather. The cedar logs repelled insects and the hard-packed adobe floor could be scraped clean every morning. The furniture for the hogan consisted of a log loom, various rolls of blankets, tanned sheep pelts, and the iron pots and skillets used for cooking. About the only articles they cared to buy from white people were axes, hoes, spades, and other farm tools, along with iron cooking utensils, shears, needles, and thread. There was one point that must ever be considered, the article must always be small enough to be carried in a packsaddle or in the wagon as the family moved its lares and penates from one hogan to another. Some articles of wearing apparel such as large felt hats for the men and brightly-patterned shawls for the women met with their approval. Any type of heavy cloth that would make into tents, wagon covers, wool sacks, or long-wearing articles of clothing were highly prized. Outside of these things the Navaho family had little use for white men's goods.

In early years all Navaho travelers rode horseback on homemade saddles, carrying ropes of hand-braided yucca or horsehair, but with the establishment of trading posts along the Río Grande River and its tributaries wagons became available. Just what these first wagons were like I do not know, but the Navahos were quick to realize the advantage of vehicles pulled by horses and soon the wealthier families were riding in wagons. After the return from the Bosque Redondo, the United States government sent an issue of red-wheeled, wide-tired wagons to the Reservation, which the Indians could buy by working a certain length of time at the government agency. This was one of the most beneficial things the Office of Indian Affairs ever did for the Navaho tribe. Nearly every Indian who had a family went to an agency and worked the months required to pay for a wagon. Some bought harnesses, but more got tanned steerhides or mulehides, which they cut into strips to make their own. They had seen canvas-covered wagons crossing the New Mexican deserts at the time of the California gold rush, in which people could live for months at a time. This seemed like a good idea, so they bent ash withes into arcs, fastened them over the wagons, and covered them with canvas. Later they were able to buy these tops ready to fit into position. In these covered wagons, whole families could travel to feasts, weddings, or religious ceremonies by using only one team of horses, but generally the wagon was a conveyance for women, children, and old folks, while the

Introduction

men rode ahead on prancing steeds caparisoned with gay blankets and silver-mounted bridles.

Although the Navahos had become acquainted with the m of the white people and the kivas of the Pueblos, they still preferred their own type of medicine lodge for religious and ceremonial purposes. Two forms of sacred structures had been built by the gods to demonstrate how these should be made in the future, and every log and stone used in the construction had been carefully noted so there would be no mistakes later. The erection of the ceremonial lodge was a rite that could brook no deviation, and this knowledge had been handed down from father to son or nephew for many generations. These hogans were often used for just one ceremony, and never for more than four.

In their manner of life, tribal social structure, and religious observances, the Navahos were unique among the tribes of the Southwest. The many Pueblo villages along the Río Grande and its tributaries, and the Zuñi, and the Hopi had been so long in contact with Spanish priests and missions that their rites had become thoroughly mixed with the Holy Days of the Roman Catholic church. Their feast days became dedicated to the Christian saints, their planting rites were celebrated after Easter week, and their harvest festivals were directed by the Church. The Navaho religion was one of the few purely primitive religions to be found in the United States.

In the first years of the tribe's return from captivity, they were too poor and too scattered to hold many ceremonies and such was their distrust of white interference that the few that were held were hidden away on mountain slopes or in secret valleys. As the years passed missions were built on the Reservation, schools were established, traders came to bring them goods, and gradually the Navahos accepted the white people as their friends. Many white visitors attended the nine-day Fire Dances or the Yeibichais, but no descriptions were ever written or data compiled. The earliest authentic account of a Navaho ceremony was made when a doctor by the name of Washington Matthews wrote a detailed account of the Yeibichai Ceremony in a book called *The Night Chant,* as told to him by a Navaho medicine man named Hathile Nah-cloie (Laughing Chanter). Matthews also collected the long legends which explained this and many other ceremonies, and the large volume, which contains this mass of religious lore, has been termed "The Navaho Bible" by students of Navaho ethnology.[1] Since 1900 many writers have added volumes on the subjects of Navaho religion, social life, history, and tribal economy, but only one or two have written of the lives, ambitions, projects, or the problems of the individual Navaho.

With so much already in print about this one southwestern tribe, I may be presumptious in thinking that I will be able to contribute something additional that will be interesting or informative to the reading public. But the stories I have decided to write do not describe the Navahos as a "primitive race" or as a "migratory tribe," for such statistics have been recounted in histories and ethnological volumes. Neither have I written of the Navahos as a tribe, but have sought to describe certain characteristics and episodes in the lives of some individuals who were our friends and neighbors during the years we owned and operated the trading post at Blue Mesa. Their problems were the same as the problems of all people—whatever the race or location—but the manner of their solving belongs solely to the Navaho. In these stories I invite the reader to visit the Navaho Reservation and become acquainted with the country, the climate, the products, and—most important of all—to become acquainted with the Navaho people who were our friends and neighbors.

[1] Matthews' *Navaho Legends* was published in 1897.

2
The First Year at the Blue Mesa Trading

To almost everyone the name "Trading Post" conjures up visions of a group of low structures of log or stone, built like a fort and located in some very isolated section of the United States or of Canada where white civilization has not penetrated. In connection with the post, they think of Indians with dog sleds or canoes bringing bundles of furs to trade for warm clothing, blankets, provisions, and perhaps for guns and ammunition, or more traps for their trap lines. There might be Indian women and their round-faced, black-eyed children, hiding behind their mother's full skirts at the approach of a white person. This would be a fairly accurate description of the first posts established in America by the French, and later by the English. It still could be a description of many of the trading posts established years later among the Indian tribes of the southwestern United States.

In the 1620's the French *voyageurs* started the fur trade in Canada with a line of forts and trading posts extending from Hudson Bay, around the Great Lakes, and down the Mississippi River to New Orleans. Quebec and Montreal started as fortressed trading posts and became great shipping ports for furs at a time when there was a demand for mink, ermine, and white fox, when men of prominence wore beaver hats. Fur was a commodity the Europeans desired from the New World at this time, and of this there seemed to be an inexhaustible supply. The problem of obtaining this fur from Indians who placed no value on either English or French currency was worked out through trade. Trade goods for the Indians were manufactured in Europe and were then shipped to America. These shipments necessitated trade centers where the goods could be handled and so fortified trading posts were established.

Trading posts were not very common in the Southwest until 1868, when the Navahos were transferred from Bosque Redondo to their own reservation. Before the time the Navahos had horses, they had been no great menace to the Pueblo villages along the Río Grande or to the Zuñi or the Hopi in Arizona. It had been customary for the Pueblo farmers to hire families of Navahos to work in their fields during harvest season and to pay them with corn, squash, and beans, and the Navahos who had farms obtained their seeds from the Pueblos by trading buckskins and eagle feathers to their medicine men. There were occasional Navaho raids in the autumn but the raiders could not carry much produce away as they were on foot and had a long distance to travel. When horses were acquired and the Navaho warriors were mounted, it became quite a different story. They could strike at a community, pick up whatever goods they found handy, and ride away before the men of the Pueblo could arm themselves.

The Mexican families who had settled in small villages around their churches during Spanish rule in the Southwest staked out large ranches, bought sheep and horses, and were prepared to make their homes in the new country. It was by raiding the flocks of these ranchers that the Navahos obtained most of their sheep and goats, but they seemed to possess a natural aptitude for the care and raising of these animals, so their flocks increased all over the Navaho territory. The use of wool also seemed to be an instinctive aptitude, for no other tribe north of the Río Grande attained the weaving skill of the Navaho women. Their sheep was a slim, long-legged breed with long silky wool almost like Angora hair, soft and fine, so that it was easy to spin into a firm silky yarn. These sheep, both bucks and ewes, had horns, some even carrying two pairs on their heads. When I first came to the Navaho Reservation nearly every flock of sheep included three or four ewes with four horns, one set curving toward its back and the other arching forward. These old-time sheep have long since disappeared in favor of larger sheep bearing a heavier fleece of wool, but with their passing, the fine, silky blankets of former years have also disappeared.

Navaho trade was established at Fort Wingate as soon as that Fort was built, and existed at Fort Defiance by 1857, for by that time the Navahos had something the traders could sell to outsiders and to manufacturers, namely, handmade blankets and wool, while the commissariats bought quantities of mutton. However, it was not until the tribe returned from captivity at Fort Sumner in 1868 that traders ventured to build their posts on the Reservation away from the protection of the soldiers. A few soldiers who had served their time in the army married Navaho girls and went to live near Navaho families. Among these were Mr. Walker, Mr. Gorman, and Mr. Keams, along with several others. There seemed to be a feeling that life at a Navaho trading post was no life for a white woman.

The first two rooms of the trading post at Blue Mesa were built before that section of New Mexico had been designated by the President as a Reservation for the Navahos. Sometime during the four years the Navahos were held at the Bosque Redondo an emigrant train of Mormons traveling north to the San Juan River camped for the night on the banks of the Tunicha Arroyo. Seeing running water, an active spring, and acres of land they thought could be irrigated, one family decided to stay and build a home below the point of the Mesa. Bringing logs from the mountains, they built a two-room cabin with adobe floor and roof, but after two years the U.S. government turned this part of New Mexico into a Reservation for the Navahos and bought this homestead. The settler and his family were glad to move to the Mormon community at Kirtland on the San Juan River where there was a church and a school for the children.

For a time the cabin stood vacant and then, about 1904, a man by the name of Mr. John L. Oliver took possession, built a square log room on the north side, and brought trade goods to barter with the Navahos. This trade did not continue throughout the year but was carried on during two months in the spring when the Indians were selling their wool and three months in the fall during the harvest and the sheep-selling seasons. So his family stayed on the farm near the San Juan River while he ran the post with the assistance of his oldest son. In 1909 this post was sold to Mr. Charles Nelson, who was a Morman living in Fruitland and who also ran the post on a part-time basis. After a few years he found himself deeply in debt to the wholesalers from whom he had been buying trade goods, and he decided to sell the place. Arthur Newcomb, then working for a wholesale firm in Gallup, went to the Blue Mesa Trading Post and stayed for several weeks to learn about the business and judge if there might be a chance for future development. He came to the conclusion that if it was handled as an all-year business it could be made to show a profit, so during the winter of 1913–14, he bought half-interest and later bought the second half. It soon became known as the "Newcomb Trading Post."

Indian trading posts in the Southwest have many characteristics in common with the earlier establishments in the North. There are the same long, low buildings of stone or log construction, with attached warerooms and living quarters. The amount of trade goods carried, although quite different, may be of equal amount and variety, with a sufficient supply to last a year. There is also a space and a shelter to accommodate customers who expect to stay two or three days while they transact business at the post. But here the resemblance comes to an end. In the Southwest we find no lakes or rivers carrying canoes filled with chanting natives, no fur parkas, snowshoes, or dog sleds. The lakes are replaced by deserts and the rivers by long mesas that are arms of the mountains reaching across the lowlands. There also are highways, not for *voyageurs* in canoes, but for plodding ponies with their gaily appareled riders who travel for days in a dusty aura of their own making. They are never in a hurry for there are no clocks and time is eternity. The Navaho trading post is unique in another respect in that its character is shaped by one Navaho product, namely wool. Just as the northern posts depended on the fur-bearing animals of the colder latitudes to create their prosperity, the Nav-

The First Year at the Blue Mesa Trading Post

aho trading posts depended on the flocks of sheep and goats owned by the Navaho Indians.

The main building of any post housed the trade room, the warerooms, and the living quarters for the trader and his family, all under one roof. At a short distance from this structure would be found the long shed or barn used to house the enormous sacks of wool after the spring-shearing time and the hay and grain that would be sold during the winter snows. Just beyond the barn could be seen the high fences of the pole corrals where sheep were sheared, or bought and sold. Then somewhere between wool barn and store stood the tall pole frame used to hold the wool sacks as they were being filled. The trader bought wool by the wagonload from wealthy Navaho sheep owners, and he would also buy a small flour sack filled with wool from some ancient Shema whose flock consisted of one or two sheep. This was all stacked in the wool barn where it would be separated and graded according to color and quality, for there were many varieties of sheep in the Navaho country. Silky wool from the descendants of the old Spanish sheep was to be kept to sell to the weavers, as well as the brown and tan fleeces from the so-called black sheep. Mohair from Angora goats brought a higher price and had to be weighed and sacked separately. At one time the government sent Merino rams to the Reservation to improve their stock, but the wool from the resulting lambs was so rough and tightly curled that it was almost impossible to spin by hand. The thumb and first finger of the spinner's right hand would become sore and often bleed, while the yarn was never straight or smooth. The result was that the rugs made with this wool were rough and full of small knots.

Other buildings connected with the barn generally consisted of smaller sheds of logs and adobe to shelter the cow and riding ponies, and there was likely to be a shed for coal and wood, and a chicken house in the back yard. The trading post had to be a self-sufficient unit which could carry its trade without assistance from the outside world in order to get through the winter months and also through the summer rainy season when the roads became quagmires of adobe mud. The needs of the trader's family must also be provided for, hence the cow, the chickens, the riding horses, the many root cellars, sheds, and storerooms.

When Arthur Newcomb took possession of the Blue Mesa Trading Post, with his brother Earle as assistant, he started a number of repairs and improvements. First there was a new roof to cover the whole structure, then a cement floor for the store, along with new counters and shelves. Last but not least, a kitchen and a bedroom were added. These two rooms were separated from the older part by a long, roomy closet and were built on the south side. One of these rooms became a bedroom and the other, which was fitted with cupboards, sink, table, and range, was the kitchen. The long closet between the two was partitioned in the middle to make a clothes closet and a bathroom. There really was not much point in having a bathroom without running water nearer than an eighth of a mile, but there was an enamel bathtub with an outlet which surfaced at the far side of the yard to water the little cottonwood tree, which I planted soon after my arrival. For the time and the place, these four rooms were an unwarranted extravagance, as trader's living quarters were generally just two rooms, one to eat and read in, and one to sleep in, since the remainder of the trader's time was spent in the store. Bachelor traders sometimes lived in one of the wererooms.

All of this took time as the building material was freighted from Gallup in wagons which traveled over dirt roads that were impassable when it rained. The store was completed first as it must be finished and stocked with trade goods before sheep-buying season in September. Many of the goods that had been on the shelves were streaked and muddy from the leaks in the old dirt roof.

One reason for not erecting an expensive dwelling at a Navaho post was because the land on which the post was built belonged to the U.S. government in trust for the Navaho Indians and could never be owned by the trader. Another was that most traders did not intend to stay many years, their object being to earn and save

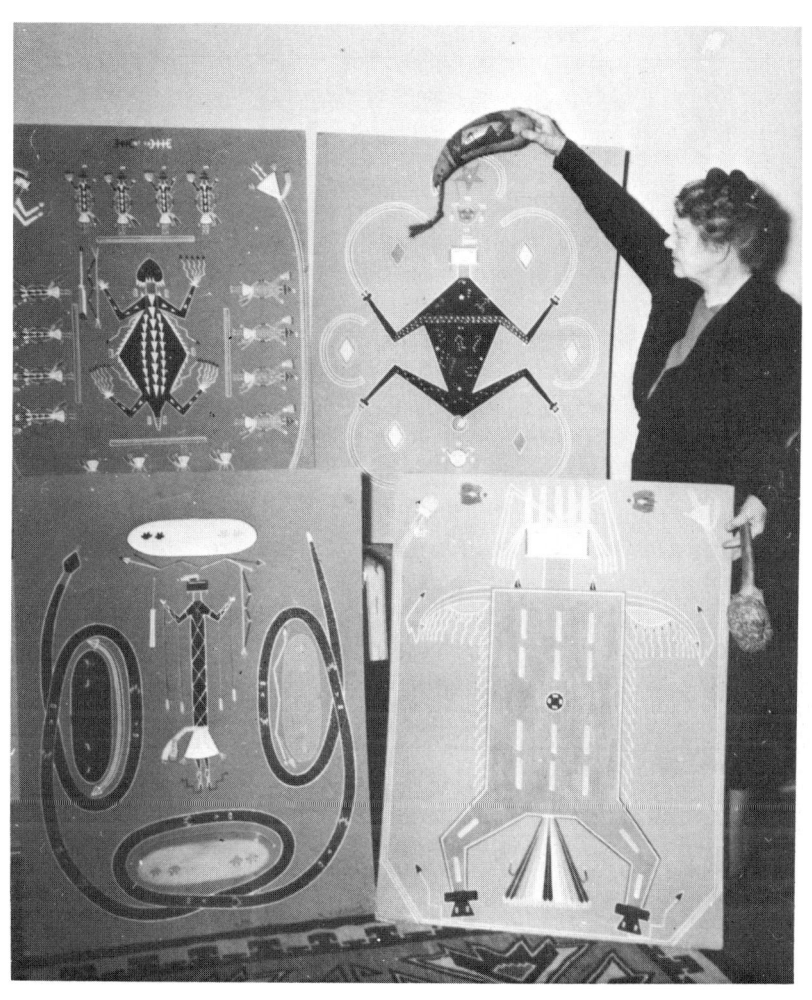

Franc Johnson Newcomb, showing a few of the sketches from her collection of 400 sand paintings.

The Newcomb Trading Post at Blue Mesa, located on the Navaho Reservation.

The First Year at the Blue Mesa Trading Post

enough money to buy a business in a "civilized community" as soon as possible.

Arthur brought me to the Blue Mesa Trading Post the day of our wedding and I prepared our wedding dinner that evening in my new home, little dreaming that twenty years later I would still be preparing meals in that same kitchen. Nor in my wildest fancy could I have dreamed of the many prominent people who would at times join us at these meals. My first view of the interior was something of a shock as I had never seen anything just like it before. The original two rooms were of logs papered with blue calico held in place with slats taken from "Four-XXXX" coffee boxes, with no attempt to conceal the lettering. The floors were of wide, badly-worn planks covered with beautiful red-grey-and-black Navaho rugs. Planks were also used to make the door, which swung on iron hinges and fastened with a heavy iron bolt. There was a small square window in each room with half-inch iron bars outside.

Heat was furnished by a huge stone fireplace that stretched across one corner and dominated the living room, as the stone face did not taper to form a chimney, but rose solid and massive to the ceiling and beyond. The furniture was new, a homemade reading table, a wall of bookshelves, a couch, two leather rocking chairs, a Morris chair, and a low footstool. With a number of books, several magazines, ashtrays, and a kerosene lamp this was really a comfortable living room. The next room was not furnished, with the exception of two wide benches and a folding cot, as this had been both kitchen and bedroom while the carpenters had been working on the new rooms. When these had been finished, the stove, cupboards, table, and chairs had been moved into the new kitchen. The two new rooms were of frame construction, the interior walls being finished with beaverboard and the floors with good, hard oak. There was new, bright linoleum in the kitchen and there were Navaho rugs in the bedroom. The bedroom furniture was simply a chest of drawers, a chair, and a bed as Arthur thought I might like to select my own furniture at a later date.

It was quite a pleasant home, but the cracks and knotholes in the old floor bothered me as I was abnormally afraid of rats and mice, of which there seemed to be hundreds scampering around behind the walls at night. Then one evening, as we were sitting around the dinner table, I chanced to look down at the floor and saw the strangest bug or worm I had ever seen crawling toward my foot. I screamed and jumped so hurriedly that my chair tipped over and I went with it. The bug was more than three inches long and fully as thick as my thumb. It seemed to have two fat sections, the front one having a round baby face on top of its head, but these features were only marks, as its eyes and sharp mandibles were under this mask. How many legs it had I do not know, as my helper, Esther, had grabbed the fireplace shovel, scooped up the intruder, and tossed it into the hot ashes in the grate. They told me it was an "Earth-Baby" but, whatever it was, I sincerely hoped I'd never see another. The Indians said its bite carried more poison than that of a tarantula, but others have stated that its bite was not poisonous. Personally, I was inclined to take the Indians' word for it.

Arthur had not wished to spend any more money on the living quarters for awhile at least, but this was too unpleasant, so he immediately ordered lumber for the flooring and beaverboard for the walls and ceiling. Meanwhile we melted and flattened tin cans to nail over all knotholes, cracks, and crevices that were large enough for even an ant to crawl through. When the lumber came the floor was matched boards laid over the old flooring, the beaverboard for the walls was nailed to a frame, and the cracks were covered with narrow lath. After that was finished, we were quite sure that even though the mice did scamper about above our heads, we were safe from unwelcome creepers and crawlers.

In the fall of 1913 there were two major events of interest to both Navaho and white people on the Reservation. The first was the Shiprock All-Indian Fair held each year during the first week of October. This was much the same as any fair held in any farming community, as there were exhibit booths in which each valley or section could display farm produce, hand-woven rugs, pottery,

The First Year at the Blue Mesa Trading Post

hanks of finely spun yarn, leather articles, and silver jewelry. There was also a school exhibit showing the work of every grade in the Navaho boarding school. This included classroom art, sewing, handmade lace, embroidery, furniture, and leather craft. Copper, tin, and silver ornaments also were shown. Mr. William T. Shelton, superintendent of the northern division of the Navaho Indian Reservation, believed that this was one way to spread advanced ideas among the older Navahos who had no formal education and little contact with white civilization.

There was one noticeable difference between this and the average county fair as there were no merry-go-rounds, Ferris wheels, shooting galleries, lotteries, or games of chance. All the amusement was supplied by the Indian Agency or by the Indians themselves.

At nine o'clock all visitors sat in the tiered stands to listen to a talk by Superintendent Shelton and to watch the school parade led by a gaily appareled school band. This was of great interest to the Navaho relatives and friends as they enjoy pageantry and music. During the remainder of the forenoon, there were contests and games such as the three-legged race, in which two contestants were tied together by one right and one left ankle so they were obliged to run on three legs. Many pairs participated and great was the amusement at the clumsy spills that occurred along the way. A sack race, a men's tug of war, a woman's tug of war, a blindfold race, and a wheelbarrow race were among the many amusing forenoon events.

After an hour's pause for refreshments, the main events began and these were the horse races. Every Navaho who owned a fast pony was there, accompanied by family and clansmen, all bringing turquoise, silver, and money to bet on the forthcoming races. Sometimes the horses were ridden by men or boys, and sometimes they were ridden by girls. There were relay races in which each rider had a string of four horses, each to be ridden once around the track. The wagon race for women was a spectacular event in which four women stood at the starting line, each holding a team with the harnesses across the horses' backs. At a signal from the starter these women ran to waiting wagons, fastening straps and buckles as they ran, backed the teams over the wagon tongues and buckled the traces. Then with reins in hand they climbed into the wagons and drove at full gallop around the three-fourths mile race track. It took a strong arm to manage the nervous horses who sometimes bolted when only half hitched, so it was not always the fastest team that won the race. On nearly every afternoon, there was at least one matched race between two horses from different parts of the reservation. Juan Kasus from Tohatchi owned a tall, white-faced sorrel that had won every race in their district, while Bi-wan Tso had bought a fast roan from the Utes at Towaoc. Betting on this race was heavy as it was a matter of north against south, and so a large pile of silver ornaments and leather goods stood on the betting blanket. The side that won was generally quite hilarious over their victory while the losing side took their losses philosophically and showed no anger, simply saying, "It wasn't my lucky day."

At sunset the barbecue pits were opened and the roasted beef and mutton placed on well-scrubbed plank tables while agency employees armed with long forks and sharp knives served all comers as they passed by. There was also a plenteous supply of large flat buns to be eaten with the meat, baked beans, and red apples. Family groups fairly covered the agency lawn as they ate and visited. Later in the evening there was a Yeibichai dance that lasted until dawn. Hosteen Klah was the medicine man who presided at this ceremony and he was known far and wide as the highest-ranking medicine man on the Reservation when it came to the nine-day Yeibichai Chant.

The last day of the Shiprock Fair was called "Watermelon Day." In all of the agency cornfields, watermelon seeds were planted between the rows of corn so the water from the irrigation ditches could water both the corn and the melons at the same time. The melons ripened and were harvested before the corn, and there must have been thousands of them as there were always more than the school children or the employees could manage to eat. On the last

The First Year at the Blue Mesa Trading Post

day of the Shiprock Fair, Superintendent Shelton had four or five wagonloads of ripe melons unloaded on the athletic field and stacked in a huge pile. Just before noon on that day, the guards sent word to all Navahos to come with their knives and take as many melons as they could eat. There was only one stipulation and that was the melons must be eaten on the grounds as none could be taken away.

The place was crowded so that there was barely room to sit. Families of four or five would have three large watermelons—each person claiming half a melon—and the tots would consume almost as much as the grownups. It was quite a sight and I am sure there was never anything like it elsewhere on the Reservation.

Arthur exhibited several finely woven Navaho rugs, but he had not been operating the Blue Mesa Trading Post long enough to have much else to show. He had not asked the Indians to bring in their best ears of corn, or their largest squash, or samples of several varieties of beans. But the next fall he knew what was expected and we both attended the fair with a fine exhibit not only of Navaho rugs, but of hand-wrought silver and turquoise jewelry, handmade leather saddles and bridles studded with silver, velvet blouses with silver buttons, and deer-hide moccasins, besides a wagonload of farm produce. Superintendent Shelton always invited several government officials from Washington to visit this yearly event, and also many business men from western cities, as he was anxious to create a market for Navaho crafts.

The second major event that took place on the eastern side of the Chuska Mountains that same year took place in November shortly before Thanksgiving. This was of national interest although it was confined to the Navaho Reservation, and was written up in practically every newspaper in the United States and possibly Canada. For years there had been no Indian wars, Indian raids, or Indian uprisings to report and then suddenly there was "The Navaho Revolt of 1913," sometimes called "The Beautiful Mountain Uprising." No wonder every newspaper in the country carried a front-page article broadcasting such comments as "The Navahos never were subdued by the whites!" and, "The only uncivilized tribe of Indians in the United States goes on the warpath!" Few people who read the newspapers knew who the Navahos were or where they were located, but they could imagine painted Indians on horseback, waving tomahawks and chasing white women and children. I wonder if they ever knew how far from actuality this was.

It really was not much of a rebellion as we have come to think of Indian revolts and uprisings, as the only Navahos concerned were one elderly Navaho patriarch, his four sons, and their seven or eight wives. No one was tomahawked or scalped, and about the only casualties were a couple of Indian policemen who were knocked about and thumped here and there because they refused to hand over the keys to the dormitory where three of the wives were being held prisoners. The affair was noteworthy in American history because it was the last time in this nation that a large force of soldiers was sent out against any Indian tribe. The ratio was somewhat uneven as there were about two hundred and sixty soldiers against old Bi-joshii, his four sons, and their wives. These were the only Navahos directly concerned but the whole tribe anxiously awaited the outcome as many had committed the same infraction of the law. The overwhelming odds did not daunt the old Indian in the least, nor did they seem to impress his sons.

Ever since his return from captivity at Bosque Redondo, Bi-joshii had lived quietly and industriously in a secluded valley near the foot of Beautiful Mountain. This mountain stood out a few miles from the Tunicha Range and was really a huge mesa with steep rocky sides, precipitous rim rocks, and a flat top. It had received its name because of its many springs and rills, its evergreen trees and its plentiful vegetation. Another fact not generally known to the white people was that this mountain was a Navaho game sanctuary. Deer, antelope, elk, mountain sheep, and even bobcats, cougars, and coyotes were safe from hunters as long as they remained on or near Beautiful Mountain. As the years passed, Bi-joshii and his family had gained wealth in the form of ponies and so they were an important family in the community. As he grew older, he wearied of caring for sheep, and being a noted medicine man much in demand for healing ceremonies, he divided his flocks among his four sons and two daughters, keeping only a token flock for himself. All of his children were married and when his wife died he gave the family home to his older daughter and built a small hogan for himself not far away.

His oldest son, Hatot'cli-yazzi, now had the responsibility of managing the greater part of the family wealth and seeing that his father was provided for. This son's first wife had died and he was looking around for another, but the girl he wanted would not leave her mother and her two sisters. Bi-joshii started bargaining with the mother and presented her with several sheep, so the outcome was that all three girls married Hatot'cli-yazzi and came to live in his hogan. Everyone was satisfied and the girls divided the tasks of herding, shearing, carding, spinning, weaving, and cooking according to their own abilities and preferences.

Sometime before this happened, Superintendent Shelton had decided to enforce the ruling that a Navaho man could have only one wife, and sent a proclamation to that effect to all parts of his section. This met with no resistance from the Navahos living in the vicinity of Shiprock, or at least there was no open defiance. Some Indians with two wives simply walked away from the one they cared the least about and left her to fend for herself and care for her children as best she could. When reproached by her parents for this behavior, they simply excused themselves by saying they were obeying orders from Washington.

However, in September of 1913 Shelton received word of the plural marriages of Hatot'cli-yazzi, son of the noted medicine man, Bi-joshii. This was a state of affairs the Superintendent would not tolerate now that it had been brought to his attention. The crime that must be punished was not the possession of the three wives, but the disregarding of the command that had been issued such a short time before. Bi-joshii had not helped matters any by asking the interpreter who came to question them what Superintendent Shelton expected them to do with two of the young wives.

"Shall we turn them out to wander in the mountains until they die?" he had asked, and then added, "No! that is not the way Navahos do things! These three girls are all members of my family, and their children are my grandchildren. I shall keep them here where they will have good care."

So Shelton sent a party of Navaho policemen out to the Beautiful Mountain vicinity with orders to bring in Bi-joshii, Hatot'cli-yazzi, and the three wives for questioning. The policemen did not find the polygamous husband who had gone to the trading post at Lukachukai Mountain, nor did they find Bi-joshii, who was conducting a ceremony some distance away. But they did find the three women and took them back to the Shiprock Agency. The Shiprock jail was a small affair which was already occupied by some six or seven lawbreakers, a short term in jail being Shelton's way of enforcing law and order. In fact these sentences were so frequent that the jail became known as "Shelton's Hotel."

This being no place to keep the three women, they were quartered in one wing of the girl's dormitory, which had barred windows and doors that could be barred and locked. Two Navaho policemen were delegated to guard this building day and night. Needless to say, Hatot'cli-yazzi was upset when he returned home and found that the police had kindnapped his wives. He, with his father, one brother, and nine other clansmen rode to Shiprock Agency on September 17 to have a palaver with Superintendent Shelton.

They were probably not too dismayed when they found that the Superintendent had gone to the county fair in Durango. This gave them a free hand without opposition, as there was no one to issue orders to halt their actions. When the two policemen refused to hand over the keys to the dormitory, there was a tussle in which the policemen were somewhat banged about and finally tied to trees, while the agency employees hid in locked houses. When the keys were found, the prisoners were released and, after gathering their belongings into bundles, they mounted the horses that had been brought for their use and the whole party rode away

The First Year at the Blue Mesa Trading Post

to the south, to fortify themselves in a sanctuary on the top of Beautiful Mountain.

Shelton, upon his return to Shiprock Agency, was fairly livid with rage to find the prisoners gone and his autocratic commands defied. He had warrants sworn out against the "rebellious Navajos" charging them with riot, assault, stealing a government revolver, and flourishing guns in a settlement. These federal warrants were placed in the hands of U.S. Marshall A. H. Hudspeth, who sent Deputy Marshall J. R. Galusha to serve them on the entrenched Indians. Galusha arrested two of the Indians named in the warrants, but the remainder of the party that had invaded Shiprock Agency had gone into camp in a fortress-like position atop 8,340-foot Beautiful Mountain, where they could hold out indefinitely against any force that might be sent against them. The two men who had been arrested were taken before U.S. Judge William H. Pope in Santa Fe, where they were found guilty of unlawful assembly and were given sentences of ninety days in jail, which sentence was immediately suspended.

Meanwhile the handful of Navahos barricaded on Beautiful Mountain had stores of corn and beans brought from the valley below. Sheep and cattle were driven up the steep trail, for there was plenty of grass and water on the flat top. Huge stones were rolled into position where they could be pushed over the edge to block all attempts by anyone trying to climb the narrow trails. It was a natural fortress where its dwellers could never be forced to surrender. There were reports that Bi-joshii had sent word to Superintendent Shelton that unless charges against them were dropped, they would attack Shiprock Agency, and the time limit mentioned was November 10. The employees at the school were very upset and several resigned and hastened to a more civilized community. But when the date arrived, no attack occurred, so I am sure there was no truth in the rumor.

As the report of this affair spread from place to place in New Mexico and elsewhere, it grew in the telling until one paper published an article stating the Navahos were in full revolt and that towns and farming communities were likely to be attacked and wiped out at any moment. Superintendent Shelton sent word to all trading posts to have firearms ready in case the rebellion spread to their sections. The traders did not know how much of this wild talk was true and made preparations to send their wives and children away from the reservation.

Superintendent Shelton telegraphed to Washington suggesting that troops be sent to the Navaho Reservation to handle the situation, and his request received instant attention. Brigadier General Hugh L. Scott, who was stationed at Fort Bliss, Texas, received orders to proceed at once to Gallup, New Mexico, where he was to await the arrival of four troops of the U.S. Twelfth Cavalry to be sent by train from Fort Robinson, Nebraska. In November, the four troops of cavalry, consisting of 240 officers and men, 5 cooks, 16 mule drivers, 256 horses, 40 mules, and 8 commissary wagons arrived in Gallup.

As soon as they were provisioned, this army started north along the road that led to Beautiful Mountain. The general started by leading the way in a car, but when this mired down in the mud of Tohatchi Flats and was abandoned at China Springs, he joined the officers on horseback. There had been several hard rains in October and November so the flatlands were muddy and the arroyos were filled with running water. As there were no bridges or other form of road construction on the Navaho Reservation, the ninety miles to Beautiful Mountain took ten days to negotiate, the greatest difficulty being to haul the commissary wagons out of the arroyos.

General Scott and his cavalry, accompanied by Deputy Marshall Galusha as guide, reached Noel's Sa-nos-tee Trading Post in the vicinity of Beautiful Mountain on November 26, 1913, and established camp on the high north bank of the arroyo, which supplied men and horses with water. General Scott ordered his men to build their own fires that night about forty to fifty feet apart so as to impress the Navahos, who were watching from the mountaintop,

The First Year at the Blue Mesa Trading Post

with the great number of soldiers in the valley. Where they found wood for so many fires the record does not say, but it is certain that the few cottonwood trees along the stream bed would soon be consumed.

The cavalry's arrival in Gallup had caused consternation among the missionaries and school people on the Reservation. No one had really believed that Shelton's "little rebellion" would be taken seriously by the authorities in Washington, but this looked like real trouble and there could be some shooting and some people killed. Everyone knew it would be the Navahos who would suffer the casualties. Father Weber, who was the priest at the Catholic boarding school at St. Michaels, Arizona, had said, "This has got to be settled before it goes any further." The next morning he started for Beautiful Mountain, accompanied by a young Navaho who was the same clan as Bi-joshii. The two rode horseback over the Cottonwood Pass[1] and down the eastern slope to Noel's Sa-nostee Trading Post. The priest asked for a conference with General Scott, and the two conferred for some time as the General was reluctant to delay action now that he had reached the scene of the trouble. But Father Weber finally persuaded him to hold his army stationary for two days; then if he, Father Weber, did not return at the end of that period with the wanted Navahos, the army could move against them.

The trail up the side of Beautiful Mountain was too steep for horseback riding, so the Navaho lad who was the guide walked and led the burro on which Father Weber rode, as he was much too feeble to clamber up the precipitous path on foot. The watchers on top probably recognized their relative, and they knew by Father Weber's attire that he was a priest, so they made no effort to stop them or to roll stones to halt their advance. Father Weber spoke Navaho quite fluently and the boy with him helped interpret the situation. The argument lasted almost the entire night, but by morning Bijoshii agreed that it would be best to surrender before

[1] Known also as Washington Pass, New Mexico.

there was any shooting during which he or some of his family might be killed. "They may put you in jail," Father Weber told him, "but that does not matter as long as your sons are alive."

The next day a long procession came down the mountain trail with Father Weber leading on his burro and Bi-joshii not far behind. The four Navahos formally surrendered to General Scott and agreed to go to Santa Fe for trial. It was Thanksgiving Day and a feast of mutton and beef was prepared for soldiers and Indians alike as the chefs had been told the Indians would not eat turkey.

The conference at the trading post was a peaceful one as the sons agreed to abide by their father's decision, although they were somewhat reluctant to do so. Old Bi-joshii held up his right hand for all to see and said, "I see blood on this hand." He was referring to an enemy he had killed on the trip to the Bosque Redondo. Then, waving the gnarled fist in General Scott's face, he added, "I afraid there may be blood on this hand again, so I come from my safe place. But I no afraid of you or your men."

In United States District Court in Santa Fe the Navahos were found guilty of "unlawful assembly" and were given ten to thirty day jail sentences by Judge Pope. These were to be served in the Gallup jail and this turned out to be something of a picnic as the Gallup citizens and the tourists were anxious to take pictures of the Navahos who had defied an army, and brought them all kinds of food and presents for that privilege. After twenty days they were taken home in a mission car and that ended the Navaho Rebellion of 1913.[2]

[2] For a more detailed account of the Navaho uprising of 1913, see Frank McNitt, *The Indian Traders* (Norman, University of Oklahoma Press, 1962), 347ff.

3
Changes and Visitors at the Trading Post

WE HAD NOT been living at the trading post long before it became apparent that there must be one or two more bedrooms. We were situated 65 miles north of Gallup, and 72 miles southwest of Farmington, and had become known as "The Half-Way Post." At this time the roads were simply Navaho wagon trails which shifted with every sandstorm or flooded arroyo, and so there were few cars that cared to attempt the trip across the Reservation, while loaded trucks could not climb out of the deep arroyos. Occasional freight wagons, each drawn by four stout horses, came from southern Utah or Colorado on their way to the Santa Fe shipping station at Gallup. Once in a while a government car carrying teachers or other employees for the Reservation's schools or the Shiprock Agency drove past our store. Most of these travelers arrived just as night was falling and many asked for meals and lodging. The freighters were glad to dine with us but slept in their wagons; the women who asked to stay the night slept on the living room couch, which was not too comfortable or private; and once in a while, when there was a storm, we had more people than we knew what to do with.

So the second summer Arthur built two stone-walled rooms a short distance from our back porch so they were inside the high fence of our yard. These rooms were finished on the inside the same as our living quarters and were furnished with good beds, dressers, chairs, washstands, and fireplaces, but there was no running water. For a time this solved the problem of lodgings for unexpected guests, but there was more and more travel and more people asking for accommodations, so every year there was something new added to the Blue Mesa Trading Post.

One September afternoon of our third year a large black touring car stopped in front of the store and a uniformed chauffeur opened its door to help a little old lady dressed in tourist's khaki descend. She was wearing a voluminous veil fastened over a visored cap, a tan duster, and huge goggles, all of which was correct motoring attire according to the latest magazines. I knew before looking at the license plates that they were from the East and my guess was "Boston," which proved to be correct. The chauffeur was a short, heavy-set man of about thirty who was plainly a Scotsman. After the two had been in the store awhile, buying a silver bracelet and a couple of turquoise rings, I stepped into the store and asked if they would like to come into the living room for a cup of tea. The man refused but the little old lady said she would be very grateful for a cup of tea. After seating her in the Morris chair, I brought a tray of hot tea, sugar, lemon, and cookies. As we drank our tea I asked if she had been on the road many days, and she answered, "Yes, a couple of weeks, for we have come from Boston." Then she told how she happened to choose this particular road. All her life she had wished to travel to new places over uncharted roads, but her mother was an invalid and required constant care. After her mother's death there was plenty of money to indulge her whim, and she was free to spend it in any manner she wished. She had bought a touring car, hired the son of the old Scotsman who had taken care of her father's stable, and the two had started West without very definite plans as to route or destination. On arriving in Gallup she had examined her road map and noticed a line marking an unpaved highway that led to the north. When she asked where it went she had been told that "it will take you through the Navaho Reservation." This appealed to her as an adventure, so she had directed her chauffeur to follow this trail even though there would be mountains and unbridged arroyos. It had been a thrilling journey.

Then she asked me how I happened to be living way out here so far from the nearest town. I answered with no intention of creating a false impression: "Oh! I have to live here. You see my husband is a Navaho Indian trader." For a moment she looked frightened and her eyes moved from side to side as though she might be looking for some way of escape. Then she drew a long breath and regained her poise. For a moment she watched me as I sipped my tea and crumbled a cookie, then she said in a small but brave voice: "Well! I am glad we stopped here. I have always wanted to know how you Navaho Indians lived." It wasn't the first or the last time I was taken for a Navaho Indian as my hair was dark and my skin was deeply tanned, but still this took me by surprise and I had nothing to say. It had been in my mind to ask them to spend the night with us, but I knew by her nervous manner she would never in the world stay a minute longer than politeness required. I also knew she would later delight in telling her friends how she had stopped on the Reservation and actually had tea with a Navaho woman. Anyway, who was I to spoil a good story?

The next year, Arthur decided that the Newcomb Trading Post was developing into a paying business and he bought the half owned by Manning & Maple Wholesale Company in Gallup. Then he had stones brought and shaped to build, on the north side, a new and larger store with two good-sized warerooms in the rear. He had thought the old store would make a good rug room, but I had other ideas and insisted that it be made into a large living room while the wareroom back of it would make another bedroom with a large closet. We had a brick fireplace built in one corner and as much of the front wall cut out for triple windows as we dared, considering the weight of the roof. The walls of cream beaverboard made a fine background for our display of Indian curios, bayeta rugs, feathered war bonnets, and Indian dolls. It was really an asset to the post as a showroom as well as a living room.

Late in November we had a letter from Washington asking when there would be a Fire Dance in our section, and, if we knew of one soon, if we could take Lord and Lady Pennoyer to witness it. There was to be such a ceremony the next week and we answered that we would be happy to have Lord and Lady Pennoyer as our guests if they would accept our primitive hospitality. Such was their desire to witness a real Indian ceremony in its native setting that they accepted at once. We sent word for them to be at the post on the twenty-fourth and twenty-fifth of November.

We had three other guests for the occasion: Mr. Burges Johnson, a professor and writer from Syracuse University; Mr. Leigh Hunt, of Washington; and Mr. Richard Nelson, of Durango. The men spent the evening discussing politics, but Lady Pennoyer retired early as it had been a long, rough ride from Denver. The next morning Lord Pennoyer was anxious to visit the grounds of the ceremony as he had his camera with him and wanted to take home many pictures of the country, the hogans, and the Indians. The five men took a lunch and were gone most of the afternoon, returning in time for a six-thirty dinner. After this was finished, I began preparations for the long, cold night at the Fire Dance. This was something Lady Pennoyer did not wish to miss, and I was anxious to do everything possible to provide for her comfort. She was a tall, blonde woman of stately beauty, and dressed much as she might have been at some hunting lodge in Scotland.

Her tweeds were impeccable, her boots were custom-made, and her long hair was coiled under a small alpine hat. The one thing that worried me about her costume was her jewelry. Morning, afternoon, and evening she wore a fortune in ruby, opal, and lapis lazuli, as well as semiprecious stones such as jade and amethyst—all set in a dozen or more rings and bracelets, which she wore on her left hand and arm and which reached from her wrist to her elbow. She wore a chain and locket of antique gold and star sapphire earrings. I was glad that the Navahos placed no value on any stone except turquoise, but there would be many who were not Navaho in the large gathering at the ceremony, so I determined that she should be so well swathed in sweaters, furs, and blankets that no one could glimpse her jewelry.

By seven o'clock that evening the thermoses were filled with hot tea and coffee, lunch boxes were packed with beef, chicken,

Newcomb exhibit at the Shiprock All-Indian Fair held in 1914.

Corn ears were piled on hard adobe floors and surrounded by a fence. Here Grandma Tsosie weaves and babysits while guarding the corn.

and cheese sandwiches, the six wool blankets (one for each) were in the car with hot soapstones, two fur robes, and three cushions to sit on. Then the six were off and I was glad of a quiet moment. I did not go with them as I had been to many just such ceremonies, and it was a cold, windy night and the fuel in the fireplaces would need replenishing often if the house was to be warm on their return. We boasted no stoves except the kitchen range and the large coal stove in the store. There were four fireplaces and in cold weather we kept them burning both night and day for once the fires were out the cold draft came down the wide chimneys and turned the room temperatures to ice. We burned logs of oak and piñon as these did not send out sparks to damage the Navaho rugs; then at night we added large slabs of coal which would burn for hours.

It was three o'clock in the morning and I had just refueled all the fireplaces when the party returned. Their clothing and blankets smelled of cedar, pine, and balsam smoke, while their faces were smoke-smudged and their eyes were red-rimmed. On a windy night when the great central fire is reaching toward the stars, the smoke whirls in every direction and is no respecter of persons. But no one ever expects to be comfortable when attending a Navaho Fire Ceremony on a cold November night, high in the Chuska Mountains. I asked Lady Pennoyer what she thought of it and she replied: "It was simply unbelievable. I would not have missed it for the world. They told me there were 2,000 Indians in attendance, but there may have been twice that many. The whole mountainside sparkled with the tiny cooking fires of the different families, and the great central fire turned night into day on the ceremonial grounds."

"Did the Indians appear friendly?" I inquired.

"They were neither friendly nor unfriendly," she replied. "They were all so engrossed in their own affairs they paid us no attention whatever."

"There had been a large medicine lodge built of logs and, directly in front of it at the east was the dance arena surrounded by a high wall of cedar branches, enclosing a space about one hundred and twenty feet in diameter. In the center of this dance floor, the trees and logs for the fire had been planted with tips pointed to the sky, and on top were more trees and brush. The medicine man lighted the fire by twirling a stick, and then the dancers came in groups to salute the fire.

"Outside the brush corral, hundreds of Indians sat around their wagons in family groups or walked about meeting friends and acquaintances. We were sitting on our fur robes as near the dance floor as the heat would permit, elbow to elbow with Navaho women who, with small fires, were boiling coffee and roasting mutton. It gave me a very queer feeling not to see one white face in the whole assemblage. It seems as though I had visited another world." And perhaps she had caught a glimpse of a primitive world that would soon change and be forgotten as the rushing tide of civilization engulfed these Indians as it had tribes of the East and the Indians of the Central States.

The next morning breakfast was late, and when it was over the two cars drove away from the Newcomb Trading Post, Mr. Johnson and his party heading north toward Durango, Colorado and the other car traveling south. This was the last large Navaho ceremony of the year and with its end, quiet settled down over the post and the Navaho families of that section.

The next summer the Indian Department built a day school quite near our post, which received its water supply from a well in the arroyo and a tank built on the point of Blue Mesa. We were permitted to pipe water from this tank to our buildings, so there was water in the kitchen, the bathroom, and the store. A couple of years later, oil was discovered at Table Mesa, which was about 40 miles north of our Post, and the oil company paved the highway with asphalt from the wells to Gallup, and also strung a telephone line beside the road, from which we had a side line.

Then, when Arthur later installed a Delco Electric Plant, we were able to have electric lights, a Frigidaire in my kitchen, and an

Changes and Visitors at the Trading Post

electrically-cooled meat counter in the store. So the Newcomb Trading Post stepped out of its status as a pioneer country store and assumed the character of a modern place of business. While I found it much easier to take care of our frequent guests, the Indian trade continued as before.

4
Billy Yazzi

THE AFTERNOON SHADOWS of the short November day were beginning to lengthen in front of our Navaho trading post as I wrapped the packages of groceries and clothing for Ahson Nez. She had been sitting quietly on the customers' bench near the coal-burning heater for more than an hour, but had waited to make her purchases until after two men had been served and taken their departure. When she was sure she could have my full attention, she approached the counter and unfolded a new brightly-patterned saddle blanket, which she had brought to exchange for the merchandise she desired. Ahson Nez knew to a penny the value of her blanket and bargained shrewdly, saying she needed much food for the chanters who were holding a ceremony at her brother's hogan. I asked for whom the chant was being held but her only reply was a shake of her head. I did not ask again as little sings and blessing rites were held for any and every occasion much as a society matron would give a tea, for a visiting friend. On these occasions all of the relatives helped with preparations and brought food and gifts.

When the full price of the blanket had been paid in yard goods, groceries, and shoes for her two small girls, she requested that something be given her *"tseegisigie"*—free—as a token of good will. How this custom started, I do not know, but when a Navaho woman sold a blanket, she always expected a gift. I added a box of frosted cookies to her pile of purchases and she nodded happily as she spread her Pendleton shawl on the floor. Placing the various items along its center, she folded the sides over each other to make a long roll, then knotting the ends together, she looped it across her shoulders to carry to her pony, waiting patiently at the hitch-

Billy Yazzi

rail, where she would tie it securely across the front of her saddle.

As she was leaving, a Navaho man entered the trading post and stopped near the stove to warm his hands. He was a tall Indian, wrapped from neck to moccasins in a brown-and-orange striped blanket and wearing a bright red silk kerchief as a headband. His dignity of manner and his strong-featured, intelligent face proclaimed him a leader among his people and a highly respected medicine man.

"*Hah La!* Hosteen," I greeted him in Navaho, and he answered in the same, "*Hah La! Hah Nee, Tsi-choie!*"—"How are you my grandmother!" This was the proper term of respect even though he was twice my age. Hosteen Klah was a medicine chanter known throughout the Navaho country as a man of great wisdom and religious power. His rites, ceremonies, and herb nostrums had effected many cures among his people and his services were much in demand. During the autumn he was seldom to be found at his own home as his trips took him to every section of the Reservation and each ceremony lasted from five to nine nights. It often happened that another ceremony in another section would require his services as soon as the first had been finished, so he would be away from home for three or four weeks. At the present time he was staying at home until the sheep and lambs he did not wish to keep through the winter months could be sold. As he brought to the store only one or two sheep at a time, this was a long process.

His face seemed unusually stern this afternoon without a hint of a smile and I was wondering what could be troubling him, when he remarked "Billy is going to die tonight!" I could not believe that I had interpreted his words correctly and asked him to repeat his statement.

"Billy is going to die tonight!" he repeated sadly. He was speaking of Billy Yazzi, his nephew, who lived in a cornfield valley with a wife and five children, and who often hauled wood from the mountains for our fireplaces, besides working for us during our busiest seasons.

"But how can this be!" I exclaimed. "He was here last week and was perfectly well then!" After much questioning, I learned that Billy had driven to the mountains to gather a load of pine and spruce logs for winter fires. On his way down a steep slant the ropes securing the load had broken and he, with some of the logs, had rolled down the slope. During this fall the stub of a dead branch had punctured his arm just above the elbow and, after penetrating the muscle of the upper arm for nearly two inches, had broken off close to the flesh. His relatives had removed the stick but they had no way of washing out the slivers and the dirt. The wound had been covered with a mixture of balsam pitch and powdered herbs, then bandaged tightly. Two days later the arm started to swell and Billy was running a fever.

A sweat house was built in the banks of the arroyo and here he was treated for two days. This sweat house was a low structure of the same shape as the family hogan and had the same eastern doorway, but there was no opening in the top. The floor was only six to eight feet in diameter so there was just room for two or three bathers to sit inside. After they entered, a helper rolled a couple of white-hot stones through the door, handed the bathers a bucket of water, and then hung two or three heavy blankets over the doorway. Handful at a time, the bathers tossed water on the rocks until the sweat house was filled with steam and the men inside were dripping with perspiration. When they were at least half-suffocated, the bathers emerged and were dried with white corn meal. This treatment twice each day generally cured illnesses caused by poisons, but Billy still had too much foreign substance in the wound for it to heal.

The family then decided to secure the services of a medicine man who lived near Chinle Valley, and who knew the Knife Chant, which was considered the proper ceremony to cure accidental injuries. A medicine lodge of poles, brush, and adobe had been built near the sweat house, logs had been piled outside for the ceremonial fires, and a healing chant had been in progress for the past three nights. This was the chant for which Ahson Nez had bought the groceries.

Billy Yazzi

"Is Billy getting better?" I inquired.

"No!" Klah replied. "He is much worse; he just lies there and groans. His arm is the size of that stovepipe and just as black!" Klah pointed to the pipe above the heater to illustrate his statement. Arthur and his helper had just come from the wareroom where they had been weighing and sacking piñon nuts to be shipped on the next freight wagon. They listened to Klah's words with much concern and Arthur asked.

"How long will this medicine ceremony last?"

"If Billy does not die sooner, it will last two more nights," Klah replied.

"Do you think Billy will live that long?" I asked. Klah made no attempt to disguise his fears.

"No!" he replied. "He will die tonight or anyway by tomorrow night."

We glanced at each other worriedly and I finally said, "We had better ride over to the medicine lodge and see if there is anything we can do!"

John, our clerk, spoke for the first time. "You do not dare interfere with a healing chant, especially when the patient is very ill. I doubt if they will allow you to enter the medicine hogan." John had lived most of his nineteen years on or near the Navaho Reservation, and he knew the customs and taboos of its people very well.

"I think they will let me in," I replied. "Since I cured Zonnie's baby they call me a 'medicine woman' and in that capacity, I am allowed to go anywhere!"

"That is all very well as far as children are concerned," my husband cautioned. "But I do not believe you had better try this time, and it is probably too late to do anything for him anyway."

John spoke again. "If he should die while you are there or even later, you will be blamed for his death. They will say that you spoiled the power of the healing ceremony." We had known of instances when the patient had died during the healing rites and the medicine man had blamed outside interference for the death. A Navaho medicine man never doubts the power of his rites and prayers to heal the patient, but the ritual must be carried out exactly and smoothly without break or deviation. A perfect ceremony will restore the patient to perfect health.

I agreed with all he said, but I was determined to go and do anything I might be permitted to do, and Arthur agreed with me. Asking John to saddle two horses, I went into our living quarters to collect the things I might need in the sickroom. In June of that same year, the head medical officer of the Navaho Reservation had stayed at our post two days and, upon finding that I was interested in the health problems of my Navaho neighbors, had ordered a supply of "safe" medicines sent me from Washington. Among these were cod-liver oil, cough sirup, zinc ointment, Epsom salts, boric power, peroxide, aspirin, and several other home remedies. This supply greatly enhanced my reputation as a medicine woman.

From the iron teakettle on the kitchen stove, I poured hot water into a gallon thermos jug, then wrapped a thick bundle of clean, cotton rags, and a couple of bath towels. I took a half-pound box of Epsom salts, boric powder, peroxide, aspirin, and cod-liver oil. Adding a deep enamel pan, soap, and a sharp pair of scissors, I made a bundle which could be wrapped in a blanket and tied to the back of my saddle. Quickly changing into Navaho costume, which consisted of two long, full skirts, a long-sleeved velvet blouse, and a scarf for my head, I was ready to go. For a wrap, I wore a heavy, wool cape, for the Navaho shawl was one garment I had never been able to manage on horseback, as it generally flapped open and frightened the horses.

The afternoon air was crisp and the horses were eager to go, so we soon covered the two miles to the medicine lodge. This proved to be a small, hastily-built brush and adobe shelter half-hidden in a bend of the mesa. Medicine lodges for most major ceremonies are large and well constructed of solid cedar logs plastered with adobe, but the structures that serve as hospital rooms for emergencies are built of small poles covered with brush, which is held in place by a plaster of wet earth. In case the patient dies, these structures can be burned with little loss.

Billy Yazzi

Several saddle ponies with heads down and reins dragging were standing nearby, a few half-starved dogs wandered about, and a small fire at a little distance from the doorway sent wisps of smoke curling upward. We knew the people in the hogan had heard the approach of our horses, so we waited until the chanting stopped and a Navaho pushed aside the door-blanket to step outside to greet us. If he was surprised to see white people, he did not show it, but asked in a gruff voice what we wanted. We did not know this Indian and I decided he must be the helper who had come from Chinle with the medicine man.

"I would like to see Billy," I told him. "May I come into the lodge?"

"Who are you?" he asked. Arthur answered him at some length explaining that we were traders who lived near the cornfields and that I was a medicine woman who had cured several sick people. After a few more questions the stranger nodded his consent and we tied our horses to the logs that projected from the woodpile. Pushing aside the door-blanket, we stepped across the sill down into the dimly-lighted smokiness of the medicine lodge. The small, circular enclosure held a surprising number of people. In the center of the room, on a pallet made of sheep pelts covered with a blanket, lay the sick man, his injured arm bundled into a cocoon of soiled rags. He lay very still, not seeming aware of any of the movement about him. His eyes were closed and his face was the color of cold, dry ashes. His only indication of life was the slow, labored breathing which came through his lips in a low moan. Around him sat or squatted many of his relatives and friends. The medicine man, his helper, and a group of chanters sat near his head, while his two wives, his sister, and her daughter sat near the pit that held the fire.

Arthur and I edged along the north wall until we found floor space on which to sit. I had brought my blanket-wrapped bundle with me, but if any of the Navahos were curious they did not show it. When Arthur had passed cigarettes to the assembled Indians, the prayer chant was resumed. I was glad the brush walls admitted an occasional breeze of fresh, cool air as the number of people in the small room depleted the oxygen rapidly and the opening in the roof was unusually small. It had probably been made small so that the room could be easily heated, but the smoke curled under the ceiling and stung our eyes before escaping through the vent.

Glancing around the interior of the hogan, I noticed two unopened bottles of medicine, with labeled directions for using, standing at one side of the door. Evidently someone had obtained these from the agency doctor but I knew they would not be used until the medicine man had completed his healing ceremony, and then it would be too late. For perhaps an hour we listened as the prayer chant kept time to the rhythm of the rattles and finally came to a close with a long-drawn *"Hah-yah-ee-ya-a."*

For a time there was a respectful silence, then the medicine man asked: "Why do you come to this ceremony? What do you want?"

I replied carefully: "We have brought some medicine for Billy and I would like your permission to use it."

When this had been interpreted by the daughter, there was an oppressive silence in the room as the medicine man considered my request. Perhaps this was the first time a white person had ever asked his permission to join in a healing rite. He said a few guttural words to his assistant and suddenly a babble of questions and answers flowed around us, with everyone seeming to have something to say. After a time the opinion of the women seemed to prevail and the medicine man sullenly granted me permission to treat the patient. It may have been that he was worried about Billy's failure to respond to his treatment and decided it would be wise to have someone he could blame if the patient did not recover.

Seating myself by Billy's side and opening my bundle, I selected the things I would use first. Arthur opened the thermos and gave him an aspirin tablet with a little warm water, while I wet some of the cloth I had brought with peroxide to bathe the arm. Then I took the scissors and started clipping and discarding pieces of the old soiled bandage. Knowing the Navaho belief that all healing must be accompanied by prayer, and wishing to conform to their pattern of conducting a healing rite, I started humming very softly a well-known hymn as I worked.

As I removed pieces of soiled bandage I threw them into a pile near the door where they could be carried out and buried. When I had washed the pitch and herbs from the arm, the wound with its ugly scab surrounded by purple flesh was laid bare and the odor was almost unbearable. I gasped for breath. "Don't faint!" Arthur commanded sharply. "You will fall on him!" I pulled myself together, but how I did wish for one good breath of fresh air.

I knew that the ugly scab must come off and still I held the scissors in my hand. Two good slashes would do it, but would my nerve hold out? There was no alternative! I moistened a wad of cloth in the boric solution, held it over the wound, then jabbing my scissor points under the scab, I slashed once and once again. The flood of matter that spouted forth was more than I could endure. Weakly, I motioned for Arthur to come and squeeze the arm while two of the Navaho women helped me to the door and on beyond the woodpile.

When finally my stomach settled back to a normal position, I walked about in the cool air for several minutes and then returned to the hogan. Two Navaho men were now working on the arm, which had shriveled to half its former size and resembled a wrinkled, gray rag. "Keep working," I told them, "until nothing comes out but good, clean blood." Emptying part of the Epsom salts into the enamel pan, I added warm water from the thermos. The clean rags furnished pads to soak in this solution and place over the wound, and also bandages to hold them in place. The whole arm was then wrapped in a dry towel. It seemed to me that Billy was much better, not quite so gray or pain-racked, and he certainly had ceased to moan with each breath.

Turning to the medicine man, I thanked him, and then added: "Continue with your ceremony and pray that he recovers, then sing some of your prayer chants for me as I desire your friendly thoughts and wishes."

When this had been translated, his answer was slow in coming. *"Yah-tuh-hay!"* "It is well," he said gruffly, and I was pleased.

Motioning to Nebbah, Billy's younger wife, to follow me outside, I gave her explicit directions as to her duty throughout the remainder of the evening and the night. The pad over the wound was to be kept moistened with the Epsom solution and never allowed to become stiff and dry. When badly stained, it was to be replaced with a clean one, thoroughly soaked and quite warm. She said she understood and would carefully obey instructions.

We walked away from the medicine lodge into the velvetry gloom of a moonless night. The stars sparkled coldly and from the mountains a chill wind proclaimed winter not far away. Mounting our horses, we rode homeward, tired and silent. The creak of the saddles and the crunch of dry twigs and grasses under the horses' hoofs made a rhythm soothing to our tense and jittery nerves. There were no other sounds, as the little creatures of the night who may have been hunting in the shrubs were silenced by our approach, and we were the only moving objects between earth and sky. I was first to break the silence. "What will happen if he dies tonight?" I queried. "Will they blame us for it?"

"Yes, I am afraid they will," Arthur answered thoughtfully, "especially the medicine man, as he will not wish to admit the failure of his ceremony."

"But will they turn against us now, when they know we have done all we could for Billy?" I persisted.

He paused a moment before answering. "Not too many years ago our lives would have been in grave danger, as some member of Billy's clan would have been appointed to destroy us. An ancient tribal law exacted a life for a life. Now they will simply shun us and no one will be allowed to venture near our trading post. We may be forced to pack our belongings and leave the Reservation."

"But he was better! His fever was not nearly as high and his breathing was almost normal!" I protested. "If Nebbah keeps the packs wet and the solution warm, he will live."

"The medicine man may not allow her to do so. He may insist

on putting your packs and the solution near the door with the medicine from the agency until his ceremony has ended. At a healing chant, the medicine man must be obeyed."

I had not thought of this possibility, but Arthur was right, and, tired as I was, I decided there was only one thing for us to do in order to save Billy's life and our standing in the community. "We must go back," I cried. "We must go back and see that he is taken care of during the night."

"Don't be foolish." My husband was as tired as I. "You have told them what to do! Now we need baths and a good night's rest."

But I insisted that we ride back to the medicine hogan.

Our horses were reluctant to turn as they were eager to reach the home corral and their evening box of oats. Our return progress was slow and dismal, but finally we stopped before the blanketed doorway and paused to listen to the deep resonance of the all-night chant.

"You tie the horses and I will go inside," I told Arthur as I slid out of the saddle. He took the reins of my horse and I walked to the door, pushed aside the blanket, and entered the sick room. The only light came from the small fire in the pit and much of the room was in deep shadow. It took me a few moments to comprehend the change in the scene I had left only a short time before.

The same number of people were seated around the room, and the same chanters were waving their gourd rattles and joining in the chant, but someone had placed a roll of blankets under the sick man's head and shoulders, raising him to a half-sitting position. His eyes were open and I thought he attempted a smile when he saw me, but it may have been only the flickering firelight. The medicine man was still waving his rattle and entreating all the powers of the heaven and of the earth to restore health to the patient. At the same moment Nebbah was applying a warm, wet pack to the wound. I could hardly believe my eyes! I had hoped she would be allowed to do so when the chanters were resting, but to have a strange medicine man accept alien treatment as a part of his ceremony was beyond anything I could have imagined.

I certainly was not needed here! Everything was being done to the satisfaction of all, including myself. There was a pause in the chant as the old medicine man saw me in the doorway.

"I came back for my scissors," I volunteered as an excuse for my presence. Nebbah handed them to me and I moved backward, dropping the blanket into its place as I stepped into the starlit night. My husband was smoking a cigarette near the cedar fire.

"We can go home now and really sleep," I said thankfully. "Billy is not going to die."

Perhaps the reader will conclude that my services were appreciated and greatly acclaimed, but this was not the case. The Navaho people are ever careful to save face and the medicine man from Chinle was given full credit for Billy's recovery. After the ceremony was finished, he and his helper were well paid and departed with honor and dignity. In discussing the affair, the Navahos agreed that I had done no harm in adding my assistance to the ceremony, as I had acted with a friendly purpose. Any of his friends would be willing to do as much. This attitude we were very happy to accept, as it assured us of a continued cordial relationship with our Navaho neighbors.

5
War Over Water Rights

THE DOOR of the trading post stood open to the noonday heat that shimmered in dust waves on the bare adobe earth outside. The last Navaho customers had departed with their sacks of groceries and the only sounds inside the store were those of the lazy flies bumbling against the windowpanes and the rustle of pen and paper as Arthur worked at his ledger. During the early part of the forenoon, he had been busy trading groceries for small amounts of wool and several hard, dry sheep pelts brought to the store by Navaho women who wished to secure their supplies and return to their homes before the heat of midday.

At the other side of the store I was busy polishing a number of silver bracelets set with turquoise, which our Navaho silversmith had finished and brought to the post the day before. These were fashioned from Mexican silver dollars and each silversmith created his own designs, often using a personal mark inside to authenticate his work. The tools with which these smiths worked were crude and nearly always homemade. The anvil, small hammers, and the dies used to stamp the patterns were fashioned from any discarded chunks of iron or steel the silversmiths were able to find, but the resulting jewelry was beautiful and unique. There was a ready market from curio stores, tourists, and Navahos, so a good silversmith often earned a better living for his family than many of the sheep owners.

Debbah, a Navaho girl, was seated on a pile of blankets trying to untangle a mass of brightly-colored rickrack that a careless customer had unrolled. There were three cards holding twelve yards each that had become knotted into a ball and must be straightened and rewound. Thirteen-year-old Debbah had been with us since February, when she had been sent home from the Santa Fe Indian School with a bad cough. Her parents lived in the upper cornfields but they were not able to give her the milk and other food she needed, so we had asked her to stay with us. I enjoyed her company and her willingness to help with whatever tasks needed to be done. Her parents came to visit her frequently so she was happy and content, which helped greatly in regaining her health.

Arthur closed the ledger and broke the silence with the remark: "It is going to be another hot day; I wish it would rain!"

"You are not the only one who wishes it would rain," I replied. "This drought has everyone worried. Klah says the Indians will hold a Rain Chant near Two Grey Hills next week, and I hope it brings us some rain." In normal years the winter snows formed a snow pack on the Chuska Mountains which, melting slowly, furnished water for irrigation through April and May. Then after a few weeks of dry weather, the summer rains again filled the arroyos, irrigation ditches, and ponds. But this year the winter had been mild, with very few snowstorms. Then the little snow there was on the mountains had disappeared during a warm spell in March. Now in April there was only a thin trickle of water in the arroyos and the ponds were nearly all dry. Rains could not be expected until the latter part of June and the sheep could not be taken out to their usual summer grazing pastures for there was no place for them to find water.

Navaho sheep owners were holding their flocks in the valleys below the mountain slopes until shearing time was past, when they would then move them into the mountains. We had bought the wool from the larger flocks early in April and now only those that numbered less than a hundred remained scattered in the lower valleys. In this area there were three or four rock springs that fed small ponds with just enough water for a few nearby families and their sheep and ponies. The dams for these ponds were built and kept in repair by these families and were claimed as their private property. Although the land of the Navaho Reservation is tribal property, the

The three wives of Hatot'cli-yazzi, Bi-joshii's oldest son, whose being put in jail contributed to the Beautiful Mountain Uprising of 1913.

Greyhair's daughter is in the process of weaving a large blanket.

rights to a certain farming and grazing area, and also rights to own a private water supply were generally respected by other Navahos. The families who owned only a few head of sheep depended on the corn, beans, squash, and melons they raised on their small farms for their winter food. They would remain in the valley until after the fields were planted, doing this during the new moon in May, then they, too, would go to the mountains for the summer. Right now they were shearing two or three sheep at a time and bringing the wool to the post in the late afternoons to obtain groceries.

During the midday heat there were no ponies at the hitch-rail, and no wagons of wool at the wool barn. The silence of the desert was a blanket that spread from the rim of bare gray rocks in the east to the tree-clad slopes of the western mountains. I had just finished polishing the bracelets when we heard the hoofbeats of a pony crossing the planks that bridged the arroyo. The pony was traveling fast and I glanced at Arthur, inquiring, "I wonder who can be coming in such a hurry?" I did not expect an answer, and we both looked out the open door to see a Navaho girl dismounting at the hitch-rail. As she turned toward the store, Arthur said, "It is Hosteen Escon's oldest daughter, Ethnahbah. I wonder why she is in such a hurry?"

It was very evident that she was in a hurry, for she was fairly running toward the door and she stepped inside quickly. Looking around the dim interior she saw Arthur and exclaimed, "Oh Hosteen, come and help us! My father he been shot and need a doctor."

We were speechless for the moment, then Arthur exclaimed, "Your father has been shot! How did that happen?"

"It was that Long Mustache," Ethnahbah stated. "He come with many sheep, and now my father will die."

"Is he still alive?" Arthur queried.

"Oh, yes! He still breathe, but he very bad hurt in the middle and blood runs all over." She pressed her hands to her stomach to designate the place of injury.

"Oh, Hosteen, can you bring the doctor quick! Quick!" And the tears rolled down her cheeks as she hid her face in her hands.

"Do you think you can carry on here while I go to Shiprock for the doctor?" Arthur asked, as he closed his ledger.

"Oh, yes!" I answered. "Debbah and I can manage the store."

Hosteen Escon and his family lived a mile or more from the post in the lower cornfields where they grazed fifty or sixty sheep and farmed a bit of valley land. They obtained their water from a small spring below which they had built a long, low dam, which formed a pond to water their livestock. Escon was a quiet, industrious Navaho with a large family, most of whom were away at a Navaho boarding school at Fort Defiance. The oldest girl, Ethnahbah, had remained at home this year to help her mother with the sheep and to learn how to weave. There were also two small boys not old enough for school. How such a quiet man as Hosteen Escon ever became involved in a shooting affray I could not imagine, and Ethnahbah gave me no chance to ask questions, for she quickly slipped out the door, mounted her pony and rode down the valley.

Arthur had brought the car and was filling it with gas and oil when two Navaho men came riding from the lower cornfields. They were neighbors of Hosteen Escon and had witnessed the shooting. Arthur ask one of them to ride to Shiprock with him to report the matter to the agent and to give the doctor first hand information. The other tied his pony to the rail and came into the store to buy groceries to supply the clan who would soon gather at the injured man's hogan. I asked how Escon was and he replied: "He is breathing better and the medicine woman has stopped the bleeding with cobwebs and the powder from oak puffballs. She also had herbs to make a brew that puts him to sleep, so he is in no pain."

After much questioning with Debbah as interpreter, I finally pieced together the complete story. It seems that the drought had started earlier on the eastern section of the Reservation, so that creeks and ponds there were about dry and the new grass had withered when it was only a couple of inches high. B'Dougal Nez, or Long Mustache, lived on the Ria Giega Wash and owned more than eight hundred sheep and goats. When it became apparent that the grazing and the water in his section would soon be gone, he visited Chee Dodge at his home on Tsonsala Mountain in Arizona, to bargain for summer pasturage for his flocks. Chee Dodge was considered the headman of the Navaho tribe and held grazing rights to a vast area in the mountains around his home and also across the mesas below. There were springs, creeks, and one lake in this territory, so it provided good pasturage even in times of drought.

A bargain was made through which sheep were to be traded for grazing privileges, but the real problem was how to move this large flock of sheep and goats across the Reservation from the very eastern corner in New Mexico to the western mountains in Arizona. Long Mustache knew that the Navaho sheep owners in the path of his march would object to such a large flock's crossing their grazing areas and drinking from their limited watering places, but there was no other way to move them. In order to overcome all opposition, he went to the Indian agent at Shiprock and asked for a paper giving him permission to move his sheep from east to west across the Reservation. The agent in charge was a political appointee from Washington who knew little about the economy of the Navaho Reservation, and who cared less. Under the old spoils system a successful senator could reward a favorite political henchman with some well-paying job in the Indian Service whether he knew anything about Indians or not. The superintendent, without asking the advice of any employee who might have understood the situation, readily made out an order giving Long Mustache permission to move his flocks from the Ria Giega Creek to the western side of the Chuska Mountains.

Armed with this authority, Long Mustache hired two herders, packed several ponies with supplies and, with the aid of two or three trained sheep dogs, started on the long drive. Leaving the Ria Giega Valley, he traversed the high eastern mesa country without opposition, as Bichai, Keeyanni, and other sheep owners who claimed that section had moved their sheep to the mountains. At the big bend of the Río Chaco he ran into trouble as several families were living here, but he was allowed to water his flock and cross to another mesa. Two days later he again approached the Chaco twenty miles nearer the mountains, where several Navaho families lived along its banks, since it still held enough water for their needs. Great was their dismay at the approach of so many thirsty sheep, but when Long Mustache showed them his "permit," they made no active resistance to his march. However, they were angry and sent word on ahead to warn farmers and sheep owners of his approach.

At the mouth of the Tunicha Creek, he left the Chaco Valley and followed the creek as it wound westward toward the Chuska Mountains. With the exception of a few seeps the creek was dry, but there were occasional small springs bubbling from the rock formations at the side, forming rills that soon disappeared in the sand. To make use of this water, Navaho families built low earthen dams by scraping away all the sand and loose earth until they came to shale or hard adobe, which served as a floor for their pond. These Navaho families were still living in the valley, waiting for the new moon that would announce planting time. There was little grazing here but the farmers had no large flocks and sheep could live for a time on last year's dry tumbleweed and this year's dry sunflower and cornstalks.

None of the valley farmers expected Long Mustache to march his flock up the cornfield area, as the usual travel route was to the north, behind a ridge which protected the farm lands from damage. But Long Mustache had evidently instructed his herders to follow the creek and take advantage of any watering places they might find. At the first Navaho homestead the small pond was ruined as there was not nearly enough water for all the animals, and even the spring was clogged, while forage in the nearby fields was trampled into dust. Two or three miles further on, was a larger pond and wider cornfields belonging to Hosteen Escon and other members of his family. They saw what had happened to the lands and water supply of Etsitty Begay, so Escon and three other men went to meet Long Mustache to ask him to change his course and leave the valley. If he refused they had agreed to join in herding his sheep away from their homesteads.

When they met Long Mustache, he showed them the written permit he had received from the Shiprock Agency, thinking that this would settle any argument. The valley farmers already held a poor opinion of the decisions made by the agent, which had already caused two bitter feuds between neighboring clans. So they simply ignored the paper and stood firm in their refusal to permit the sheep to cross their land. There were three shepherd dogs with the large flock, and Hosteen Escon had with him two larger dogs, part collie and part German police. As soon as these dogs approached each other, there was a fierce dogfight, and soon one of the shepherd dogs was stretched out dead. Seeing this, Long Mustache pulled out his revolver and shot one German police dog through the head. Hosteen Escon moved toward the fighting dogs just as another shot was fired, and fell to the ground with a bullet in his abdomen. Whether it had been Long Mustache's intention to shoot Escon, or whether he had meant to shoot the other dog, no one seemed to know or care. The fact remained that he had seriously wounded Hosteen Escon and if death resulted, his life would be endangered by clan reprisals. In the general confusion, the herders turned the sheep north to take them out of the valley and away from the farms. They would reach water by nightfall at the sheep dip near Two Grey Hills where the government had built a dam which formed a lake.

The relatives of Escon carried him to his hogan and called a medicine woman, then Ethnahbah mounted her pony and rode to the post to ask Arthur to bring the agency doctor. She may have decided on this action without consulting her parents as they would have preferred a medicine man from their own tribe, but she had spent some years at the Shiprock school and knew the agency doctor.

Long before this Navaho had completed his account of the shooting, I had become aware of the arrival of several Indians on horseback. A group of six from the east, another four or five from the south, then several from other directions. I noticed they wore headbands instead of hats, while the absence of coats exposed the cartridge belts and the holstered guns. Every horseman carried a gun of some description, although there was a law forbidding Indians' carrying guns, and traders on the Reservation were not permitted to sell them either guns or ammunition. But the traders off the Reservation and the stores in the nearby towns were not governed by these restrictions, so the Navahos were well supplied with both.

"What is the meaning of this?" I asked Dinnae Tso. "Who are all these men?" He had been watching the riders through the open door, and replied: "They are members of Hosteen Escon's clan, also his relatives by marriage. They will kill Long Mustache if Escon dies."

"Oh, no! Oh, no!" I cried. "Long Mustache is armed and will not hesitate to kill several of them. Then they will kill just as many in return and there will be no end to the killings. How can we stop them?"

Grasping his arm, I guided him to a spot outside the door where we could talk to the horsemen. "Tell them," I commanded, "that Arthur has gone for the doctor and that Hosteen Escon is alive. Then tell them that they are to stay here until the doctor arrives." Dinnae Tso delivered my message and some of the men nodded their consent, but others turned away and I heard one man say in angry, guttural tones.

"Who is this white woman who tells us what we must do? We are here to wait for Hosteen Escon's brother from Tohatchi, and when he comes we will go. Then we will see who can shoot the straightest."

"You have not eaten since morning," I said, willing to try anything that would create a delay. "I will make you some coffee." This offer met with blank silence but I hurried into the house to fill the kitchen range with wood and coal. The ten-quart enamel bucket was nearly full of water and I set it on the stove to heat for coffee. The five loaves I had baked that morning using Mormon yeast, which makes the lightest bread with the largest loaves of any bread in the world, still lay on the kitchen table. As these loaves were much too soft to cut with a knife, I broke them into chunks that filled a large dishpan. Then opening several quart cans of tomatoes I poured them into smaller pans and added generous scoops of sugar, this being the Navaho way of serving tomatoes. As soon as the water was hot, I added the coffee in a cheesecloth bag, then Debbah and I started carrying things out through the store door—coffee, sugar, pans of tomatoes, bread, enamel cups, and tin spoons from the store. A free lunch was not to be ignored and soon all of the horses were tied to the hitch-rail and the war party was squatted on its respective heels around the box that served as a table. Each held a tin cup in one hand and in the other a crusty chunk of bread with which to dip up the tomatoes.

"Oh, dear!" I said to Debbah, "I do wish Arthur would come with the doctor. He has been gone a long time!" But it was not Arthur who came into view at that moment; it was Escon's brother riding a foam-flecked horse with flaring nostrils and heaving sides.

"Now they will be on their way!" I exclaimed, but the brother rode into the group and they evidently explained the situation to him. Tying his horse to the rail, he, too, helped himself to coffee and bread. As the empty cups were being piled into an empty dishpan, I wondered how I could cause a further delay. Stepping behind the store counter, I took down three cartons of cigarettes, and, going outside, gave several "smokes" to each man. I knew they would smoke each cigarette until the fire touched their lips and that would take some time.

We could hear the car toiling up the sandy valley trail before we could see it and we walked a little way to meet it. As it crossed the plank bridge we saw that the doctor and Arthur were in the front seat but it was not until it reached the gas tank that we could see the occupant of the rear seat. A bed of sheep pelts and blankets had been made in the back of the car and on this lay Hosteen Escon, apparently fast asleep. Arthur and the doctor stepped out of the car and came toward the store, while the Indians circled the car, staying at a respectful distance, but where they could see the injured man. His face was gray from loss of blood but his breathing was regular.

"How is he?" I asked the doctor after we had exchanged greetings.

"He has lost a great deal of blood and there is some internal bleeding, but the bullet did not damage any vital organ and is now lodged in the pelvic bone. I think we can take it out and have him walking around as spry as ever in a couple of weeks."

"I wish you would have someone explain all that to his relatives," I told the doctor. "But for goodness sake, do not let them know that you must operate to remove the bullet! They would call a medicine man to suck it out through a hollow reed."

Arthur laughed and said, "They have their own methods of removing foreign objects from the body." Then he looked around to locate an interpreter.

"He is under sedation," the doctor volunteered. "I thought the trip would be easier on him that way."

When Arthur had secured an interpreter for the doctor, I asked him what was happening in the cornfields and he said: "There are still a good many angry Navahos milling around the place, but Long Mustache has moved his sheep over the ridge and is hurrying them toward the mountains. Someone has dragged the dead dogs away and buried them and things will soon quiet down."

I asked the doctor if he would care to wait a few minutes while I prepared something for them to eat, but he replied that they would get started now, as he wished to have his patient in the hospital as soon as possible. However, he said that if coffee would not be too much trouble, he would appreciate a cup. By the time the car was filled with gas, oil, and water, the coffee was ready to serve with a plate of oatmeal cookies. As the car disappeared in its own dust, I watched the Escon clansmen arguing about their next move and it was plain that several still wished to ride against Long Mustache, but finally, one by one, they mounted their ponies and rode toward their own homes. They were not happy about it, and still thought that Long Mustache should be punished, but decided to await the outcome of the hospital treatment.

Then they were all gone. Arthur, the doctor, and Hosteen Escon were on their way to Shiprock. Dinnae Tso and his brother headed back to the cornfields. The members of the war party went to their separate hogans. The sun had set and silence settled over the desert. With Debbah's help, I locked the store doors, then went into the kitchen to view devastation. My beautiful bread was gone to the last crumb and the sink was piled high with dirty cups, pans, and spoons. Most discouraging of all was the fact that there was no water with which to wash them. The tears came into my eyes and rolled down my cheeks. "I wish I was back in the schoolroom teaching little black-eyed Navaho babies to spell *C-A-T*," I mourned.

Debbah patted my arm comfortingly, "But this is lots more exciting," she said. I had to agree that she was right.

6
Ahsonchee the Brave

DURING THE SUMMER that Ahsonchee was ten years old, the family was living on the eastern slope of the Chuska Mountains just below Cottonwood Pass. Her father, Hosteen Begay, was engaged in the task of cutting and trimming pine logs with which to build a new hogan, to be located near the Two Grey Hills where he held rights to five or six acres of farm land. The old hogan in which the family had lived for some years had been damaged by the wind and water of a summer cloudburst while the family was at their summer home in the mountains. No Navaho dared enter the damaged structure, which had been claimed by the evil wind spirits, and it could never be repaired or lived in again. So now Hosteen Begay must build a new hogan of absolutely new materials, as far from his old one as his land permitted.

The Begay family consisted of Hosteen Begay, his wife Ahson Begay, their ten-year-old daughter, Ahsonchee, two boys seven and five years of age, and little Jolie, the baby girl. Their summer abode under the tall pine trees was little more than a long, pole shed thickly covered with branches of pine and spruce. The doorway faced the east and there was a stone fireplace and chimney opposite the door, to use when the weather was cold or stormy. There was another fireplace outside, as most of the family activities took place outside the shelter. The roof had been plastered with a coating of adobe mud to keep out the rain and also the heat of warm summer afternoons. It was a pleasant summer home, with a sparkling mountain rill not far away, and, in a marshy swale not far below was a large garden patch where they planted melons, squash,

Ahsonchee the Brave

and potatoes, which grew without irrigation. The higher slopes furnished plenty of forage for the sheep and horses.

Ahson Begay had erected her log loom for rug weaving under the spreading branches of a nearby piñon tree, and worked at her weaving while her husband toiled with ax and saw. All of the children except little Jolie did their share. Ahsonchee herded the sheep to make sure they did not wander too far and fail to reach the home corral by dusk, for there were bears in the rim rocks and even an occasional cougar. The two little boys gathered sticks and pine cones for the fires and brought buckets of water from the creek, then amused themselves by trying to catch the saucy chipmunks, or by hunting for wild strawberries and currants. It was a wonderful place for small boys.

The high brush corral for the sheep and goats was quite near the home and the shepherd dogs were penned with the sheep at night in order to sound the alarm if prowlers came too near. The horses, too, were brought home at night and safely housed in a pole shed, as cougars were known to attack horses as well as sheep, but the coyotes and bears generally slipped away when the dogs started barking. There were no firearms in the shelter, and Hosteen would not have used one anyway as there was a strict taboo against killing either a coyote or a bear. His method of repelling marauders was to grab a burning stick from the fire and chase the animal away.

By midsummer a large pile of pine logs was cut, trimmed, and ready to move down the mountain. A crude sled, much like a toboggan, was built, to which three logs at a time could be chained and dragged to the new location. The distance was not too great, but after leaving the mountain slope, it was slow work dragging the unwieldly sled over the crooked trail, so one trip each day was all that Hosteen Begay could possibly accomplish. There were sixty ten-foot logs for the six sides of the new hogan, and then there were many shorter logs and long poles to be used in the dome-shaped roof, all of which must be handy before work on the house began.

The summer days passed rapidly and by early September the logs were assembled, with the addition of several stout planks to frame the door, the smoke vent in the roof, and one small square window. Erecting a new hogan had always been a community affair, the same as a barn-raising in Wisconsin a generation ago. So a day was set, a yearling calf was killed, quantities of beans were boiled with chili peppers, and a wagonload of roasting ears and melons was brought to the building site. In every community there was one man known as "The Builder" who was asked to supervise the construction of hogans and ceremonial lodges. He seemed to be able to judge the weight and quality of the logs so there would be no bulging or lop-sided walls. The morning of the appointed day, this man arrived early to mark the heaviest logs, which would be used for the lower part of the structure, then the next in width, and finally the smaller ones for the top. The earth for the floor had been cleared and tamped solid, then grooves were dug for the first layer of logs. The logs were ten feet long, so the six sides would be nine feet in length, and after this first row was solidly in place, the door frame was nailed to it. Many hands were busy chipping notches near the end of each log so they would fit closely together, others carried the logs to the builders in the order by which they had been numbered. Circle by circle, the wall rose in the air so well grooved there was hardly a crack between. By noon, the walls, the doorframe, and the window frame were in place and everyone was glad to rest and enjoy the feast that had been prepared by the women. Pans of meat boiled with potatoes and onions, beans, corn bread, and coffee formed the main part of the meal. Dishes were few, with the exception of enamelware cups and tin spoons, the hard, crusty bread serving as ladle and bowl to hold the stew and the beans, while the hot ears of corn could be held by the husks in which they had been roasted.

As in older times, the men squatted or sprawled full-length on the ground to partake of this food at their leisure and converse at the same time. There were many children running around, most of them holding a small ear of roasted corn in one hand and a piece of meat in the other. The babies were safely strapped to their cradleboards where no harm could come to them while their mothers worked around the cooking fires.

After the melons had been sliced into quarters and passed to the men, the women sat on the ground in puddles of brightly-colored skirts, nursing their babies and keeping watch of the other children, while enjoying their own share of the banquet. There was no need now to bring wood or water, or to stir the food in the kettles; the fires would slowly fade to ash as they enjoyed every tasty morsel and exchanged neighborhood gossip. Homemade cigarettes would be enjoyed by everyone before the afternoon work was begun.

The dome-shaped roof with the smoke vent slanting to the east was yet to be laid and this was probably the most difficult task of all. The men were divided into groups to handle the different tasks. One group selected the poles in the order they would be used, the long ones first and then the shorter ones as the dome narrowed to its apex. Another group carried these poles to the men standing on the walls, who fitted them carefully into place so as to hold the next slanted tier. The poles of this roof were tightly laid and the larger cracks were wedged with strips of wood. All of the logs and poles must be laid before sunset, for the hogan was a symbol of the sun and must not be built at night. The September days were short and the men worked hurriedly, so well before sunset the last log was laid and the last crevice filled. Then the workers and their families took their departure in wagons or on horseback, to follow the dusty trails to their own homes.

The Begay family was living in a temporary shelter near their new home at the eastern side of the cornfields. All of the outside plastering was yet to be done and this would be a thick coating of adobe and blue clay mud. The roof would have a thick coat of this same plaster, then before it could dry and crack, it would be covered with earth several inches in depth. Hosteen Begay dug a pit in which to mix the mud and twisted a rawhide rope with which to pull the buckets of mud to the roof. With two helpers to fill the buckets and operate the ropes, he was able to plaster half the dome in one day. The next day they worked steadily and were almost finished when, as he was lifting one of the heavy buckets, his foot slipped and he fell, the bucket going first. It was not a long fall but he came down sideways across the rim of the bucket and broke his hipbone.

The helpers carried him to his home, then mounted their horses and went to get a medicine man who knew how to set broken bones. The neighbors were soon informed of the accident and came with gifts of food and offers of help. Some of the men completed putting the mud on the roof and said they would cap it with earth later. When the Navaho specialist arrived, he tied a heavy stone to Hosteen's foot and when the leg was straight, he wrapped the patient's hips in a wet goathide, which would shrink as it dried and hold the bone in its proper place. When this was done it was decided that he must have a healing ceremony to drive away the evil spirits that had caused him to fall. No one told the traders in the valley about Hosteen Begay because he did not wish to be taken to the white man's hospital. He told his wife: "The white man's hospital is a Chindee hogan where very sick people go when they are about to die."

She agreed with him saying, "Their relatives take them there so they will be buried in a box in the white man's cemetery; this saves the relatives much trouble and expense."

Hosteen said, "This broken bone will soon heal, but I had better have a ceremony so the same thing will not happen again."

There were several ceremonies from which to choose but they decided on a Hochonji [devil-chasing] Chant, to last three days and nights. A messenger was sent to contact the right medicine man to find out when he could come to hold the rites of exorcism. This would not be a major ceremony and would be attended only by relatives of the family and the nearest neighbors, so extensive preparations would not be necessary. One goat would furnish sufficient meat and everyone who came would bring corn, melons, squash, or loaves of hard bread. A neighboring family loaned them the use of a hogan in which no one was living at that particular time, and as soon as the articles stored inside had been removed, it was ready. A chanter who knew the Blessing Rite held his ceremony to bless the hogan and all who would enter during the three days and nights. He then started the central fire by means of the whirling stick, and this fire would be kept burning, either inside or outside the hogan until the last prayer was chanted and the last rite performed.

Hathilie Tzee-Zhin arrived a day early as there was much to be done and much material to be collected before the ceremony began. He would need small branches from cedars, spruce, piñon, and balsam trees, and he would need thirteen different herbs to boil for the emetic. These included yarrow or milfoil, meadow rue, pennyroyal, wild mustard, and many others. Leaves would be needed from five varities of yucca and these were to be cut with a prehistoric stone knife or a sharp piece of obsidian from the eastern side of each plant. The long fibers from the leaves of the Spanish bayonette would be used as ropes to bind the patient. Dodge weed, grama grass, wild buckwheat, rock sage, and red willow would produce the ashes with which to mark his face, while pine charcoal mixed with mutton tallow would make the paint to be used for the Blackening Rite.

The rites of the first night were short, consisting of chanted prayers, an act in which a masked assistant shot tiny arrows with obsidian points over the patient's head from four directions, and lastly the drinking of herb medicine. It was over by midnight; the visitors departed, and the participants slept.

The next day the medicine man, his helpers, the patient, and other men took turns in the sweat house for ritual baths, while the women ground corn meal for ceremonial mush. The second night was much the same as the first with the addition of the Thunder Stick Rite. Among the sacred articles in his medicine bundle, the medicine man carried a stick called "bull roarer." This black stick was about eight inches long, by two inches wide, and half an inch thick. At its wider end three round bits of turquoise were set to represent eyes and mouth, and to the smaller end was fastened a long cord or thong. As this night's rites came to a close, the medicine man's assistant carried this stick outside and, whirling it rapidly, made a sound like that of low thunder. This was heard first from the north, then the west, south, and east in turn and was supposed to banish any evil spirits that might be lingering outside the medicine lodge.

The next morning more helpers were needed as a sand painting was to be made on the hogan floor. Fine tan sand was spread as a background and then three painters, each using five colors of ground sand, made as a central design a likeness of the hero, Nalyeinezgonnie, the Enemy Slayer of myth and legend. In the four directions, eighteen-inch mounds of sand were piled to represent mountains and each of these was covered with sand of different colors: black in the east; blue in the south; yellow in the west; and pink (mixed red and white) in the north. When this painting was completed, the medicine man erected eight yucca leaves in each mountaintop; long yucca in the east; wide-leafed yucca in the south; slim leaves in the west; and horned yucca in the north. The butt ends were buried in the sand and the points stood up, so if there had been more of them, it would have resembled a picket fence. They really did form a symbolic fence to bar all evil influences from entering the painting.

Two assistants brought Hosteen Begay into the hogan and set him on the design representing Enemy Slayer, in the center of the sand painting. A chorus of voices intoned the prayers of healing as the medicine man performed the healing rites. First he pressed the patient's body with feathered prayer bundles from head to foot, then reversing the direction, he pressed the bundles from the soles of the patient's feet to the top of his head, then made the motion of tossing them out through the smoke vent in the roof. Sand taken from the painting was pressed to the patient's body with the same ritual, then came acts of massage to arms, limbs, and head which ended with the two sitting back to back as the medicine man sought to strengthen the patient's spine. Herb infusion was then administered both internally and externally, after which live,

The boys have brought barrels of water from the spring and the women have brought their empty buckets to be filled.

B'Dougal Nez (Long Mustache), who shot Hosteen Escon and nearly started a clan war.

glowing coals were placed before him and sprinkled with herb incense. A fragrant, blue smoke arose, which the patient inhaled to clear his mind and to banish all fear of a repetition of the accident. The ceremony completed, the patient left the medicine lodge and the sand was scraped into a blanket to be disposed of outside, so the hogan could be readied for the evening rites.

This last night was the most important of the three-day ritual as the prayers and rites cleared the patient of all evil influences and restored his mind and body to health and happiness. The medicine man had many small articles to prepare for these last rites. There were yucca crosses of four kinds; there were sixteen kewthawns made of sections of hollow reeds, to be filled with tobacco and bits of turquoise, which would be placed at a distance from the hogan as a sacrifice to the immortals; then there were the herb infusions; and then the body paints were to be mixed.

So the chanting started late in the evening, and as this was a moonless night, the stars stared coldly through the opening in the roof. The medicine man and the patient sat to the west of the central fire with all the required fetishes and paint spread before them, while a group of five or six chanters sat against the south wall. The remainder of the hogan was crowded with relatives and visitors as there was some curiosity as to how the rites would be conducted over a patient who could not walk. For a time there was only the chanted prayers, which were accompanied by a rattle made from a crane's skull solidly beaded to represent feathers and eyes.

In half an hour or more, the medicine man laid out his clay paints and proceeded to mark designs on the patient's body and face, after which he took a bowl filled with black paint, which had been made by mixing mutton tallow with charcoal, and with the help of his assistant, he painted the patient's body completely black. His face was striped with white, red, and black paint. After this blackening there was a long period of chanting and then dozens of long yucca strands were placed beside the medicine man. One by one he knotted these strands together and bound the resultant rope around Hosteen Begay's feet, legs, body, arms, and head—always being careful that each knot was on the outside of some joint and the last one securely tied on top of the patient's head. As he sat there on the sand painting, he was thoroughly enmeshed in a net of knotted yucca, with every knot representing an ache or a pain.

After the proper number of prayers had been chanted, the medicine man picked up his obsidian knife and made the motions of cutting the upper knot, then quickly untied it, and slipped the strands down to the patient's shoulders. Again he made the motions of cutting the knots and deftly untied them to push the strands down around the arms. This continued until all of the knots had been cut and the pile of yucca strands lay at the patient's feet, to be picked up by an assistant and carried out of the hogan. This completed the Hochonji [evil dispelling] Rites and those that followed were called the Restoring to Beauty Rites. These were the anointing, the drinking of herb medicine, the eating of pollen, the tying of a sacred bead and a prayer feather to the scalp lock, and breathing the incense. A basket of corn meal mush was brought in and the patient ate a pinch from each of the cardinal points and then from the center. This was then passed to the chanters and the helpers. Now the patient was helped to his own hogan and was free to eat the same food as the others in his family, but the ceremonial paint must stay on for four days and nights.

I saw Hosteen Begay some weeks after the ceremony and he still could not walk on that foot. The bone had been splintered and refused to heal properly, so a friend had gone to the mountains to secure oak poles, which had been hardened in hot ashes and made into a pair of crutches. These he used for more than a year and after discarding them he still walked with a limp and could do no heavy farm work or caring for the sheep. Ahsonchee and her mother assumed the extra tasks, leaving the herding to the two boys and their dogs. So it was these two women who carried water to the mud pit and plastered the outside of their new home with thick clay so that the logs could hardly be seen. Ahson bought a small pane of glass to seal the window and hung a heavy blanket over the doorway. The hogan was now complete, but no Navaho family would think of living in a new structure until a House Blessing Ceremony had been held. Hosteen Hathile, who was Ahsonchee's uncle, came to conduct the rites that would dedicate the home and bless all those who were to dwell therein.

It was a long ceremony and as soon as the sun was up, all the family, the relatives, and the friends came and sat in a circle around the wall. The medicine man started the central fire by means of the "whirling stick," and the fuzz from the cliff rose was used to catch the first spark. Then four kinds of wood were added, each from a different direction. It was the medicine man who whirled the fire stick, but it was Ahson Begay who held the fuzz to catch the spark and then added the splinters of kindling, for this fire was a symbol of the life possesed by the hogan, which now belonged to Ahson Begay. Hosteen Hathile then placed oak twigs above the door and on the rafters in the four directions, intoning a prayer for the structure's strength and stability as he did so. All of the assembled Navahos joined him as he started the House Blessing Chant, during which he sprinkled pollen four times around the circular floor, four times up and down each wall, and four times around the ceiling, and lastly, a handful through the smoke vent in the roof. This pollen had been a mixture of pollens from wild flowers along the valley floor, grass pollens from the mesas, and tree pollens from the mountains—it was called "earth pollen." He now opened another small buckskin bag which contained corn pollen, pollen from melon and squash blossoms, and bulrush pollen. This he sprinkled over the family and the friends who had come with gifts to take part in the ceremony, and he ended by placing a pinch of pollen in each person's mouth.

The new hogan was now ready for occupancy and everyone lent a hand to bringing the family's possessions from the temporary shelter to the new dwelling. This was accomplished by noon, and, as a dinner had been prepared, all stayed to eat and admire the new well-built hogan.

Autumn on the Reservation was a time of feasting, holding religious gatherings, and ceremonial rites, but it also was a time of hard work in gathering the harvest, storing food for the winter, selling surplus sheep, and hauling firewood from the mountains. Hosteen Begay was too lame to accomplish much of this labor, but after Ahsonchee had harnessed the team to the wagon, he would drive through the cornfields while she and her mother would walk on either side breaking the ripened ears from the stalks and tossing them into the bed of the wagon. When the corn was harvested, it was taken to a well-fenced enclosure where it was spread on the hard adobe ground to dry. When the bean vines were pulled, they were stacked on a canvas floor and, when thoroughly dry, were pounded by a flail to shell the beans. Then the vines and chaff were raked away and the beans were sacked.

Hosteen Begay could not flail the beans, nor could he dig the pits to store the squash and melons, so these tasks were performed by the women, but he could husk corn, so day after sunny day he sat in the enclosure husking and piling the bright ears separately according to their color. White was to sell at the trading post, blue was to make ceremonial mush, red was to sell to the tourists, and variegated was to feed the farm animals. When the crops were finally harvested it would be time for the fall roundup and the horses and cattle that had grazed on the mountains during the summer would be brought down and turned into the fields where the dry cornstalks and bean vines would provide fodder when the snow covered other feeding grounds. As Hosteen Begay could not go on the roundup, he hired a neighbor lad to go in his place.

The Tunicha Mountains provided summer pasture for all of the Navaho stock on the eastern side of the Reservation. With the high slopes of mountain herbage, the long mesas and plateau grassland accompanied by a never failing supply of water, the Navaho sheep and cattle grew fat and ready for market before the first winter snow arrived. But the Navahos were not the only ones who benefited by the excellent summer grazing on these mountains that reared their rocky peaks twenty miles to the west of our post. There were three or four cattle ranches to the east of the Reservation and when a summer happened to be unusually dry these ranchers would drive a herd of steers and young cattle across the Reservation line, skirt the Navaho farm lands, and scatter the animals on the mountain slopes. Here they would graze until roundup time in the fall when a bevy of mounted cowboys accompanied by a chuck wagon would scout the mountainsides to collect the cattle that wore their ranch brand. They carried branding equipment with which to mark all calves that had been born during the summer.

The Navahos objected strenuously to having these herds pastured on their land. They claimed the cowboys branded many Indian cattle and drove them off the Reservation. The cowboys argued that the few they took from the Navahos never could equal those belonging to their ranch that the Indians had butchered and eaten during the summer. The argument finally reached official ears in Washington, and orders were sent saying that in the future no outside cattle would be granted grazing privileges on the Reservation.

It was the October before this regulation had been made that a group of cowboys and their chuck wagon stopped at the post to ask the shortest and easiest route to the mountains. The main highway in front of our store ran north and south. However, the branch that turned west toward the mountains made a sharp turn around our buildings, skirted the steepest point of the mesa, then climbed the south slope to its level top, where for ten miles it was almost a straight line. Then there was a climb to a higher level which we called "second mesa" and this led to the first mountain ridges. On the eastern side of the Chuska Mountains there were four long mesas spreading from the base of the range like four fingers of a gigantic hand, and the longest of these was Blue Mesa, named from its strata of blue clay, which the prehistoric Pueblos had used in making pottery. The ruined homes of these "Anatsazi" [Ancient Ones], could be found at several places on the mesa and dotting the higher elevations along the valley floor. It was this early civilization that had built the first dams, irrigation ditches, and farm dikes which now had been rebuilt for Navaho use. The Blue Mesa Trading Post, *Pezh-doclish-dezii*, was located under the point of the long mesa, with the Tunicha arroyo on the north and five miles of valley land stretching to the south. It had been built by a Mormon trader who later moved to the San Juan River Valley where he owned an irrigated ranch. We purchased the post in 1914 and the Post Office Department named it Newcomb.

A week or so passed and we had half forgotten the cowboys and the roundup taking place on the mountains, when about noon of a crisp autumn day, a Navaho man strode into the store exclaiming: "The cattle are coming! The cattle are coming! Bring everything into the house!" By that time we could hear the crunch of gravel and the bawling of the thirsty animals, but we thought they would follow the arroyo and pass by on the north. However it was only minutes before we knew they were coming down the mesa by way of the wagon road, but it was too narrow for so many stampeding cattle and hundreds dashed over the point and down the steep sides directly behind the buildings. Here the herd divided and those at the south stormed through the yard, leveling the back and front fences as though they were matchwood, snapping my clotheslines and carrying away towels, diapers, and one of Arthur's best shirts on their horns. The hitch-rail was on the north side and two Navaho ponies tied there broke their straps and raced away ahead of the cattle. A team of fat, aged horses hitched to a light wagon was engulfed by the stampede and ran in its midst until the wagon overturned and they were halted by its weight.

A cowboy stopped to ask where they would find water, as the arroyo was almost dry. Arthur told him there was a dam and a good-sized pond about half a mile farther on. Then they were gone and there was nothing but the dust and the wreckage to bear witness to their passing. I walked out into the yard to retrieve whatever was left of my laundry and to estimate the damage. The fences and clothesline poles were flat on the ground; one hen with eight little chicks, which had been penned in a coffee box near the porch, had been trampled into the dirt. That seemed to be the extent of the damage.

As I started back to the house, a wagon drove up to what was left of the hitch-rail and its occupants climbed out. Two small boys made a beeline for the trading post door while the man tied the team to the post and, noticing his limp, I knew it was the Begay family. Ahson Begay lifted little Jolie to the ground so she could follow her brothers, then with Ahsonchee's help, she started unloading the stiff, unwieldy goat pelts they had brought to exchange for groceries. Just as Ahsonchee was picking up a goat pelt, she saw a wild, long-horned steer leap out of the arroyo and head straight for the little girl. Her mother saw it too and called frantically: "Lie down, Jolie! In the ditch, Jolie, in the ditch!" Like a little brown partridge or a baby rabbit, the child obeyed its mother's cry of fear and threw herself flat in the ditch that had been made by the road scraper at the side of the road. It was only about sixteen inches deep, but the child hugged the bank and although the steer hooked at her he hit the ground and his momentum carried him some distance away. Here he stopped and turned to locate the child, but Ahsonchee was running toward him waving a stiff, dry goat pelt. One target was as good as another and this one seemed more threatening, so the steer lowered his head and charged this latest enemy. He tossed the goat pelt high in the air and threw Ahsonchee several feet to one side where she crumpled to the ground. The steer turned and seemed undecided whether to charge the goat pelt, which was nearer, or the motionless girl. The two cowboys who had been following hard on the animal's trail, made good use of this minute of hesitation, and one circling lariat settled around its horns and the other around its hind legs. As the two horses jumped in opposite directions, the steer hit the ground with a bone-jarring thud that left it stunned and breathless, and the cowboys were able to tie its feet together so that it was helpless.

Ahson Begay picked up little Jolie and carried her into the store while the rest of us ran to see what we could do for Ahsonchee. Wrapping a blanket tightly around her, the men picked her up and brought her into the house. I had a tourniquet ready to bind her upper arm to halt the flow of blood and, as I tightened it in place, after the long sleeve of her blouse had been cut away, I could see that the arm was badly shattered. This was no slight injury that I could treat, and Arthur started for the garage to get the car. After the arm was bathed in an antiseptic solution, I wrapped it loosely in soft towels and then, to keep it stationary during the trip, I bound the upper part of her body in a sheet. A bed was made for her on the back seat, while her mother and Jolie sat in front with Arthur, as Ahson Begay insisted on accompanying Ahsonchee to the hospital.

Hosteen Begay and the two boys exchanged the pelts for groceries and then drove to their home where they told the neighbors of Ahsonchee's accident and hired one of them to take care of their stock while they were away. Early the next morning they started the long dusty ride to the agency.

They put the canvas top over the wagon and filled the back with hay and provisions as they would be traveling two days and stopping at Sulphur Springs one night. There they would feed and water the horses, cook their own food, and sleep in the wagon bed with the horses tied to the wagon. They could take no chances of having the team driven away by prowlers.

Ahsonchee was in the hospital four weeks and when I next saw her I was happy to observe that her arm was as good as before the injury. Her wrist and elbow moved normally, and she flexed her fingers normally so there had been no crippling or stiffening of joints. I was glad of this because Ahsonchee would be called upon to card much wool and to weave many rugs and blankets during the years ahead when she started caring for her own family.

7
Reservation Dust Storm

THE TRUCK which carried the U.S. mail the 140 miles from Gallup to Farmington generally arrived at our trading post about noon and unloaded our mailbag, along with the sack that would go by a mail carrier to the Indian School at Toadlena. This was a weekly service we looked forward to with much eagerness as it brought papers and letters from "home," and was about our only contact with the outside world. The driver generally stopped long enough to drink a cup of coffee and eat a piece of homemade pie, relating the local news and the condition of the roads as he did so.

It was a day in early May when Arthur received an official looking envelope that excited my curiosity. It was from a girl's riding academy located in the Green Mountains of Vermont. The letter stated that their summer season was about to open and they would like to have us send them twenty Navaho saddle blankets of uniform size, weight, and approximate coloring. The order ended with: "Please ship by insured express as soon as possible." Arthur handed the letter to me with the remark: "They seem to think this is a rug factory where any amount of rugs of a stated size can be turned out at a moment's notice. I suppose they think we hire the Navaho women to do the weaving in order to get cheap labor."

I smiled as I read the order, thinking of our Navaho weavers with no two looms of the same size and no two rugs ever woven with the same patterns. The outstanding feature of any Navaho rug or blanket was its individuality.

There was no possibility of putting twenty, or even ten, Navaho weavers to work on this order as it was early in May and lambing season was in full swing. During the cold weather of January and

February the Navaho women worked at their looms to use up the last of the yarn they had stored, but April and May brought lambing, shearing, and planting so the looms were dismantled and stored. The families moved from winter hogans to summer camps adjacent to new pastures and the cornfields they would start irrigating. Even the grandmothers stopped carding and spinning as they would be in charge of the babies and small tots while the mothers worked in the fields with their men.

But here was a bona fide order sent in good faith and if we could furnish the saddle blankets they needed we would be likely to receive future orders which would help us market many Navaho blankets. Arthur led the way into the storeroom where rugs were piled according to their size and quality. There was a pile of some sixteen or twenty saddle blankets and these Arthur started unfolding and measuring, one by one. Some were much too large and there were three only half-size, while a couple were too narrow. Finally five were laid to one side as being approximately the right size, weight, and pattern. "Well! that's a start," Arthur remarked as he folded the others. "Now we will see what we can buy from neighboring traders."

As soon as the store was closed, and our dinner and chores disposed of, the three of us—Lynette was then nine months old—climbed into the big, black Hupmobile and drove eight miles up the cornfield valley to the Ed Davies trading post where we found two saddle blankets of the right size and colors. Then we drove to the foot of the mountains seven miles west to buy two more rugs from George Bloomfield. We now had ten saddle blankets that answered the buyer's description and Arthur decided to ship them to Vermont with a letter stating that another shipment would soon follow.

During the week we visited the Sheep Springs Trading Post where we found that Mr. Goldsmith had just sent all of his rugs to the Manning wholesale house in Gallup, but at Naschiti Trading Post we found two very nice ones. We still needed eight more before we could make the final shipment.

We had visited all of the nearer posts and Arthur decided his next try would be at the Red Rock Trading Post located in a cornfield valley twenty miles west of the great spire of rock known as Ship Rock Peak. We had heard that the weavers of this valley wove exceptionally fine saddle blankets.

Although this trading post, which was owned by Mr. Stallings, was only sixty miles from us, it was not a trip we could make in an evening. For thirty-five miles we would be traveling on a graded dirt road that led to the government Indian School at the Shiprock Agency, but before crossing the bridge over the San Juan River, we would turn to the left and follow a wagon trail toward the Carrizo Mountains. For twenty miles this road wound its way between high hummocks of adobe clay, through sandy gullies, and around jutting rocks, climbing a long slope to circle the great pinnacle of Ship Rock. The tail to this pinnacle was a long dike of black rock that stretched miles to the south but had one opening where the road could cross. This trail then descended to a wide valley and an arroyo which at times carried a roaring flood of red water. On the far side of this valley, the road wound along the foot of the mountains until it came to the Red Rock Trading Post.

Sunday morning dawned bright and warm, with only a bank of low black clouds over the top of the western mountains. I looked forward to a pleasant outing in the beautiful Carrizo foothills with their brilliant red rocks crowned with the green of piñon and pine. As I packed a substantial lunch basket with food for two meals, I decided it might be wise to pack a pasteboard carton with emergency rations. I took our camp coffeepot, a fry pan for bacon and eggs, dishes, and extra food. For Lynette I took two quart-sized thermos jugs of fresh milk, a dozen oranges, and also one baby-bottle filled with milk and wrapped in oiled paper and a towel. There was a gallon thermos of drinking water, a bag of diapers, a large pillow for a bed, and my brightly-patterned Pendleton shawl in case it should turn cold on the way home. As I walked toward the car with my arms filled, Arthur remarked, "It looks like you intend to be gone all summer."

I smiled and answered with our favorite phrase—"You never can tell!"

Billy Yazzi was herding our horses to the arroyo for their morning drink and as he passed I pointed to the long purple cloud in the west and asked, "Is it going to rain today, Billy?"

He studied the sky intently for a moment and shook his head before answering, "No rain. Plenty big wind!"

April and May were the months in which we could expect wind and dust storms, which were always disagreeable but caused no real damage. "We will be near the mountains," I told him. "There is never any dust where there are trees."

He looked at the sky again and shook his head, then he followed the horses to the corral.

It was ten o'clock when the car was finally serviced and loaded. Besides the boxes and bags I had stowed on the back seat, there were two wool army blankets, a five-gallon can of gasoline, cans of oil, and a towrope to help us out of possible sand traps. The two extra tires were always carried in the trunk, and all of this was standard equipment for any journey across the Reservation away from the main traveled highway. The Hupmobile was large and slow, but its engine was powerful and we could climb steep slopes and pull through ditches that would stall an ordinary car. With the store locked and barred, and with Billy Yazzi to guard against prowlers, we started on a jaunt we expected would be carefree and wholly enjoyable. But, as I had previously remarked, "You never can tell."

That morning had been warm but, as midday approached the air became brittle with a dry heat not usual so early in the summer. At times little gusts of hot wind stung our faces and danced away across the desert in waltzing dust spirals. We paused at Sulphur Springs to eat our lunch and to fill the radiator, and here the first long sigh of the approaching storm passed over us. The sky had turned a copper color and the sun was a pale disk behind a haze of yellow dust. After we had eaten, Arthur decided to put on the side curtains which were made of leatherette and isinglass, saying as he took them from under the back seat, "This looks like a bad dust storm but we will be out of it when we leave the lowlands and climb toward the mountains."

By the time the curtains were in place, Lynette had finished her milk, orange juice, and crackers and was taking her nap on the pillow on the back seat. I had packed away the remaining food and had taken one of the army blankets to fasten across the inside of the car on the windward side to keep out the dust. It would seem that we were prepared for the worst the wind and dust could bring us. However, we were aware that this was no ordinary storm and we had many miles to cover before reaching the mountains and a shelter of trees.

"We must hurry," Arthur remarked. "It will not be long before the smaller arroyos will be filled with sand." How the motorist on the Reservation hated the small sand-filled arroyos that appeared to be good hard road! Sometimes they were narrow and the front wheels would sink to their axles, and sometimes they were wide enough to accommodate all four wheels. In any case the sand was bottomless and it took several stout Indian ponies with long lariats to pull the car to solid footing.

Visibility was decreasing and twenty miles per hour was the top speed to be achieved on this dirt road. It was one o'clock when we came to the side road that would take us west toward the mountains, and after we turned the wind came from the rear. The sharp rattle of sand against the car and the effort to stay in the road was not so noticeable now, but we made no better time as this was a Navaho wagon trail boasting no upkeep whatever. It was a long gradual climb to the black wall of jagged rock that formed the tail of the mighty dragon whose horned head was now lost in clouds of dust.

A bend in the wall formed a windbreak and we stopped the car to allow the engine to cool and to wash the dust from our throats with a drink from the thermos. I poured a cup of milk for Lynette and Arthur held the blanket over us as she drank. Suddenly a wild gust of wind opened the blanket and sand came into our faces to make a crust of dirt on the baby's wet lips and a scum on the milk. Luckily I had put the cork and the cover on the thermos so that the milk was not ruined. Again I pulled the blanket over our heads and Arthur started the car, moving at not more than a crawl, as this last bit was a steep climb.

The rock dike was not more than twenty feet in thickness and then we were looking down the slope to the Carrizo Creek. This valley now was a funnel which carried a dense cloud of red dust and sand sweeping toward the north, into which our wagon trail disappeared completely, and all other landmarks were blotted out. I looked at it in shivering dismay. "We can't ever drive through that!" I exclaimed in a shaking voice.

"We will have to try," Arthur answered. "We cannot go back, and this will not blow itself out until midnight."

"If we could only reach the mountains," I cried. "They would be some protection."

Just then a vicious blast shook the car and the sound of cracking isinglass followed. Our curtains, which up to now had been some protection, shattered into bits and sailed away on the wind to parts unknown, leaving only a few shreds of tattered leatherette clinging to the frame. Almost immediately the fabric of the car's top tore loose from the front bar and three long black strips flapped in the rear like the bedraggled tail-feathers of some enormous crow. If we had been driving a lighter car it would have gone rolling across the landscape like the native tumbleweed, but with the top and the curtains gone, the wind did not get much purchase against the heavy body of the Hup.

Now, indeed, we did feel the full force of the wind and the sting of sand and sharp bits of gravel it swirled through the air! For a moment neither of us had anything to say, then Arthur spoke, "You had better take Lynette and sit on the floor between the two seats. You can never keep yourselves covered with the shawl here, but there you will have some protection and can cover your heads." It was a struggle to open the car doors, but finally Lynette and I were settled on blanket and pillow between the seats, with my shawl drawn over us for a tent. Here we were fairly well protected from the wind, but as the car had hard tires we seemed to be in direct contact with every rut and stone it passed over.

Arthur was wearing his slicker with the hood pulled over his forehead and the straps over his mouth. Even so, the sand stung his face and it was well that his eyes were protected by wide amber glasses, for the dust was blinding as he drove into the valley. Moving along slowly when a portion of the trail was visible, stopping when the headlights failed to penetrate the dust, it seemed that we were trapped and smothered for hours. In reality the distance was only a little more than half a mile, but I hope I am never again called upon to travel another half-mile as long as that was.

As we climbed the grade and came nearer to the mountains, the force of the wind diminished and, although still blowing a stiff gale, it seemed like a mere zephyr in comparison with the tornado we had just passed through. Lynette and I reoccupied our place in the front seat and we continued our way along the foothills for another slow twenty miles. The arroyo running past the Red Rock Trading Post was a wide shallow stream of water floored by hard red shale, which provided a solid crossing, but here, too, a down draft of violent wind brought a wall of red dust. This was not such a wide blast as had filled the Carrizo Valley, so we drove through it without difficulty.

On the second bench beyond the arroyo stood the long stone buildings of the trading post, the store and its warerooms coming first, and then house and sheds, with the corrals well in the rear. I was glad to see the solid stone walls, which could never be shaken by even the wildest blasts of wind, and I looked forward to a peaceful night in their protection. We stopped in front of the store and Arthur honked the horn. When no one came to answer the horn, Arthur went to the door and knocked loudly, but still there was no one to welcome us. Then we drove around to the side and he knocked on the door of the house without receiving an answer. The Stallings family were Mormons and had gone to Fruitland that Sunday to attend church services.

"They are not at home!" Arthur stated, and I started to laugh—a laugh that turned to streaming tears and long shuddering sobs of complete exhaustion.

"Stop crying!" Arthur commanded sternly, as he feared hysteria. "This is not the end of the world."

"It might as well be," I sobbed. "There is no place to go." But Arthur had glimpsed an open shed at the rear of the store and now drove the car into it, then hung our canvas over the front opening. It was not a solid structure and shook with every blast of wind, while the dry cornstalk thatch rattled and the dust seeped in at every crevice. But we were protected from the full force of the wind and I walked back and forth beside the car to bring some circulation back to my knees before pouring the milk for the baby. When she was busy with her bottle, we took time to open the lunch box and enjoy our chicken sandwiches, peach pickles, and coffee. It was surprising how the food cheered us and gave us a brighter outlook.

"This is a valley of cornfields," There must be Navaho hogans not far away. We had better drive up the valley and see if we can locate one." I was in no hurry to brave the wind and dust, but finally we were again in the car moving slowly along a rutted wagon road that seemed to lead nowhere. Darkness had arrived early, as the twilight was blotted out by dense red dust which our headlights failed to penetrate. Not more than a mile had passed when we dimly discerned three or four hogans not far from the road we were traveling. Arthur stopped in front of the largest and honked the horn. In a few minutes a tall blanket-wrapped Navaho stepped out to survey us with evident astonishment. Arthur greeted him in Navaho, "*Hah La Tse Kis*," and then asked if we might come into his hogan. Without answering he turned and disappeared behind the door-blanket. When he returned, his wife was with him and it was evident that she must make the decision as the hogan was her property. She was a substantial woman of about forty-five, with shrewd black eyes and a generous mouth.

Again Arthur asked for shelter and had an immediate answer,

The water supply brought for a Navaho ceremony.

Occasionally a hogan is built of squared logs, like the one here with Arvil Witt standing at the door.

for she had seen that I held a baby in my arms and this was no night for a woman with a baby to be out in the storm. Holding the blanket to one side, she motioned me to enter, saying, as I climbed out of the car, "*Hucko, hucko, toadeena,*" meaning for me to hurry as the dust was drifting into the hogan. I was only too glad to hasten inside and drop the shawl I had been holding to protect Lynette and myself. I nearly fell as I stepped over the doorsill, as the inside floor was fully fourteen inches lower than the outside ground level. It was fairly light in the hogan as a cheerful fire burned in the fire pit in the center of the room and someone had just added splinters of dry pine, possibly to get a better look at the unexpected visitors. I heard Arthur ask the man where he should put the car for the night, then I was shown a pile of blankets where I was to sit.

The family in the hogan consisted of the mother, whose name I later learned was Ahson Hochee, two boys who were now outside helping Arthur and their father, Hosteen Hochee, unload the car, two girls about eight and ten years of age, and an ancient grandma who sat near the fire. The floor of the hogan appeared to be round but was really eight-sided, the cedar logs that formed the sides being not more than ten feet long. The interior was larger than I had expected, being about seventeen feet in diameter, with a square smoke vent in the center of the dome-shaped roof, and a blanket-covered door at the east. The central fire pit was surrounded by flat hearth stones on which stood a large black kettle, two iron skillets, and a coffeepot. Other utensils for cooking and serving food were stored in a box-cupboard nailed to the wall. Around the walls and hanging from wooden pegs were all the family possessions. These included a couple of saddles, bridles, suitcases, many sheep pelts, blankets, and shawls—in fact, everything they considered essential for family comfort. Near the north wall stood a large loom which held a half-completed Navaho rug. The top of this loom was fastened to the ceiling and the lower end of the poles were buried in the floor, which was red adobe, pounded almost to the hardness of cement. This loom stood away from the wall about three and one-half feet so the weaver could work on the rug from either side.

Arthur and the Navaho men brought everything from the car, even the two seat cushions, the canteens of gas and water, and the towropes. Our lunch boxes, thermoses, bags, blankets, and canvas made a large pile just inside the door, and if the family was curious as to the contents they gave no such indication. In fact they accepted our presence in their dwelling as though entertaining white guests was a daily occurrence.

When Arthur entered the hogan and was seated on a folded sheep pelt, Ahson asked if we were hungry, and would we care for coffee and corncakes. It would not be good manners to refuse so Arthur told her that we were not hungry but would enjoy a cup of hot coffee. The coffeepot was placed on a bed of glowing coals, and soon enamel cups of scalding brew were passed to everyone except little Lynette. I rummaged in the lunch box and handed Ahson a small can of condensed milk, which she opened with a large butcher knife.

Now there were questions and answers: "Where were we from? Why did we come? Was the road very bad? Who were the Navahos near our post?" And so on they went. Every time the two girls looked at Lynette they burst into giggles and were shushed by their mother. This was the first time they had ever seen a baby with curly hair, and Lynette's soft brown curls, after being covered so many hours, were plastered tight to her head like a cap. They thought perhaps the wind had twisted her hair into loops and it would straighten out when it was combed. Then Arthur thoughtlessly ran his fingers through his hair and it fell back in tight curls. The girls laughed so hard they were ashamed and hid themselves behind the loom, to escape a reprimand from their mother.

At any other time I would have enjoyed asking questions and listening to family history for I was sure Grandma was one of the "Old Ones" who had gone on the "long walk" when the soldiers had taken the Navaho tribe to the Bosque Redondo. I was equally sure that Hosteen Hochee was an important medicine man in this community as I had noticed dried herbs and medicine bundles hanging from the ceiling. But I was fairly numb with fatigue and could think of nothing but fixing a bed for the baby and a pallet for myself. The north side of any hogan is generally reserved for the women, and this was no exception. I asked Arthur to tie one side of the canvas to the loom post and the other to the doorframe so as to provide the baby and me a nook in which to sleep. I knew the two girls spread their bedding behind the loom and grandma slept near them, so the north side was a long, narrow bedroom. Arthur brought one of the car seats inside this nook and tucked the bottom of the canvas under it. This, with my folded shawl and a small pillow, made a very comfortable bed for Lynette. All of our bags, boxes, and thermoses were placed in the narrow upper end where I could reach them if I needed milk for the baby in the night. Ahson handed me a large, heavily fleeced sheep pelt, which I folded lengthwise and placed between the baby's bed and the wall. Then I removed my shoes and my dress, pinning it to the canvas partition, and after applying cold cream to our wind-blistered faces, I wrapped the army blanket around me, fluffed the pillow, and stretched out with one arm over Lynette's covers. No bed of rose petals or of eider down was ever more acceptable and I was asleep before I had finished my prayers.

I awoke two or three times during the night, but only long enough to see that Lynette was covered and to change position. With the first morning light slanting through the roof opening, I sat up listening to the quiet movements of the family and wondering why it was so still. Then I realized that the wind had ceased to blow and the morning was beautifully calm. "What a relief," I thought as I lay back on my pillow for a moment; then Lynette pushed her blanket aside and sat up. The breakfast aromas of coffee and hot panbread made me realize that it was time to be up, so I reached for the thermos of water, the soap, and towels. When I had sponged and dressed Lynette and fixed her bottle, I removed some of the dust from my own person and donned my shoes and dress. I had opened the second quart of milk, and now I was worried for fear the milk supply would not last until we reached home.

With Lynette in my arms, I pushed aside the canvas and said "Good Morning" to the family. Five men, including Arthur and the two boys, were sitting in a half-circle, enjoying roasted mutton ribs, hot panbread, and coffee. Shema was patting dough into flat, round cakes and Ahson was sitting near the fire frying them in a skillet of hot grease. The two girls looked at Lynette and again burst into laughter as her wet hair was curled tighter than ever. I handed the baby to one of the girls. They were happy to hold her, as they wished to see if they could straighten her hair and great was their glee when the soft brown locks coiled around their fingers. I went to our food box to get a box of cookies to add to the meal, then I sat down to wait for breakfast. This was not served until the men had finished and had left the hogan. Perhaps they did not wish the men to know that they had saved the best ribs for themselves, anyway there was much laughter when I gave them sugar for their coffee and a can of peaches, the general attitude being that "what the men didn't know wouldn't hurt them" and no one was going to tell them what they had missed.

By the time I had finished my breakfast and had packed our belongings, the car was ready to go. Arthur had pulled the torn fabric of the top forward over the frame, tying it there with twine and wire. It was an odd looking top, but it would provide us with some shelter from the sun on our homeward trip. We shook hands with the Hochee family and said goodbye with all the warmth of long-established friendship. Arthur offered to pay for our night's lodging, but Ahson shook her head in refusal, so I gave her everything from my lunch box except the milk and a couple of oranges.

It was a short ride to the Red Rock Trading Post and we were glad to see horses tied to the hitch-rail and Navahos walking about. Mr. Stallings was in the store and was surprised to see white people so early in the day. He had returned early that morning but his wife and family had stayed in Fruitland. Arthur told him the purpose of our visit and the two men went into the rug room to look at saddle blankets. I wandered about inside the store, interested in the trade goods on the shelves and in the jewelry in the display cases. At the further end of the long room were the heavy articles—the saddles, leather, harness parts, hardware, and implements. Then came a small section holding skillets, enamel dishes, and household articles. The central shelves held groceries with emphasis on canned peaches and tomatoes, plug tobacco, boxed cookies, and crackers. The nearer end held dry goods, bolts of white duck, calico, sateen, and beautiful shades of velveteen. There was one shelf of expensive Pendleton shawls, and another of heavy shoes for all ages, men's shirts, Levis, and sheepskin-lined jackets. On the shelf above this were large, felt sugar-loaf hats, much prized by the men of this section.

This arrangement of trade goods was only slightly different from that of our own post, although the emphasis here seemed to be on clothing for men, while our grocery department was larger and carried a greater variety of canned goods, fruit, and smoked meats. As I went back to the car I saw the men approaching with arms loaded with rugs. Arthur had bought six red, white, and black saddle blankets and two much larger rugs with unusual designs. These were all folded and placed on the back seat, then covered with the canvas to protect them from the dust. We said goodbye to Mr. Stallings and crossed the arroyo, which now was almost blocked with sand. The road was no better going home than it had been coming, but now we could see the ruts and the sand traps and could manage to avoid the worst places.

Arthur still lacked two blankets to fill the Vermont order, and so he decided to stop at the Tocito Trading Post to see what Mr. Foutz might have. While Arthur was in the store, I carried Lynette to the top of a small knoll that held the hot spring for which the post was named. At first we saw no water, then it rose slowly in the crater and boiled over the rim to form two small streams on the north side. I had been told that years ago it had spouted up as high as a man's head and the water had been steaming hot. But my informant said its spirit was growing old and feeble now so that it barely came over the rim. I never knew just what minerals it contained, but it was evident that the whole knoll had been formed by lime and other minerals deposited by the water.

Arthur secured the two saddle blankets he needed and there were no more stops before arriving at our own post. Billy Yazzi was glad to see us and reported little damage from the wind. The cornstalk roof of the cow shed had almost entirely disappeared and a few of my largest hens were missing, but this was not as bad as we had anticipated. It was wonderful to be safely at home again, although every article in our four-room home was covered with layers and layers of adobe dust. When I thought of all the dishes to be taken from the cupboards and washed I refused to agree with the statement of an elderly friend, "There is nothing cleaner than dust blown from a long distance!" Well perhaps it carried no germs, but it still looked like dirt to me.

In accordance with his promise, Arthur shipped the second bale of ten saddle blankets in less than ten days. I would have enjoyed sending a history of the purchase of these last ten with them but doubt if anyone would have put much credence in my story. Probably those who received the blankets would always believe that the Newcomb Trading Post was a Navaho rug factory that could put out twenty hand-woven saddle blankets in ten days.

8
Laura Thapaha

IN THE HISTORIES of all nations and tribes of people, there are certain years that encompass events, either tragic or momentous, which cause that year to stand as a marker on time's calendar. For the Navaho Indians and all other inhabitants of the Reservation, 1919 will always stand as a year of tragedy. That was the year of the great epidemic of influenza that swept across the whole United States and proved especially disastrous to the Indians. Government reports state that one-fifth of the Navaho tribe perished during the winter months, but we who lived on the Reservation were sure that the percentage was much higher. The government could make an estimate of the loss of human lives, but no estimate or accounting could ever be kept to list the children who had been orphaned, the destitute mothers of small children, and the aged invalids left without family or support.

Missionaries, welfare workers, and traders worked tirelessly to bring order out of despair; to collect the orphans and place them in government boarding schools; to take invalids to hospitals; and to provide food and medicines for the destitute. But the task of making permanent adjustment was accomplished by the Navahos themselves. One Navaho mother adopted her sister's four children, which increased her family to nine; Klah's sister took the five children of her oldest daughter; another family opened its doors to a crippled brother and his two small boys. And so the adjustments were made and there was a new sense of tribal unity and efficiency.

Before the flu epidemic Laura, her mother, father, grandmother, two sisters, and three brothers lived in a cluster of round log hogans near Black Rock Spring, about a mile east of our post. The father owned a few acres of cornland, a small flock of sheep, and also several ponies. Laura's mother was a good weaver and, with Grandma to do the spinning, she could earn a fair income so the family lived comfortably but with little to spare. Naltsos, the oldest son, was seventeen that year and we hired him to bring our mail from Tohatchi, a distance of forty-five miles. He made the ride once each week, allowing two days to go and another two days to return, then a three-day rest for the pony. In winter it generally took six days instead of four; in either season we received our mail once each week. Betsy, the oldest girl, had attended boarding school and spoke English fairly well. She helped her mother with the weaving and the care of the baby who was just learning to walk when the flu arrived in our valley. I did not know Laura as I had seen her only on occasions when she came to the store with her mother. She was slimmer than most Navaho children of nine and her eyes were larger, with a velvety brownness that caused me to name her "Pretty Girl" long before the school gave her an English name.

During February of 1919, the flu spread like wildfire across the Navaho Reservation, and no one could keep track of the stricken families. This epidemic had struck the towns around us in the fall of 1918 and many of them had been put under quarantine, so it did not reach us until a few months later. I had been in hopes it would miss our valley entirely, but it came when our winter weather was at its very worst and when Navaho food supplies were at their lowest. Rain, sleet, and ice had covered the grazing areas and the wind seemed to come from the arctic regions.

Klah had been on a trip to Durango, Colorado, during two weeks in September, and when he stepped off the stage and staggered into the trading post, we knew that he was a very sick man. We asked him to stay with us but he wished to go to his own home where he had herbs to make brews for his own cure. He said he knew what it was because there had been an epidemic of this same sickness forty years before and his grandfather had died of it. Arthur packed a box of groceries for him and took him home in our car, then drove to the hogan where Klah's sister lived to tell her he was ill. We did not see him for a couple of weeks but the relatives assured us that he was recovering. So when this epidemic made its appearance on the Reservation in February, he was not afraid of it. He gathered his family and members of his clan into neighboring hogans where he could visit them every day. His treatment was simple but quite effective as his was the only family in all that section that did not suffer heavy losses, the only fatality being Althbah's baby, which was about five weeks old. Klah did not come to the post during the weeks the epidemic was raging, but he had given me the powdered roots of quinine and sassafras to make the bitter tonic he used for all his patients, and he had given me an herb fumigant to sprinkle on the open fire. These I used faithfully and also changed our menu to corn bread, goat's milk, and fruit as I was much too frightened to disobey his orders. My housemaid, Louise Bicenti, my baby, and I came through without even a cold, but Arthur had come into contact with influenza in the store and was ill for ten days.

    The history of Laura's family through this bitter winter was told to me by Mr. Brink, the resident missionary who lived near the Toadlena school, and by Laura herself some years later. It seems that Laura's father had left about Christmas time to look for work in some of the little towns along the San Juan River. As he never returned, it was thought that he was one of the many who died during the epidemic and were hastily buried without identification. The baby girl came down with it first and was buried in a cliff crevice high on the east side of Rock Mesa. Her body was wrapped in a blanket, along with her toys and extra clothing, then pushed far back into the crevice and a wall of stones erected in front of it. The weather had turned bitter cold with frequent storms of sleet which covered everything with ice. The tasks of bringing wood and water to the hogan and of caring for the sheep were exhausting. Naltsos saddled his pony and started on his trip to Tohatchi for the mail, but must have stopped at Sheep Springs to water his horse, as his body was found on the bank near the spring. Betsy became delirious and wandered away from the hogan but her footsteps led her across the ridge and into the valley where Klah was making daily visits. He saw her wandering about, took her into a warm hogan, and made her drink herb tea. She recovered from her illness but when she was well enough to walk about, her family had disappeared.

Grandma was taken sick next and realized that she had only a short time to live. She and Laura's mother walked to the cave where the baby was buried and took down the stone wall. Then Grandma wrapped her shawl about her and lay down beside the child, with only a bowl of water and a few corncakes near her hand. Laura's mother rebuilt the wall of rocks and went home, leaving her mother in her last resting place. There were only four of the family left in the hogan now—Laura, the two small boys, and the mother. The mother, who had been going without food in order to give the children the little there was, awoke one morning so sick and dizzy she could not rise from her pallet. She told Laura to get the old gray horse that never wandered far from the spring, put on its saddle and all the blankets the children had used for bedding, and then to make a package of cornbread to take with her. Then she was to put the two boys, aged six and four, on the horse, close the hogan door, fasten it with the leather thongs, and pile all the poles and loose brush she could find against the outside; then they were to ride to the home of the missionary.

Laura did everything exactly as her mother directed, crying silently as she did so, for she knew she would never see her mother again. The three children arrived at the home of the missionary late that night and were taken in, fed, and put to bed on cots they kept handy for just such emergencies. The next day the missionary and his Navaho helper went to the hogan and gave the mother a Christian burial and then burned the hogan. A passing horseman told them of seeing the body of Naltsos lying near the spring so they drove to that place and performed the same service for him. In spite of months of contact with sick Indians, burying the dead, carrying some patients to the hospitals and others to their relatives, these two devoted men never contracted the flu. The missionary said, "We were too busy to be sick, but we never stopped praying."

As soon as transportation could be arranged, Laura and her brothers were sent to the Episcopal orphanage, the Good Shepherd Mission, near Fort Defiance. The next fall Laura was sent to the Indian boarding school at Phoenix but the two boys were kept at the orphanage until little Stephen was six and Stanley was eight. I had named the two boys when Stephen was about two and just learning to walk. He had stubbed his toe and had fallen into his mother's cooking fire, burning one arm from wrist to elbow, and the hand with which he had grasped a glowing coal was charred so deep that the tendons and one bone could be seen. It was a terrible burn and when they brought him to me, I decided to keep him for a while so I could change dressings often. In order that he would not become lonesome and cry in the night, I asked to keep his brother also, and that was when I had given them their names. In the long run, it was not my salves and unguents that cured the burn, but some mush-poultices of pounded and boiled seeds that Klah brought for me to use. This may have been flaxseed or it may have been seeds from any number of plants that grew on the dessert or the mountain. Anyway there was only a thin scar in later years.

It was six or seven years before I saw Laura again. Then one late afternoon in April an Indian school bus from Phoenix, Arizona, stopped in front of the store and four teen-age girls descended, were handed their suitcases and other possessions, after which the bus turned around and drove away in the direction from which it had come. We had been expecting these girls as we had received a letter from the Phoenix Indian Agency saying that four girls were being sent to their homes as they had contracted tuberculosis and the school had no facilities for their care. It had also asked us to notify their parents of their expected arrival so they would be met by relatives at our trading post.

This we had done and now there were many Navaho men and women standing outside the door waiting to greet the four girls.

Klizhin, his wife, and four children put their arms lovingly around Nell, took her suitcase and bundles, and guided her to their wagon, not wishing others to witness their emotion. Several of the Allemigo family gathered around Rosalie to welcome her arrival, while others were clustering about Betty Nez, but there were only two to greet Laura, although Klah and his sister stood by to take her home if there had been no one. Her grandparents on her father's side were there to offer her a home. Grandma and Grandfather Grayhair had a hogan and a few acres of land just across the arroyo to the north, and we employed him as the choreboy and handyman around the store. Grandma was known as an excellent weaver and was especially good at spinning fine yarn, so she was employed by many busy Navaho housewives to spin the yarn they needed for their weaving. Their hogan was small and I wondered where Laura would sleep, so when the others had taken their departure I had a chance to talk to her. I told her that we had a small bedroom back of the kitchen that she could occupy if she wished to stay with us. But she decided to go with her grandparents at least for awhile and so her grandfather picked up her suitcase and they walked across the bridge and into the sunny cornfields.

These four Navaho girls had all been kept at the Phoenix Boarding School two years after their formal education had been completed, on the pretext of giving them partial manual training. They worked in the laundry, the bakery, the sewing room, and they continuously scrubbed walls, floors, toilets, windows, and stairs. The school management did not wish to let these girls go as they were better workers and were more dependable than the Pimas or the Papagoes. However, the climate and the low altitude did not agree with Navaho lungs and all four picked up tuberculosis germs, but still they were not sent home to the high, clean mountain air of the Reservation.

Then Nell, who was working in a basement laundry room, gave birth to a baby and, with Rosalie's help, killed it by hitting its head with the heel of her shoe; then she carefully hid it under piles of soiled bedding. The school matron found it and sent Nell to the hospital, but too much damage had been done and Nell had only a short time to live. By this time Rosalie and Betty were hemorrhaging occasionally and so, as the school did not wish the records of their deaths on their books, it was decided to send them home. When Laura heard that her three friends were leaving, she was panic-stricken. The Navaho girls had banded together against the sly persecution of the many girls of other tribes, and Laura could not face the situation alone. She refused to eat and became so weak that she fainted while scrubbing the dormitory stairs, so the matron asked that she be sent back home with the other three, as a sick girl would not be of much use anyway.

Nell died two weeks after her return, and Betty lived two months, but Rosalie lingered on until nearly Christmas time. I asked her mother how she was, and was told that she was too weak to walk and knew she was dying. She was not afraid to die but she was crying continuously because she wished to be buried in a coffin and not in a wrapping of blankets. Arthur told Ahson Allemigo to tell Rosalie not to cry, that she would have a coffin. It was a very stormy winter and the mountain roads were hazardous, but we went to Toadlena to ask at the carpenter shop for wide boards with which to make the box. The shop was bare of any kind of boards, but three of the employees volunteered to go to the government sawmill high on the mountain near the rimrocks, start the engine, and saw the required boards. The sawmill road was blocked with snow but the Indians had kept a narrow trail open, so the men went on horseback.

They were gone three days and at the end of that time the boards were ready to tie together and skid down the mountain trail. At the shop the carpenters fitted the boards together to make a coffin, which was painted white, then padded and lined with white outing flannel from the school commissary. The next day a team was hitched to a long, homemade sled, which took the box to a place near the Allemigo home, and Rosalie was told that it was there. Perhaps she had been waiting for this news, for she died the next day and was placed in the coffin, which was then sledded to the Toadlena cemetery.

Laura remained with her grandparents during the summer months while they were living on the mountains and also when they returned to the cornfields in the fall, as they needed her help in the work of gathering the harvest of corn, beans, squash, and melons. But when the nights were growing cold and a scum of ice covered the pond, she decided to live with us. Dorcas Morieto had been my housekeeper for more than a year and lived near enough to spend the nights in her own home. When a new day school was built near Crownpoint, Dorcas and her husband were hired as matron and caretaker, so late in August they moved to this new school. Laura came to live with us in September and was a member of our family for three years. She was quick and efficient with the housework and was also a good interpreter when I took her on my trips to the various Navaho ceremonies, but she was more interested in the Navaho way of living. She realized that she had been away from her own people so long that she had forgotten how they earned a living, or how they cooked their food, or managed their households. So, as soon as her work was finished in the afternoons, she would walk to her grandmother's hogan where she was learning to card and spin the wool for weaving a rug. Or she went to the home of some neighbor to watch them grind the corn for *tortillas* or corncakes. There was much for her to learn and she wished to be as proficient as the girls who had not been so long at boarding school.

One day in mid-January, as she was helping me prepare our noonday meal, she said, "There is going to be a moccasin game in the cornfield tonight. Do you think you would like to go?" I had heard of moccasin games ever since I had been on the Reservation but I had never been invited to attend one. My Navaho friends knew that I was interested in any religious gatherings and to these I was invited, but a moccasin game was quite different, being to the Navahos much the same as bingo is to white people. All of the missionaries who had lived on the Reservation had made some attempt to discourage Navaho gambling and games of chance, but to the

Navahos there was no point in playing a game unless there was something to be won.

During the long, cold months of January and February not many ceremonies were held, but groups gathered in the larger hogans to listen to long legends as related by some elderly person who had gained a reputation as a storyteller. And sometimes a group of men would gather to chant ceremonial songs so the younger men and boys could learn the old chants. But most frequent of all were the groups who met to play games. In the olden days, there were many games of dice played in different ways, since sometimes the dice were made of small, square stones and sometimes from flattened sticks. Most of these dice games were now forgotten and only two remained in common use, for both men and women. One of these was known as "Guess the Number," and in this forty-eight marked sticks were used. Sides were chosen, and the side that held the sticks hid a certain number; then, after being given a quick glance at the remaining sticks, the opposite side tried to guess the number of those that had been hidden.

The other game called, "Hide the Ball" was also known as the moccasin game. In playing this game, four, tall, red deer-hide moccasins are buried in a long pile of loose sand with only about four inches of their tops showing. Players are divided into two groups and a coin is tossed to see which side will be first to hide the ball, which is generally an agate not much more than an inch in diameter. A blanket is held in front of the line of shoes while the ball is being hidden and then the shoes are loosely filled with sand. When the blanket is taken away, the members of the other side approach and examine the shoes and then retire for consultation. A choice is made and one man is given a stick or cane with which he hits the shoe decided upon. Immediately the shoe is taken up and the sand emptied. If the stone is inside, the guessing side wins a certain number of counters; if it is not, they have three more chances before sides are changed. There are 102 counters that must be won by one side before the game ends. Some nights there are no winners and then the game continues through the next night since it cannot be played in the daytime. It was supposed to have been originated by the birds who fly at night playing against the birds that fly during the day. If the night birds won there would be no day, while if the day birds won there would be no night. After four nights of playing, the counters were about evenly divided and so each twenty-four hours was divided into day and night. Because of the criticism the Navahos had received over playing this game they seldom invited a white person to attend or even told them when one was to take place.

I asked Laura where the game was being held that night and she said, "In Nethie Shorty's hogan, which is the largest of any in the cornfields."

"I do not believe they will let us in, and anyway we are not invited," I objected.

"Oh, yes, you are!" she replied. "I asked if I could come and bring you and Mr. Newcomb with me and Nethie said she'd be glad if you would come."

I laughed, as it was evident that she wished to go and knew we would not allow her to go alone. "Well, we will see what Mr. Newcomb has to say." Then I went into the kitchen and baked an extra-large batch of fat, molasses cookies.

While we were eating our evening meal I asked Arthur if he would care to attend a moccasin game that evening. His answer was, "Well, why not! It might be amusing." If we were going I wanted to know a little more about what we might expect and so, while Laura was washing the dishes, I went into the store and asked one of the older Indians what would be the proper course of procedure for white guests who wished to take part in the game. I was told that each should have a coin ready to pay our hosts as an entrance fee, and that we should take either money or a piece of silver jewelry to place as a bet that our side would win. They did not need to tell me that any gift of food would be welcome as this month was the "Hunger Moon" both for the flocks, which were now living on dry cornstalks or drifted tumbleweed, and for the Nav-

A summer, open-faced shelter near the cornfields, with Hosteen and Ahson Morieto.

Baking bread on a cold morning. This hogan was built extra-large for a Mountain Chant. The logs were set upright and then plastered with adobe.

aho people—many of whom were thankful to have a handful of parched corn as their day's fare. Hunger and privation was the heritage from all past ages and could be endured with fortitude, for there was always the next autumn, with its feasts of corn and mutton, to which they could look forward. It was the multitude of ills, such as tuberculosis, diphtheria, smallpox, measles, whooping cough, flu, and whisky, which had arrived with the coming of the white man that brought death to the body and spirit of the Navaho and from which they had no immunity.

Darkness arrives early at this time of year, and by seven o'clock the three of us were in the car and on our way to the hogan which was two miles from our post. As we approached, we could see by starlight a number of horses standing here and there around the hogan, so we knew that many of the players had arrived before us. We each had a quarter to pay the entrance fee, and Arthur had a number of silver dollars jingling in his pocket for the bets, while I had a silver bracelet, and Laura had a ring set with turquoise.

Our entrance into the hogan was no surprise as Keedah had told them we were coming, so we paid our fee and were told to draw sticks to determine which side we would be playing with. Laura and I drew one side and Arthur drew the other. Then we handed our bets to the man in charge of the game and watched as he put them in a sack with the others, tied the sack, and buried it at the end of the mound of sand. Placing a blanket over the spot he proceeded to sit on it. I smiled a little at these elaborate precautions to insure the safety of the bets. There seemed to be no hurry about getting on with the game; perhaps they were waiting for latecomers so there would be no interruptions. After a time of visiting, with many jokes and much laughter, the shoes were buried in the long mound of sand and a blanket was held in front of them while one group placed the ball well down in a toe, then filled all of the shoes with sand. As soon as the man started to hide the ball, the chant began, as the Navahos do not enjoy carrying on any community labor or entertainment in silence and all activities have prayer chants to accompany them. There are more than forty-eight chants that may be sung while the moccasin game is in progress. Most of these are dedicated to the spirits of the bird-people who originated the game and are supplications for luck to attend the side that is doing the chanting.

When the blanket was taken away, the members of the other group examined the shoes saying: "It's in this one," or "It's in that one." Finally, when several had decided on one shoe, the leader hit that shoe with a short stick. The shoe was removed and the sand shaken out to prove that the ball was not there, so the guessers lost five points. Then the blanket was again held up, the shoes were placed in different positions, and again our side selected a shoe. This time we won and our side was given a number of counters. I did not see how it could be possible for either side to win, as the counters were handed back and forth, but I was informed that soon someone would have a run of luck in which the counters would all come to one side, and then the game would be finished for that night. This did not happen while we were there and after one o'clock, when Nethie and her sister served us with hot coffee and the molasses cookies I had brought, we decided it was time to go home. Why anyone, even a missionary, would seek to abolish such a quiet and well-regulated form of entertainment was a mystery to both Arthur and me.

Laura spent the next year partly with us and partly with her grandmother, learning to string the warp on the loom and then to weave in the woof to make a Navaho blanket. Late that fall she brought us a small three by five foot rug and wanted me to keep it as a present because it was the first rug she had completed all by herself. I was glad to keep it but insisted on paying her the regular price a blanket of that size would bring. She took the money to buy more wool and immediately started work on another rug, and I knew that someday she would become an excellent weaver, able to earn her living with the craft that was a recognized accomplishment of her people.

The next autumn I decided to spend the school year in Long

Beach where Lynette could attend secondary school and have the advantages of music lessons and other activities not possible on the Reservation, and Laura went to live with her grandparents. When we returned in the spring we found she had married Tom Sherman and had a hogan of her own on a small plot of corn land given her by her grandfather. Tom did occasional odd jobs for the day school at Newcomb and Laura kept busy weaving rugs to exchange for their groceries. After little Lauretta was born, I kept a crib ready for her and Laura brought her every morning when she came to help with my housework. We had a high chair for her and often kept her for two or three days when Laura was working in the fields. Lauretta was two years old when we again left the Reservation to be near a good secondary school, and when we returned Laura was expecting another child. She still came to work for me at times and often brought little Lauretta to stay with us for several days at a time, as Laura was finding it difficult to work and buy the right things for the child to eat.

One day Laura looked so drawn and worn, I asked if she would let me take her to the hospital at Shiprock, but she did not wish to go and said she would be all right in a few days. Then Arthur's mother came to spend a few weeks with us and one morning I asked if she would like to go for an auto ride. She enjoyed riding around the Reservation to see the Indians at work, so she, the two girls, and I started out across the cornfields. I had not seen Laura for a week so I decided to pause at her hogan to ask how she was getting along. She saw us coming and came across the irrigation ditch to greet us. She said, "I am glad to see you. I was going to send my grandfather to ask you to take me to the hospital."

It seems that her grandmother wanted her to go, as she was afraid to have the baby born at home, so I said, "I'll be glad to take you. When do you wish to go?"

She answered, "Today."

I was surprised and thought a moment and then said, "If Mother will take care of my girls and the house, I will take you today."

Arthur's mother said she would be glad to be of any assistance possible. So I said, "All right. Get your suitcase and shawl and get into the car."

It took her only a short time to dress and pack the things she would take, then we returned to the post where we left the car at the gas pump to be serviced, and I carried Lauretta into the house. She would be happy with Lynette who loved taking care of her. I put on a suit, selected a scarf for my head, then made a box of sandwiches and filled a thermos with hot coffee. It was then eleven o'clock and I expected to be in Shiprock for our evening meal.

The forty-five mile trail to Shiprock was just a winding dirt road with some sandy stretches and three deep arroyos with trickles of water in the bottoms, which were always something of a problem. One was never sure that the car would be able to pull itself up the opposite bank. It was a slow and bumpy trip but we were in front of the hospital before sundown. A couple of nurses came to help Laura up the long steps to the door. As she reached the top Laura turned and said, "Thank you, Shema! I am certainly glad to get here."

I told her that I would see her in the morning before I went home, and then I drove to the little hotel.

The next morning after I paid my bill and had the car filled with gas and water, I drove to the hospital. I stopped at the desk and asked the nurse, "How is Laura this morning?"

She looked at me with a smile and said, "Laura is fine, and so are the twins."

"Twins!" I gasped, and my knees shook so that I collapsed into the nearest chair. "When were they born?"

"About twelve o'clock last night," was the reply. I was simply speechless. Laura must have been holding on with all her might during that long, bumpy ride from the post. What if we had stalled in one of the arroyos. How could I have coped with twins? My heart thumped painfully.

"May I see them?"

"You can look through the glass at the twins," she replied. "But

Laura has been given a sleeping tablet and will sleep most of the day."

They took me down the hall and I peered through the glass at two small, white bundles with incredibly wrinkled faces, and again I felt almost too wobbly to stand upright. As I turned away I said to the nurse, "You will never know how thankful I am that they are here in those clean, white beds, for it just might have happened in the car." "How long will you keep them here?" I inquired.

"We expect to keep them about three or four weeks," she informed me, "until we are sure that she will be able to care for both of them." And I thought to myself, "They will be well cared for and well fed for four weeks and that should give them a good start."

9
Election Day at the Trading Post

OBJECTS IN THE SQUARE, low-ceilinged, log trading post were rapidly growing dim as the short November twilight faded into night. I spoke to the two customers who were standing near the glowing, round-oak heater, "It is dark in here. Wait just a moment and I will light the lamps." Taking a handful of matches, I climbed onto the high counter and, after several attempts, succeeded in lighting the swaying kerosene lamps that hung from the hand-hewn log rafters. In the flickering glow, the shelves with their neat bolts of calico and velveteen lost their horizontal rigidity and assumed more comfortable positions. The gay wrappers on the cans of tomatoes, peaches, and beans, and the bright cloud of kerchiefs hanging in the corner, the tiers of striped shirts, and the Pendleton shawls appeared quite sober and subdued. Along the walls the dark wavering shadows of the water kegs, the cooking utensils, and the bulky saddles, which hung from the ceiling rafters, gave the trade room an animated and rather ghostly atmosphere. There was never much light in the low-ceilinged trade room, but in summer the door was open to add to the light admitted by two small, heavily-barred windows. Now, in early winter, the lamps must be lighted almost before the sun had set and even then the corners were in darkness.

"I can take care of you now," I said in Navaho. "What will you have?" I had hoped to be through with the trade before this hour of the afternoon, but there were still two plump Navaho matrons with three small children, waiting to exchange bundles of dry pelts for groceries and household supplies. Pelts and hides of sheep,

Election Day at the Trading Post

goats, and sometimes of cattle constituted one of the lesser sources of Navaho income and were generally brought to the store by the women to be exchanged for groceries. In fair weather they were dry and stiff and not too hard to handle, but during a stormy period they came to the store limp and bloody, with an odor quite beyond description. Wet or dry, I found weighing and stacking these pelts an unpleasant part of trading.

Hurriedly weighing the pelts on the wareroom scales, I tossed them into a corner and returned to the cash drawer to count out each woman's pay in nickels and dimes. Ordinarily a Navaho customer ponders at length before making even a five-cent purchase, but tonight there was no delay. Flour, sugar, coffee, bacon, canned tomatoes, tobacco, and candy were quickly purchased, divided, and tied in separate flour sacks to make two long bundles that could be strapped to the backs of the high saddles. There was no time spent in pricing the goods or indulging in neighborhood gossip. To their way of thinking, it was not wise to be too far from home when the long shadows of night came creeping over the land. Only owls, bats, and coyotes cared to wander about after the sun had set.

In Navaho legends, the spirits of evil never roamed about to do their mischief in the bright light of the sun. But as soon as the sun's face was hidden behind the western mountains, these "Chindees" emerged from their hiding places and wandered along the paths and trails seeking any belated traveler. Unfortunate indeed, was any Navaho whose path they crossed, as he would become subject to fainting spells and epileptic seizures or he might develop some mental disorder.

As the solid plank door slammed shut behind the retreating backs of my customers, I drew a long breath of relief. Now I could close the store for the night and turn my attention to my baby and to my neglected house. Little Lynette, not quite a year old, was fussing for her supper, bath, and bed; the housework had received no attention since early morning; and the outdoor chores were waiting, as the horse and chickens must be fed and the cow must be milked and shut in her shed. It would be hours before I could call my day's work completed.

Early that morning, after doing the chores at the barn and bringing our daily supply of wood, coal, and water, my husband Arthur had eaten a hurried breakfast and then filled the car with gas, oil, and water before starting on a trip of eighty-five miles to the county seat. It was the first Tuesday after the first Monday in November and he wished to reach the courthouse in the town of Aztec in time to cast a vote for Woodrow Wilson. For although our post was on a U.S. Reservation, we held the status of New Mexico residents. The first forty-five miles of the road he would travel boasted no bridges over the deep arroyos and no smooth asphalt to cover the patches of drifting sand. If the car did not develop engine trouble or if an axle did not break on some steep grade, he would arrive at the county seat around the noon hour. After voting, the afternoon would be spent buying and loading the car with trade goods and visiting with other traders who were in town to cast their votes, so I did not expect him home until well past midnight.

All day long I had endeavored to wait on the customers who came to the store, also to attend to Lynette's needs, and keep the fires burning in the round, oak heater and in the two fireplaces that heated the house. It had been a long, lonesome day, as I was not accustomed to being alone with the care of the post. Generally there was a Navaho girl helping in the house and a handy man in the store. But this week Keedah had gone to attend a "sing" held over his sister and Esther had gone to the Mission School at Ganada to enter classes for nurse's training. Now as day faded into darkness, I was glad to be finished with the work in the store. Walking around the high counter, I was about to raise the long, iron bar with which the door was bolted at night and slide it into the slots when slowly the heavy door swung open.

There, on the threshold, not more than three feet away stood the largest and ugliest Indian I had ever seen. His huge, blanket-

Election Day at the Trading Post

wrapped figure filled the entire doorway, but I glanced through the window and saw a small car parked by the metal barrel that served as a gas tank. He was not a Navaho and noting the two long braids that hung over his shoulders, I knew he must be either Ute or Apache. In the wavering light of the swinging lamps, his pockmarked face and crafty, hooded eyes might have belonged to some medieval ogre. For a moment my heart seemed to stand still and the blood in my veins turned to ice. All the tales I had ever heard of the cruelty of the Utes and the Apaches crowded into my mind. Stark terror must have been written on my face, but luckily it was too dark for the stranger to observe my expression. In the five years we had lived on the Reservation, I had never had the slightest reason to be afraid of any of the Indians I had met. In fact Arthur and I both felt that we were protected by a surrounding wall of friendly people. But this feeling of friendship did not include the Utes or the Apaches, whose Reservations were north of us.

After the first minutes of stunned silence, I found my voice. "What do you want?" I asked, and was surprised that my voice was so calm.

"My car—no gas. Where your man?" The Indian stumbled into the store as he spoke, and with him came the sour smell of bootleg whisky, which did little to allay my fears. He gave me an ugly glance and then let his eyes roam over the trade room, seeming to miss no smallest detail.

I never should have allowed him to come inside the store, and now I thought, "He is still half-drunk and if there is anything to be done, now is the time to do it!" The iron bar, which I held in my hands, was long and heavy. "Shall I try to hit him with this?" I thought. "Or perhaps I can push him back far enough so I can slam and bolt the door!" But I knew I was not strong enough to move him as much as one small inch, and any such action would only serve to make him angry.

He had asked for gas, and there was no gas. Arthur had pumped the last gallon from the iron barrel-tank that morning. If this

Indian's car was entirely out of gasoline, it certainly created a bad situation for me.

"We have no gas." I told him. "You go to the next store, they have plenty."

"Car no gas; car no go," he stated flatly. "Me stay here. Me hungry."

"I will give you something to eat," I offered. "You eat in your car. I must lock the door now."

"Not eat outside, too cold!" He walked farther into the store. "You got whisky?" His eyes were searching the shelves.

"No! we never have whisky," I told him, "but I will make you some coffee." His request for whisky had told me that his supply was exhausted and his mind would not be inflamed by further drinking. But drunk or sober I could not trust him out of my sight. The only thing that kept him from robbing the store of cash and valuables was, or so I imagined, the fact that there was no gas. He could not move his car away from the store and so he would make himself comfortable and wait until morning, as he knew there was no need of haste.

I was helpless and he knew it. He had quickly sensed that I was alone and his manner had become insolent and domineering. All I could do was to delay his coffee and supper as long as possible in hopes that my husband might come home earlier than I had expected.

"Come into the house," I said. "I will have to build a fire in the kitchen before I can get your supper." I could hear the baby crying as I closed and bolted the door, turned out the kerosene lights, and lead my unwelcome guest into the living room. Lynette's baby crib stood at one side of the deep stone fireplace, while on the other side were two deep Morris chairs. The logs and coal in the open grate had burned down to a bed of glowing coals, leaving the room in semi-darkness. With her Raggedy-Ann doll clutched tightly in her arms, Lynette watched us with round, inquiring eyes as I piled more wood on the coals and motioned my guest to a Morris chair. As he looked around the living room and saw the baby in her crib,

Election Day at the Trading Post

I think his ugly mood softened somewhat as all Indians are fond of children and Lynette's brown eyes and dark, curly hair were unusual in that region. He gazed at her tear-streaked face for a moment and then said, "She hungry. You feed. I wait!" Then he sat down heavily in the nearest chair.

Picking up the baby, I carried her into the kitchen and put her in her high chair near the table. The kitchen was dark and cold. I lighted the kerosene wall-lamp and then took kindling from the woodbox to start a fire in the range. Starr, our Jersey cow, was bawling in the corral. She was hungry and it was long past her milking time, but I dared not leave the house to do the outside chores.

Handing Lynette a Graham cracker to keep her busy until her food was warmed, I filled the teakettle, opened cans of tomatoes and sweet potatoes, put them in the oven, and set the table. From the cooler on the back porch I brought home-churned butter, cold beef, and applesauce, to which I then added thick slices of home-baked bread and a plate of cookies. I hoped my unwelcome guest was hungry and would spend a long time at the table and then perhaps he would fall asleep afterwards. I thought of taking Lynette and leaving the post while he was eating, but the nearest Navaho family lived a mile away and I could not expect any travel on the highway at this time of night. It would be better to lock and barricade the bedroom door, push the dresser in front of the window, and pray that it would not be necessary to use the pearl-handled revolver hidden behind my mirror.

He could take the money from the cashbox and whatever clothing he fancied, but what would happen when he found the five-gallon can of kerosene? Would he set fire to the store? I did not believe he would as he could gain nothing with his car out of gas.

As Lynette was finishing her mush and milk, I put the food on the table, poured a large cup of coffee, and told the Ute that his supper was ready. I heard him rise from his chair and walk across the living room. Then, just as he entered the kitchen, the opposite door that opened on the back porch swung open and there, silhouetted by the night, stood another tall, blanket-wrapped figure almost as large as the Ute and with features just as rugged and weather-beaten. But, Oh! what a friendly smile!

"Hosteen! Oh, Hosteen!" I cried. "I am so glad to see you!" I choked on the words and tried not to shed tears of relief. This was something I had never believed would happen, as Navaho families generally close their doors or their door-blankets tightly at night. There are no windows in their hogans and if travelers come or go outside, they do not see, nor do they wish to know who it may be. But Hosteen Klah was not guided by the usual superstitions as he had many prayers he could use for his protection so to him night was no more to be feared than was the day. He often walked about his home in the darkness to see that the sheep were safe in the corral or that there were no prowlers.

The presence of Hosteen Klah changed the whole situation and no angel from heaven could have been more welcome at that moment. During our five years at the trading post, Hosteen Klah and his family had been our neighbors and our best friends. He had accepted my husband as a member of his clan; he had sung the Blessing Chant over my baby when I brought her home; and now he had come to act as guard until Arthur's return. "I see car. I come!" Klah stated, and I knew that he had been aware of my husband's absence and, when he noticed that the car did not leave the post, was afraid to leave me alone with the stranger.

The crafty eyes of the Ute darted from Klah to me and back again until I could imagine he was forming some plan to dispose of both of us, and I shivered as I considered the size of the knife that I was certain was concealed beneath his blanket. Hastening to place another plate on the table and to fill another cup with coffee, I motioned the two Indians to be seated at opposite ends of the small table. Then, opening the drawer that contained my kitchen cutlery, I selected the longest, sharpest knife it contained and laid it beside Klah's plate.

"Take this," I said, "as a gift to your sister." I did not believe Klah would ever use it to harm anyone, but I knew he carried

Election Day at the Trading Post

nothing of the sort and I wanted the Ute to know he was armed. An ounce of prevention might avert a tragedy. Now that I was relieved of the responsibility of watching my unwelcome guest, I could go about my delayed chores.

Lifting Lynette from her high chair, I carried her into the bedroom, undressed her, and tucked her into sleepers, then fixed her crib for the night. A few minutes of rocking and she was fast asleep. As I went through the kitchen and out the back door, the only sounds from my guests were those of rapid and noisy eating. There would be no conversation between them until every morsel of the food I had set before them had been eaten and every brown drop had been drained from the coffeepot. On Klah's part, this was courtesy to his hostess and his way of expressing appreciation of the food that had been served; the Ute would eat heartily because he had not eaten since morning.

As I walked out of the warm kitchen, I found the night air frosty and the stars large and bright in an inky sky. A gusty north wind pushed me hurriedly along the path to the barn. I opened the corral gate and drove the cow into the shed where I could do the milking as she was eating her bran. The milk almost filled the bucket as this was well past her usual milking time and, after it was strained, I would need an extra pan to store it in the water cooler on the back porch. A measure of corn and a bucket of sour, skim milk fed the pig, then I closed and latched the chicken coop, and gathered an armful of diapers from the clothesline. I still must bring an armload of kindling for the breakfast fire, but the coal and wood that had been brought that morning would have to suffice. I had learned not to go into the coal shed in the dark as there were snakes hibernating in the crevices between the larger chunks of coal.

When I entered the house with my armload of kindling, both men were seated by the fireplace keeping close watch of each other and talking occasionally. This conversation was either in the Ute or the Apache language, neither of which I understood. As I passed near them on my way to the wareroom, I said, "We have no beds for you but there are plenty of blankets." There was no answer but the eyes of the stranger glittered evilly and I thought his lips twisted into a sneer. To me, he seemed as dangerous as a coiled rattlesnake and I wondered if Klah was carrying the knife I had given him. Then I wondered what would happen if Klah went to sleep. I resolved to remain awake to be ready for any emergency.

From the rug room I brought a number of Navaho blankets and piled them on the floor near the fire. Then going into the bedroom, I partially closed the door and took the revolver from its hiding place. Whirling the cylinder, I found that three chambers were loaded, and I decided to show the Indians that I was armed. Pulling the low, bedroom rocker into the doorway, I wrapped myself in a warm shawl and sat where I could keep watch. An hour passed and the Indians spread the rugs on the floor and seemed to sleep, but I sensed that both were awake and alert to every sound and movement. The fire died to coals and the coals turned to ash as the clock ticked away the minutes that turned into hours. My back ached and my arms grew numb, as the cold wind crept under the door and searched the cracks around the windows. But I was too tense to sleep or even become drowsy.

This was one of the few times in our years of residence on the Navaho Reservation that I realized how far we were from people of our own race, and how complete was the silence that surrounded us. I firmly resolved that never again would the baby and I be left alone at the post for any length of time. If there was a "next time" things might be worse and it was not likely there would be a friendly Navaho to come to my rescue.

It seemed that I had been sitting there forever when, from a distance, I heard the purr of a motor. Soon the garage doors slammed open and I drew a long sigh of relief. Arthur was home from the county seat.

10
Ruins and Rattlesnakes

THERE WERE TWO THINGS of widely divergent characteristics that were seemingly indigenous to our section of the Reservation and could be found almost everywhere in what I deemed to be superabundance. One was animate and the other inanimate, but neither could well be disregarded or treated with indifference. If a person traveled off the highway or away from well-traveled trails, he was sure to encounter one or the other and sometimes both together before he had gone any great distance. The ruined dwellings of a prehistoric people whom the Navahos called Anat-sazi [Old Ones] were scattered everywhere over mesa and valley, while practically every bush, gopher hole, or rock pile sheltered a family of snakes.

The Navaho Indians who shared the same terrain had long ago decided to leave these two things strictly alone and to stay as far away from them as possible. If a Navaho happened to be walking along a trail and saw a serpent on the path ahead, he stopped and waited to see what the serpent was going to do. If it did not appear to notice him, he detoured at a respectful distance, coming back to the trail farther on to continue his journey. But if the snake hissed at him or whirred his rattle, the Navaho turned and went back home as his journey would only end in bad luck if he continued. When it came to prehistoric ruins, the Indians built their hogans and mapped their trails as far away from them as possible, and no one would think of venturing near one after the sun had set. The burial mounds of the Anat-sazi were only a short distance from the tumbled walls of the houses and in many places the bones had weathered to the surface of the ground. These were supposed to be harmless in the daylight but could turn into evil spirits or Chindees at night.

Snakes were never killed, no matter how alarming the circumstances, and that was one reason why they were so numerous. I asked Klah why the Navaho men did not get together and declare war on the rattlesnakes and at least reduce their numbers somewhat. He answered, "There are many reasons why the Navahos do not kill any kind of snake, and these reasons have been handed down to us through many generations." He proceeded to relate a long list of reasons why snakes must not be killed. "In the years before the Navahos or the Pueblos had sheep, they depended on corn, beans, squash, and many wild plants for their food supply. These would all have been destroyed by the field mice, cutworms, gophers, and ground moles if there had been no snakes to keep these pests under control. The Old Ones kept snakes as pets and their progeny still inhabit the ancient ruins and the underground kivas. The snake has a powerful spirit that never dies. In the winter the snake lies cold and stiff, but when the days grow warm his spirit returns and he is alive again. The snake has command of the moisture in the ground and directs the water to the roots of the trees, shrubs, and grasses, and also to the newly-planted seeds in the fields. If the snakes were gone, the ground would become dry and hard so that nothing could grow. This has been the teaching of wise men for generations and we know it is true. You white people come from a different land and do not know the rules for this one, but it would be well if you did not kill the snakes that sometimes come around the store or all snakes will soon be against you." Some of this was self-evident and Klah believed all he had said in his effort to warn us against future bad luck.

Of course we were trying to pattern our actions to accord with the laws and traditions of the people in whose country we lived, but it was not always easy to do so. When a beady-eyed rattler stuck his head from behind a bolt of blue velveteen and challenged Arthur's right to sell a few yards for a Navaho blouse, I am afraid that Arthur forgot Klah's warning and ended the argument then

Navaho farmers build a dam in the lower cornfields.

Laura's grandmother, Ahson Greyhair, was part Pueblo.

and there. Later in the spring, when I found one in the hen house greedily devouring my tiny fluffball chicks, I picked up the hoe and chopped its head off without any qualms whatever.

We had three root cellars dug back into the mesa, roofed with dirt-covered logs and walled with unchinked stone. In one of these we had large bins for corn, oats, potatoes, apples, and other farm produce we wished to protect from frost during the winter months. The field mice and pack rats that entered through cracks in the walls played havoc with almost everything, so Arthur cut a hole in the door to permit the cat to enter at will. Things were better for awhile, until the Navaho dogs killed the cat, but still we did not have much trouble with mice or rats and we wondered what could be killing them. One day when Arthur quietly opened the cellar door, he saw a mother skunk disappearing behind a potato barrel and he had the explanation. It was several days before we could think of a way to move Mama Skunk and her four babies out of the den she had dug in the back wall without annoying her to the point of ruining our supply of apples and potatoes. We decided to wait until we discovered her outside and somewhat away from the buildings. So Arthur and I took turns at night watch.

Three nights later Arthur saw the skunk emerge from the root cellar and start walking leisurely down the tote road that led to the barn. She paused at the door of the hen house to sniff and dig at the dirt in hopes that the door might have been left unlatched. Then she continued her ramble, headed for the horse shed where spilled oats often attracted mice. Arthur took his gun and I carried the flashlight, which we scarcely needed in the bright moonlight. We were glad she had decided to circle the corral and was on the far side when Arthur shot her. Even so, it was some time before we could forget her when a south wind blew.

For a time the mice and rats carried away quantities of corn and piñon nuts without interference. Then one morning Martin Aloysious, who helped us in busy seasons, brought Arthur a box covered with a window screen, in which lay a three-foot bull snake. "Put this in your corn cellar," Martin said, "and you will have no more mice in your corn." He explained that the Navahos liked to have bull snakes stay near the pits or caves where the winter harvest was stored. Arthur decided to keep the snake as an experiment but I cannot say that I welcomed this new addition to our ménage with anything like enthusiasm. I said, "Well, if you want a snake underfoot every time you open the cellar door, it is all right with me, but just be sure you keep him on your side of the premises."

He was a beautiful specimen of snakedom, wearing a bright gold undergarment overlaid by a delicate pattern of shiny, brown lace. His eyes of black jet watched every move we made without one blink and seemed to see in every direction at the same time, so I named him Argus. This was immediately shortened to Gus by the men, and Gus he remained to the end of his stay. Gus would have been the perfect answer to the mouse problem if he had been content to live in a hermitage, but he was not. He had no sooner become accustomed to his new habitation, with its abundance of mice and the morning saucer of milk, than he decided to invite his wife, her sister, and several cousins to come and live with him to share his good fortune. They were all about the same size with exactly the same markings, but they were not as tame and hid themselves when they heard someone approaching.

Gus grew rapidly and was soon about four feet in length and from three to four inches in thickness. He seemed to know that he was a privileged personage, for he never fled from any of us nor made any motion toward us, but stayed a safe distance and kept wary watch of our movements. Sometimes Arthur saw one of the others and would remark that Gus was getting slimmer but, never seeing two at the same time, he was not aware of the increase in our wareroom population. One morning when I was watering my plants on the front porch, and was standing near a box that had once contained mountain leaf mold, a yellow head emerged from the box and hissed at me. I was startled but recovered my breath to say, "Now look here, Gus! You know you belong in the wareroom and not here on my porch. I was afraid that something like

Ruins and Rattlesnakes

this would happen." Then I stormed into the store to tell Arthur he would have to take Gus back to the wareroom and keep him there.

"He can't be out there." Arthur stated. "I was just in the cellar and Gus was under the corn bin." "Well he is," I said positively, "and I do not want him there, and besides, he hissed at me!" "Oh, all right," Arthur answered. "As soon as I finish this report I will get him." But when he looked in the box the snake was gone and Arthur was sure I had imagined seeing him there. The next day after lunch, I went to the hay barn to get my saddle and bridle for a horseback ride. As I was in the darkest corner unlocking the huge chest that held all of our riding equipment, I saw a gleam of gold the full length of the chest and just back of the lid, and there was Gus. His sharp, black eyes were watching every move I made, and it seemed to me that he was twice as long as he was the last time I had seen him. I picked up the hayrake and started pushing him off the chest, talking out loud to calm my shaken nerves. "Really Gus! You are getting to be a horrid nuisance, and I think you enjoy frightening me halfway to death every few minutes. And besides that, this is no way to earn your bread and milk." He did not seem to be in any hurry to leave, but glided majestically down to the floor and out of sight through a large crack.

When I told Arthur about it he said, "Well that is queer! I could almost swear that Gus has been in the wareroom all day." "Well then he must have a twin brother!" I remarked, and suddenly we both knew that must be the answer and we both burst out laughing. "I guess you will have to put a bell on Gus," I suggested. "I would like to recognize him when I meet him, and not become too friendly with a half-dozen of his kith and kin." I shivered when I thought of the huge monster I had pushed from the harness bin. "Strange snakes are not too safe to have around." "I doubt if they are strange by this time," Arthur argued. "I have had a feeling for some time that we were pretty well-policed by snakes." "Well, why didn't you do something about it?" I demanded. Arthur laughed. "I figured they were only helping Gus," he replied, "and after all, he has been worth his weight in ducats since he has been living in the corn cellar, and a good workman deserves a little consideration." "Well," I declared, "the next time I am almost bitten by one of the horrid things, I am going to chop it into little bits, if it's the last thing I ever do." But no one agreed with me and so they all stayed, growing fat if not too friendly, and I never approached a partly open door or a shadowy corner without a stick in my hand and a lump in my throat.

That summer we decided we would spend three weeks on a motor trip to visit my relatives in Wisconsin, leaving Arthur's brother, Earle, in charge of the post. It was midsummer and most of the Indians who traded with us had moved to the mountains so trade was light. I think Arthur must have forgotten to tell Earle about Gus and his relatives, for when we returned there were no snakes anywhere about. In their places were two large gray cats and three kittens. They all had short, crooked tails and long tassels on their ears; their fur was silver-gray with tiny, black spots. Any Navaho dog with good sense would think twice before starting an argument with either of the grown ones. Earle called them manx cats, but I was sure either their father or their grandfather had been a bobcat from the mountains. They were not house cats and never did become very tame but they handled the mouse problem in a scientific manner and even ate small rattlers when occasion offered.

There were a great many snakes in and around the cornfields, so the women and children who husked the great piles of corn ears were always on guard against picking up an extra long ear that might be one of the snakes that crawled through the piles looking for mice. One day Shema's girl came rushing into the store gasping, "Come quick! Come quick! There is a snake in our hogan between us and the baby." Arthur ran to the back of the store for a garden shovel, and I picked up the long pole with a steel hook on the end that we used to bring goods down from the highest shelves. It was not far to Shema's hogan and we ran all the way, but the daughter explained as we ran that the intruder must not be killed in the hogan and that we must try not to make it angry or it would bite the baby and the family would always have bad luck. Just how we were to manage this, she did not say. We pushed the doorblanket to one side and looked in. Sure enough, a good-sized rattler was coiled on the floor between the door and the central fire pit while the sleeping infant, safely bound to his cradleboard, was propped against a pile of blankets and sheep pelts beyond the fire near the west wall. It would be fairly simple to step to the door, kill the snake with the shovel, and carry it away, but how to remove it alive was another matter.

It was a low hogan with a square smoke hole in the roof, so Arthur climbed up the back and, reaching down through the smoke hole with the long pole I had brought, gently nudged the snake toward the open door. Little by little he urged it along until it reached the sill, which was about seven inches high. Here the snake decided to turn around and crawl toward some sheep pelts next to the wall, but I pinned it down with the shovel until Arthur came with the pole. Then, between us we scooped it up and carried it to the arroyo where we were glad to drop it over the bank. There were many Navahos watching by this time and all were glad to see that we had not harmed the snake. An elderly Hosteen took out his buckskin bag of pollen to bless the hogan and banish all evil influences that might have been left by the snake's presence.

We had lived at the Newcomb Trading Post more than a year before we were aware that our store was situated in the center of what once had been a thickly populated farming community. Two thousand or more years before our arrival, and long before the advent of the Navaho Indians, these valleys, mesas, and mountain slopes had supported a population well in excess of 8,000 people. This seemed quite impossible as the present census listed only 125 families with an average of five persons in each, scattered about so as to make use of every natural resource that could be developed. The meager water supply now irrigated only a fraction of the fields that once were cultivated; the trees and shrubs had completely disappeared from mesas and valleys; while springs, lakes and rivulets were now filled with sand.

The Navahos tell of three periods of drought lasting respectively four, seven, and fourteen years, the first being so long ago that even the legends are vague. The second had lasted seven years and had encompassed the entire Southwest, scattering the Indian tribes in all directions. Some of these abandoned the dry lake regions and journeyed east, crossing deserts and dry mountain ranges, to reach higher mountains and larger rivers. It is quite possible that the Navahos came into Arizona and New Mexico at this time, in clan groups of ragged, half-starved wanderers searching for water and food. Here they found the great pueblos along the Gila, the Colorado, and the San Juan rivers. But these people too, were suffering from the protracted drought, the lessening water flow, and consequent diminishing food supply. Hunger and disease had reduced their population, and those who remained were degenerating into sluggards and gamblers.

But what appeared to be ruin and starvation to the once wealthy Pueblos may have looked like plenty to the ragged Navahos. They were glad to build their humble shelters near the great apartment houses and work the fields or herd the flocks of turkeys for just enough food to keep themselves alive, and to obtain feathers from the turkeys for weaving into blankets. Up to this time, the wandering Navahos had lived off the land, gathering seeds of millet, sunflowers, and beeweed and also hunting such small game as rabbits, gophers, and prairie dogs. They had possessed no knowledge of agriculture and here they came into contact with planted fields for perhaps the first time. Some of their legends speak of corn growing out of ponds and lakes and they came to the conclusion that this corn belonged to the "Water People," while in reality, they were seeing the irrigated fields of the Pueblos for the first time.

The Navahos sent their young men to work for the "Stone-House-People" in order to learn the correct methods of sowing and planting, and also to memorize their elaborate religious rituals.

Gradually the drought grew worse and the great stone houses were abandoned to crumble into ruins when the inhabitants fled to seek less hostile surroundings. The Navahos who had learned much from these "Wise Ones," and who were still few in number, moved towards the mountains to make use of mountain springs and rills and to plant their stolen seeds in the moist swales.

Our valley must have been used as a highway and its mesas and promontories as temporary places of abode for all the tribes that moved from north to south as migration followed migration. But these people had disappeared and the Navahos found an unoccupied terrain and immediately claimed it as their Promised Land. Although hundreds of years had passed, all of these early tribes had left evidence of their passage and of their residence in this valley, so archaeologists have found this an interesting section to explore. They have found the sunken circles of the pit houses, the buried pole huts of the migrant hunters, the adobe walls of the pre-Basket Makers. They have found skulls flattened both front and back, marking a race of Indians with peaked heads, and skulls flattened at the sides. There are ruins of cliff houses in the canyons, and community dwellings on the mesas; in fact there are traces of many eras of prehistoric men. On two promontories there are stone monoliths put in place by some ancient race that no one has been able to name or even guess much about. On the promontories overlooking the Tunicha Valley stand several huge stone slabs, the exposed portion of which measure about the height and width of a large door, and are from ten to twelve inches in thickness. How deeply they are set into the ground, I do not know. Arthur started digging the earth away from the foot of one, but after reaching the depth of four or five feet, abandoned the project as being too dangerous. No ethnologist who visited our section could give us any idea of why these slabs had been erected, who had shaped and set them on end, or when it had been done.

Another mystery we uncovered was a burial pit containing three skeletons of enormous size, located on the mesa near Two Grey Hills. By measuring the leg bones, it was estimated that these men had been at least eight feet tall. Perhaps these were just freaks of nature and then, who can tell, there may have been giants in those days.

Several years before we bought the Newcomb Trading Post, the Hyde brothers had been operating a research center and a trading post in the Chaco Canyon and were exploring all of the ruins they could locate. In 1897 their workers found ruins all along our mesa and in the cornfields, which yielded some very unusual pottery and many skeletal remains. But, as there were no ruins of great apartment houses like those in the Chaco Canyon, they did not work here for any length of time. Then the Nordenskjöld party came and dug long enough to obtain 280 pieces of pottery, along with numerous other artifacts. In 1918 we discovered a much larger ruined village on the end of the mesa east of a gap, which was a split in the high mesa wide enough for a road to traverse. We sent word of this find to the American Museum of Natural History, which immediately commissioned a party directed by Earl Morris to explore and excavate this site. During 1917–18 nine months of excavation netted them 864 pieces of pottery and 72 skeletons, besides barrels and bales of smaller relics such as stone and bone knives, beads, bracelets, shell ornaments, flint axes, arrowheads, and drills. All of this was crated and shipped to New York to be stored in vaults, which were almost as inaccessible to the general public as the original burial mounds in New Mexico.

The expeditionists had paid the Indians to point out all the mounds and caves that contained prehistoric ruins and then had explored each one thoroughly. Surprisingly, the greatest amount of pottery and relics they discovered came not from the larger ruins, but from the burial mounds of the small four-to-five room farm houses that dotted the valley. These had evidently been built and occupied during a lengthy period of peace and plenty when farming conditions were excellent. The walls were not extra-thick, and rooms never exceeded eight or nine at most. Each house opened on a patio at the east, which was outlined by the remains of a high stone wall. The trash heap, which was also the burial ground, was generally found just north of the gate. There were no traces of the high walls that would have been built if the inhabitants had lived in fear of enemy raids. It was evident that these houses had been occupied generation after generation as the burials were made one over the other in as many as four tiers. Also, the floors showed different layers of earth and silt and different types of pottery shards were found. All these dwellings were dated several hundred years prior to the cliff houses at Mesa Verde or the extensive Pueblo ruins at Aztec.

The pottery found in these early dwellings was interesting as it seemed to be going through a period of free art, wherein the potter was allowed to fashion his ware into any shape or pattern that might suit his fancy, quite different from the conventional forms and designs found in the Mesa Verde pottery. Of course the majority of large pieces were ordinary bowls, water jugs, cooking pots, and ladles, but others that may have been made for ceremonial use or for children's toys, were shaped like turtles, gophers, eagles, frogs, ducks, and even an occasional snake. Years later, when a fire destroyed our post, I had in my collection twenty-two ducks, ranging in length from two to twelve inches. We searched the ashes after the fire and found three of the smaller ducks, along with ten small bowls and pitchers, the others having been destroyed by falling timbers.

The last expedition led by Earl Morris in 1920 had certainly explored everything that faintly resembled a ruin, and as we drove about the country on our Sunday afternoon jaunts, we saw knolls and sides of mesas that might have been laid open with a bulldozer. But even so all the pottery had not been found, nor all of the ancient ornaments that had been placed in the burial mounds, and sometimes expedition workers had thrown away small bowls and tiny pitchers as they shoveled away the dirt. We sometimes took our lunch and spent the day near these diggings, sifting the dirt that had been thrown out and digging along the edges of the pits that had been left open. I carried a large sieve and a trowel, while Arthur carried a short shovel and a whisk broom. These ancient people had been buried with quantities of personal ornaments, as well as with their work implements, and with bowls of food. Sometimes I would find hundreds of small white beads, or perhaps beads of black jet with a few pieces of odd-shaped turquoise that had been strung with them. Once I sifted out all of the five-inch bone beads that had formed the breastplate for some ancient medicine man. And once I found ten shell bracelets that had been carved from a conch shell. Large and medium-sized pottery had been taken away, but we found the small pieces just as interesting. There were tiny two-inch bowls, jugs with two handles, pitchers, and ladles that had evidently been toys of the children buried here, and there were small mugs and bowls for individual use. I decided to call my collection "Prehistoric Miniatures," and by 1923 I had 900 pieces on display. The Crown Prince of Sweden who, with his party, stopped at our place for lunch on his way from Mesa Verde to Gallup, pronounced it one of the most interesting collections he had ever seen.

One afternoon as we were exploring one of these old diggings along the top of the mesa, I needed a place to put each bead as I sifted it out of the soil, so I placed a thin, flat stone about two feet in diameter on three stone legs to make a bench. I walked about, far and near, sifting dirt from different areas and then placing my findings carefully on this bench. There were two small arrowheads, fourteen or more beads, several pieces of moss agate, a turquoise earbob, a turkey-bone whistle, and several chunks of green quartz. Deciding to move to another area, I walked over to the bench and, using both hands, picked up the flat stone that held my collection. As I straightened up, there, between the three stone legs, was coiled a gray rattler, watching me with beady eyes. I stared at him and he at me, and neither of us moved a muscle. "Well," I finally remarked, "you could have bitten my ankle a dozen times when I came near and you refrained from doing so, although I imagine it was a great temptation. I salute you as a gentleman and a scholar. Now if you will excuse me for taking away your roof and leaving you in the hot sun, I shall not trouble you further." Hastily I took my departure. As I looked back he was gliding away between the rocks and I was glad to see him go.

As we became more interested in collecting, we tried to locate a few ruins that had not been explored by the waves of ethnologists and pothunters that had swept across our area, and great was our joy when some Navaho would direct us to some unexplored cave or mound that had been overlooked. On one such occasion, an Indian who lived near the Río Chaco said he had found a cave in the canyon wall with a large Anat-sazi house in it. He had climbed up high enough to look into the cave and he could see no signs of white people having been there. Most of the walls were still standing and some of the smaller rooms at the back were still enclosed. We asked if we would need ropes to reach this cave and he replied that the fallen stones and rubble from the outer walls had made a slope that would not be difficult to climb.

The next Sunday we started early, with baskets of food, drinking water, a five-gallon can of gasoline, shovels, ropes, and two carton boxes filled with crumpled papers in which to pack any pottery or other "loot" we might find. Circling Sunflower Lake we climbed the steep side of East Mesa and drove along its level top for twelve or more miles. Then our guide pointed to a break in the rim and said it was a road leading down to the valley of the Río Chaco. It proved to be more like a sheep trail than a road and, although we slid down it without much trouble, I wondered how we would climb back up again. The Río was almost dry and we found a place to cross where there was no quicksand. Then it was less than a mile to the rift in the cliff where the ruin was located.

The car could go no farther as our trail had completely disappeared, so we walked up the little side canyon and were quite thrilled when we saw, up near the rimrock, a long, low cave with an arched ceiling. No wonder this ruin had never been discovered as it sat near the rear of the cave and could be seen from only one direction, and then just at a certain angle. I looked for a trail up the canyon wall but if there was one in former years it had now scaled off leaving smooth rock. It is true that the rubble had slid over the edge to form a slope, but this was of such steepness that the rocks and loose earth were ready to slip and start a small avalanche at a moment's notice. For this reason we could not climb in single file, but each must find his own path so as not to be hurt by stones dislodged by the one who went first. It really was not a climb one would attempt as an appetizer before breakfast.

When we finally reached the ledge that held the ruins, we found the cave much longer and deeper than had been apparent from below, while the ruined house was longer and contained more rooms than we had expected. The front had been six or seven rooms long, and in the center it was four rooms deep. The arched top of the cave, which served as the ceiling, was not high so there was only one story. The whole front wall had crumbled and lay in heaps on the plaza or had slid over the rim, but the second wall was broken only in a few places and the wall back of that was intact. We walked around, looking it over from the front plaza. "There is nothing in these first rooms," Arthur stated, "and if there ever was, it is all crushed now by the fallen walls." We were a little hesitant about stepping through the breaks in the next wall to examine the second tier of rooms but, after using our flashlight and listening for rattlers, Arthur went into one room and I stepped over a pile of rubble to enter another. My little ray of light did not dispel the shadows but some illumination came from above and I soon discovered a number of large cooking pots partially buried in the dust, lying on the floor near the fire pit. I was sure they were lying in the same positions in which their owners had left them when this dwelling had been abandoned centuries ago, and I realized that I was the first person to enter this room since its original inhabitants had fled. There were three large pottery jars lying among the fragments of others that were broken in the dust.

Calling Arthur to come and see what I had found, I walked farther into the room and stooped to brush the dirt off the largest pot and to loosen it from its bed. It was about fourteen inches in diameter and sixteen inches tall and was lying tipped halfway on its side with the mouth pointing away from me. I grasped the largest bulge in both arms, backed out through the opening in the wall, and started picking my way among the fallen stones. I saw Arthur coming toward me and heard him suddenly yell, "Put that thing down and come here quick." I sensed the urgency in his voice and thought he might have slipped on a rock and sprained his ankle. But I certainly was not going to drop my precious thumbnail pot and watch it break—not after it had lasted at least a thousand years. Near me I discovered a hollow between two rocks and into this I carefully placed the pot, still in a slanting position, with the mouth pointing away from me. Just as I turned to make my way to where Arthur was standing, my eye caught a movement at the lip of the jar and I saw a snake's head emerge, and pause as if measuring the distance to the ground below. I gave two quick leaps, and when I looked again, the snake was twisting its way down the slope of rubble. I could see that it was a slim, gray sidewinder, the villian of the snake family, as they do not coil or rattle before striking. They simply draw their heads back and strike without giving the least warning.

Needless to say, I did not go back into that room or into any other. Arthur and the guide brought out all of the whole pieces and many of the fragments, which we later glued together to make three almost complete bowls. We did not stay to search the ruin much farther as this was mid-November and we were afraid there might be snakes hibernating in all of the dark corners.

As it was, we were late getting home that afternoon, as the car refused to pull the steep grade up the side of the mesa and Arthur walked half a mile to the nearest hogan to hire a team to pull us to the top. But this did not dampen our spirits in the least as we both knew that we had just found the prize pieces of our whole collection, two of them being black-on-red and another being a dark yellow ocher color, while the larger ones were thumbnail cooking pots. This color of pottery did not belong in our section and how it came to be there no one knew. We could surmise that a group of prehistoric people were following the Río Chaco as they migrated from north to south and, upon finding a bordering field that could be irrigated, decided to build their hidden home in the canyon. They had not been here many years when some unlucky event caused them to flee to some distant place. But we had no scientific data to prove this and it was simply our personal explanation.

11
The Gift of a Child

THE YEAR when Lucy first came to work for me, the Department of Interior in Washington had decided to build a Navaho day school just around the mesa point south of our post. This was to be for children attending the lower grades and was for the purpose of providing schooling for small children under ten years of age. Up to this time, nearly all Navaho children had been taken away from their homes and placed in government boarding schools at the early age of six years. But this day school was also an attempt to interest the Navaho parents in sending their children to be educated in "white" schools. There was a schoolhouse with two class rooms, a dining hall with a large kitchen where noon meals were to be served, and three residencies for the employees. There was one house for the superintendent and his wife, who were the two teachers; there was another house for the welfare nurse who was paid by the Quaker Indian Welfare Association; and still another house for the stockman who supervised sheep-dipping and other government farm activities over a wide area.

The majority of the Navaho parents in the valley were greatly pleased with the new day school and sent their children with surprising regularity, so that the attendance was between forty and fifty pupils. However, there were a few families who refused to have anything to do with it. They argued that it was better for their children to stay at home and learn from their parents how to earn a living with sheep and weaving than it would be for them to go to school to learn to read and write. I could appreciate their way of thinking as many return students who had been away for years found it difficult to adjust to Navaho life on the Reservation.

The superintendent was of the opinion that if he could get these objecting parents to visit the school, he could overcome their objections. So, as a Thanksgiving celebration, he planned a school field day with a noon picnic for all valley residents who cared to attend. We thought it a very good plan and helped all we could with the details. When the day arrived, Navaho wagons loaded with people and cavalcades of horseback riders assembled around the school. The forenoon was given to the school exhibit of classwork—sketches, clay modeling, wood carving, and other handicrafts—this being a form of education that all of the parents could understand. Following these displays, there was a flag drill led by a drum corps of six drummers, as these Indian children needed little training to capture the rhythm of the drum. Then there were games and children's races, after which the parents were conducted on a tour through the classrooms, dining room, kitchen, and craft workshop to see for themselves how the children were taught and how they were cared for during the school day.

The noon picnic was served on long plank tables set at the outside of the dining room near the kitchen door. On the tables were four or five immense dishpans filled with sliced bread, three immense kettles of mutton stew with thickened gravy, a wash boiler full of pinto beans, and a tub half-filled with sliced onions. Further on there were baskets of apples, pans of sheetcake, and buckets of coffee—all ready for the visiting Indians. Enamel cups and tin plates were provided and the food was served buffet style. Arthur, Lucy, and I stood behind the plank tables with the school employees and helped serve the food as the Indians walked past holding out their plates, on which we put three slices of bread, with a slice of meat and a dipper of brown gravy, two or three onion slices, and a cup filled with beans. Then an apple, a four-inch square of cake, and a cup of sweetened coffee comprised the serving to each individual, large or small. As a person was served, he walked away to find his own family group and enjoy a leisurely meal discussing the school and exchanging the latest gossip. It was a sunny day and the air was like summer, so no one was in a hurry, and I believe we

Laura demonstrates how full a Navaho skirt should be.

Grandfather Greyhair is shown making a saddle, which is how he earned his living.

The Gift of a Child

served 150 Navahos, besides the several who had volunteered as helpers.

The planning of the afternoon program had been turned over to the men living in the vicinity of the school and they had decided to hold a *"Nah-hoe-hii,"* commonly called a "Chicken-Pull." This was a competition greatly enjoyed by teen-age boys and young men who took pride in their excellent horsemanship, but it was no sport to be indulged in by anyone who was not slim and agile.

A committee of ten older men had been appointed to act as judges and to arrange the details of the contest. They had taken the "chicken," which, in this case, was a canvas sack containing four dollars in nickels, to a level space of hard adobe and buried it so that only six inches of the sack's top was above the ground. The loosened earth around the sack was pounded and stamped so that it would not be easy to pull the sack from the ground. Any number of horsemen up to twelve could take part in the contest to see who would be first to pull the prize loose and then ride away with it, but this must be done while riding full-speed past the place where it was buried, and must be accomplished with just one grab.

Twelve youths, mounted on spirited horses with only blankets for saddles, lined up fifty feet from the sack and at the drop of the starter's hat they were off in a mad scamper to be the first to make the grab. With one knee hooked over the horse's back and one hand grasping its mane, the rider reached with his other hand to grasp the few inches of canvas showing above the ground, but at the crucial moment some other rider would slam into him so that he would lose position and miss the target. It seemed that no one could move quickly enough to gain the prize, and then it became apparent that the best-trained horses gave their riders an advantage. A horse that would wheel quickly and gallop back toward the sack would eventually allow his rider to win, and soon a lad riding a small bay pony held up the sack at arm's length to show that he had the trophy. But it did not belong to him until he had ridden his horse twice around the track with the others in full pursuit, trying to take it away from him. He had a head-start and completed the course, stopping in front of the judges to hand them the sack.

The sack was still in good condition, so the judges left the nickels where they were and handed the boy four silver dollars, the value of the sack's contents. Then the committee walked out onto the field and carefully selected another hard spot in which to bury the sack for the next game. An entirely new set of boys and horses were waiting to enter this competition and the former riders walked their horses up and down to allow them to cool off. There were three prizes offered and so three games were played. The superintendent of the school had donated four dollars, Arthur had given another four, and the Navaho men had collected the last four from among their own numbers, so that the "Chicken-Pull" could last throughout the afternoon. This game had come into the Indian country from Old Mexico, where certain tribes of Indians buried live chickens with only their heads above ground; but the Navaho Indians did not raise chickens and they did not believe in killing them or anything else that wore feathers, so they buried a sack containing silver jewelry or pieces of money instead. Nickels were used to make the sack have weight and next to horse racing, this was the sport most enjoyed by Navaho audiences.

The school field day was a success in more ways than one—the first being the pride the children had exhibited when showing their new accomplishments to their parents and the second being the good will established between the school employees and the people of this Navaho community. More children were soon enrolled and more parents started using the community laundry and the blacksmith shop.

At this time Althbah, Lucy's aunt, had two children, a girl of two and a baby boy, while her husband, Jim Manuelito, had built a three-room log cabin in the center of his farm, which was really the nicest Navaho house in the valley. Jim was a man who worked hard at any job that came his way and Althbah was an excellent weaver so they were a prosperous family. Lucy had been orphaned by the flu and when she had finished the ninth grade at boarding

The Gift of a Child

school, she came home to stay and had lived with Althbah and Jim to help care for the children. Then when Lucy came to help me with the housework, Althbah had asked Jim's grandmother to live with them so there would always be someone to keep an eye on the babies. This old woman had curvature of the spine, but this did not prevent her from taking care of the babies or from spinning the fine yarn that Althbah needed for her weaving. With Grandma taking charge, Lucy felt free to leave her aunt's home and live with me.

That winter the girls and I went to Phoenix to live through the school year and Lucy went with us. It was not a pleasant winter as there were heavy rains and the house we had rented must have been sitting on an old earth-filled marsh. After the second rain my Buick, which was parked in the driveway, sank into the mud until the chassis was partly buried. No crane or truck could pull it out because the drivers could find no solid footing for themselves, so there it stayed for two weeks. When a scarlet fever sign appeared on the front lawn of the house next door and a measles sign about four doors away, I telephoned Arthur to come and take us home. But we had not moved soon enough as both girls came down with scarlet fever shortly after our return to the Reservation.

Lucy went immediately to see Althbah and her family, bringing sad news when she returned as there had been an epidemic of whooping cough while we were gone and Althbah's baby boy had not lived through it. The little girl, Zonnie, had recovered although she had been very ill, and had lost all of her plumpness so that now she was a thin, little girl with large, sad, brown eyes. Zonnie was now the only one left of Althbah's four children, as the first two had died in infancy and, needless to say, she was the pet of the whole family. Althbah made her several little velvet dresses and tied bright ribbons in her hair so she always looked like a Navaho doll. When she refused to eat corn bread and mutton, Jim bought apples, canned peaches, cookies, and candy at the store. I began to wonder if she had forgotten how to walk as, when they came to the store, someone always carried her in their arms. Perhaps because of this attention, she lost her shyness and would come to us as readily as to people of her own family, so we became very fond of the child.

That summer brought unusually heavy rains which were greatly appreciated by the farmers and sheep owners. The ponds filled, the arroyos ran steady streams to irrigate the fields, and the grass grew high on the mesas and the mountainsides. So the sheep grew fat and there was hay to be cut for winterfeed. When the Navahos came to the store to sell their blankets or their sheep pelts they would say, "This is the way it used to be before the last long drought." Only the old people remembered those days. "Before then there was always running water, many ice-cold springs, and grass as tall as a man's knees." The lambs we bought from the Navaho flocks that fall were large and heavily fleeced. As the Indian trade continued to be brisk late into the autumn, we decided not to leave the Reservation that winter but to hire a private teacher for the girls.

My young cousin, Delia Purdy, had taught secondary school in Wisconsin the previous year and now agreed to come to New Mexico to teach our little school. We were informed that if our school could have an enrollment of eight or more pupils, we would be classed as a district school and part of the teacher's salary would be paid by the county. So we enrolled the four Taylor children from the Sheep Springs Trading Post eight miles south of us, and three Navaho children from the Clyde Beaal family in the cornfields. There was a two-room cabin east of the highway that had been built by the foreman of the road crew and it was now vacant. This we cleaned, painted, and sketchily furnished for a schoolhouse, so for one year there was a public school at Newcomb, New Mexico.

With Lucy to do most of the housework and Delia to take charge of my two girls, I was able to spend much of my time helping in the store, and this left the men free to work at the corrals buying lambs or in the warerooms weighing and buying piñon nuts, which were plentiful this year as also were Navaho farm products, espe-

The Gift of a Child

cially corn and beans. By mid-October we had bought more than 400 lambs and wethers, which must soon be delivered to the buyer at the stockyards in Gallup, a distance of sixty-five miles. The year before we had hired Navaho herders to take our flock across the mountains to Thoreau, where they were to be loaded into stockcars, but an early snow and sleetstorm had caught them on the way. Some of the lambs died and the others lost so much weight from lack of grazing that there was a heavy loss on the whole transaction. This year Arthur had decided to hire stock-trucks to transport the sheep to Gallup for, although the cost was higher, there would be no loss of weight en route.

The first truck to be loaded was a new double-decked stock-truck that could carry forty sheep on the lower deck and thirty on the upper, so that six or seven trips would take all the sheep we had to sell. The sheep were soon loaded and Arthur and Kee followed in our car to arrive at the stockyards when they were taken from the truck to be weighed. The road to Gallup had been graded and asphalted, but it was only a single track in width, so there were still two or three dangerous grades on curves going over the mountains. The loaded truck looked narrow and top-heavy to me, as it drove away from the corral, but it was the first one I had ever seen and the two truck drivers laughed at my fears, saying that it was perfectly safe. All went well until they reached the mountains when, just as they were rounding a steep curve, they met a car coming down. As they turned off the asphalt their outside wheels sank into the soft dirt and the truck listed so badly that the sheep were all thrown to the lower side. The driver set the brakes and both men jumped out to try to hold the car from tipping further. But the truck was too heavy and the load was now all on one side. Slowly at first, and then with a "plop" it turned on its side, then over onto its top, and finally came to rest on its other side, leaning against the embankment. Arthur and Kee arrived just in time to see it turn over and stop at the bottom of the gulch. They backed their car down the grade until they found a side road that led into the gulch and they could drive to the wreck. It was certainly a most disheartening sight! All of the lambs on the top deck were dead and the majority of the others were either dead or badly injured, so that they would need to be killed.

Arthur sent Kee to find the nearest Navaho hogan to ask them to send messengers to every hogan in the valley, asking for men and women to come and help. These workers would be paid with fresh mutton. As they removed the lambs from the lower deck, they discovered eighteen or twenty that had not been hurt, but the remainder had suffered broken legs or backs and were immediately dispatched. Then Arthur drove to Gallup to hire a stocktruck to take the uninjured lambs and the pelts of the others back to Newcomb.

While he was gone more than thirty Navahos came to help with the skinning of the dead sheep, and when he returned with the truck, there was a large pile of pelts to be loaded. These were roped into the front end of the truck while the live lambs occupied the rear. Arthur also had twelve dressed lambs wrapped in a canvas and tied on top of the pelts, which he took back to the store to give to his own customers. The remainder were divided among the workers. There are many taboos among the Navahos against eating meat from animals that have been killed in an unusual manner. Those that have been killed by lightning, wind, flood, eagles, coyotes, or any other predatory animal may not be used as food, but there is no taboo against eating mutton from sheep that have been killed in an automobile accident. All of the residents of that valley feasted on mutton for three or four days. This accident did not prevent Arthur from shipping the remainder of his sheep by truck, but these trucks were not double-decked.

Our district school was a decided success and before Christmas arrived, Delia had coached her pupils in a program that pleased everyone who attended. There were Christmas carols and a playlet of the tale of the Three Bears, complete with costumes, stage furniture, and even real mush in the porridge bowls. There was also a pageant of the shepherds visiting the manager, which was rendered quite realistic by the two pet sheep belonging to Ena and Eskay

The Gift of a Child

Beaal. The program was so well carried out that Delia was asked to give a repeat performance at the Toadlena Indian School to add to their Christmas exercises. In return we were invited to partake of their Christmas dinner and to assist in handing out the many gifts that had been sent to the Navaho children by several welfare organizations in the East. Two truckloads of clothing and gifts had arrived from the East in early December in response to the efforts of Mr. Brink, the missionary for our section, who lived near the school. There was a quantity of clothing and household goods, but one truck was entirely filled with toys, and these were now given to the children. I was glad when the festivities were over and our part of the program had been pronounced a success, as I had been in charge of the carols and the background music and had spent most of my time on stage seated at the piano. On our way home I said to Arthur, "I think everything went off very well. Don't you?" He answered, "Well, yes, I guess so! But next time I wish you would see to it that your stockings were mates!" My private little balloon of egotism never did have a chance of sailing very high.

At the post we had a tinsel-trimmed tree in the living room with gifts for the family, the helpers, and Delia's scholars, but there were no candles or electric lights as we could take no chances of having a fire with our limited water supply. Years later our post did burn completely to ashes with nothing of value saved, but luckily, there was no loss of life. We did not hold a barbecue for our customers this year, or hand out toys to the children as we knew they would all receive food and gifts at Toadlena. But we did fill 250 paper sacks with treats to give away. Each sack contained an orange, an apple, a popcorn ball, candy, peanuts, and a couple of frosted cookies, and we had prepared enough to give to every man, woman, and child who came to the store.

It was barely daylight when the first wagons stopped at the hitch-rail and whole families came into the store to receive their packages. Then they paused a few moments to visit with friends from a distance before climbing into their wagons and continuing their ride to Toadlena. We were glad to have them come early as we wished to close the store at noon and join the trek to the Navaho school.

It was midmorning when Althbah, Jim, and little Zonnie came into the store. I did not notice them in the crowd until Zonnie came to the gate that barred the customers from entering behind the counters. She shook the bar and I asked Lucy what she wanted. Lucy replied, "She wants to see the tree." We took her into the living room and she gazed happily at the tree for a few minutes and then said something to Lucy so rapidly that I did not understand. Lucy translated, "She says she has come for her doll." We had no toys to give to any of the Indian children, but Lynette was standing beside me and said, "I will get her one of mine." She soon returned carrying a flaxen-haired doll, dressed in white with a red jacket and cap. She placed it in Zonnie's outstretched hands and watched the look of joy on the little girl's face. Then Zonnie looked up and said, "This is my baby, my very own baby!" Then she turned to run through the store to the wagon where her grandmother, well-wrapped in shawls, was seated in the back on a pile of hay. She wanted her grandmother to be the first to see her new doll.

The last week in December, we all packed into the car, bag and baggage, and drove to California to attend the Rose Carnival and to visit with friends and relatives. Arthur's mother lived in Long Beach and there we rented an apartment and stayed three weeks. On our return to the Reservation we were told that Grandma Jim had passed away during our absence. She had tried to lift the pole that barred the corral gate and the effort had brought on a hemorrhage that caused immediate death. Little Zonnie was heart-broken and kept asking when her grandmother was coming back. Every morning as soon as she was awake she would ask her mother if Grandma had come home. She missed her sadly as it had been Grandma who had dressed her in the mornings, watched over her during the day, and crooned her to sleep at night.

The weather, which had been mild during January, suddenly turned bitterly cold with blizzards of snow and sleet. If it was a

The Gift of a Child

trial for us, it was a hundred times more so for the Navaho families, living in one-room hogans and trying to care for the livestock huddled in the open corrals. There were frozen hands and feet, and near-famine conditions in many Navaho homes. Then, to add tragedy to misery, an epidemic of measles swept across the Reservation. Among white families, measles is seldom a fatal disease, but to the Navahos it is fully as deadly as diphtheria or smallpox. These germ diseases had not been known to the Indians before the advent of the white man, so no immunity had been developed and nearly all cases of measles turned into pneumonia, for which they had no cure. It was a sad time for the Navahos of our valley, as many families lost two or three children and no one knew which child would be taken next.

One morning when Arthur unlocked the store door, Jim and Lucy were standing there waiting to come inside. I knew by the expression on Lucy's face that something was very wrong. "What is it?" I asked Lucy. "What has happened?" She bowed her head on my shoulder and said in a choked voice, "Little Zonnie is dead!" "Oh! no! I cried. "That just can't be!" But Jim nodded with tears streaming down his cheeks. "We have come to buy burial quilts and clothing," he stated. I asked Lucy to tell me about it, and she said that Zonnie had been taken ill three days ago but had seemed to be getting better. Then last night her fever had climbed very high and she had become delirious. Suddenly the fever broke and she talked to them, asking for her doll and her string of red beads. She held these for a few minutes, and then asked for a drink of water. Althbah had held her up as she gave her water from a spoon. Before she had swallowed the water, she looked toward the door and an expression of joy came over her face as she held out her hands and said, "Grandma! Oh, my Grandma! You have come to take care of me!" As she fell back, Althbah gathered the frail little form into her arms and tried to talk to her, but the eyes were closed and her breathing had ceased. Althbah refused to allow anyone to take the dead child from her arms and was still holding her close to her breast when they had left the hogan to get the burial robes.

But Klah would give Althbah an herb tea that would put her to sleep; then they would prepare little Zonnie for burial.

This must take place before sundown as it was the general belief that when the breath left the body, it became empty of spiritual life and unseen evil spirits who roamed about at night, could enter and turn it into a ghost or Chindee. Klah's family were not as superstitious as many of the other Navahos in our district, but they did adhere to the traditional forms and customs for all the major events of life. Klah explained that if these traditions were abandoned, they would have no laws or precepts to guide them, and these ancient customs had been followed for many generations.

Jim and Lucy bought three heavy quilts for wrappings, shoes, stockings, and red velveteen for a new dress which many willing hands would cut and sew before sunset. They also bought hair ribbons, a flashlight, and ten silver dollars to make sure that Zonnie did not enter the next world in poverty. Late that afternoon a sad pilgrimage was made to Rock Mesa with little Zonnie wrapped inside many quilts and blankets—along with her entire wardrobe of dresses, her doll, her beads, the ten silver dollars, and the flashlight. Then Althbah's heart and home were indeed left desolate. Weeks passed and Althbah did not come to the store. I asked Lucy how she was, and if they had gone to the mountains. Lucy answered, "No! They are not going to the mountains this summer as Althbah is not very well. She does not want to do anything, but just sits and cries and cries. Her mother is living with them now and is afraid she is losing her sight."

At the close of the school year, Delia had departed for her home in Wisconsin and as September approached, I planned to rent a house in Farmington for the school year. As Lucy was helping me sew and pack to go, I asked what she was planning to do during the winter, as she had not wished to go with me. I was quite surprised when she informed me that she was planning on going to Cortez, Colorado, 100 miles to the north, to take a job as waitress in a cafe. "But can you go that far away?" I asked. "What will

The Gift of a Child

Althbah do without you?" "Oh! She is better now," Lucy answered. "She has started weaving again so her work will keep her mind busy, and her sister, Daisy, will stay with her while I am away."

I was back and forth between Farmington and the store all that winter but I did not see Lucy again until June. One sunny morning she walked into the store wearing a full Navaho skirt, velvet blouse, and red deer-hide shoes, while her hair was combed in Navaho fashion with a bun at the back. I was surprised to see her in this garb as she generally was dressed the same as white girls, and I was more surprised to see that she was noticeably pregnant. As she came through the gate into the living room I asked, "Lucy, are you married?" She smiled at me a little ruefully and answered, "No, I am not married." "But Lucy," I exclaimed, "you are going to have a baby." "Yes," she replied. "I am going to have a baby in about three weeks." I finally accepted the fact and told her, "You had better come here to stay so that I can take you to the Shiprock hospital in time." But Lucy shook her head. "No, I am staying with Althbah, and my grandmother will be there with a midwife who is very good with newborn babies.

A month passed and I was told that Lucy had given birth to a son. After the traditional days of seclusion had passed, I went to visit them taking clothing for the baby and fruit for the family. As I entered the cottage, I noticed that it was Althbah who was holding the infant while Lucy came to greet me. The baby was wrapped in a pink baby blanket and a white, knitted shawl, but I could see its little, round head covered thickly with black hair, and I could see its fat, little face. It looked so important lying in Althbah's arms, that I immediately named him "Little Chief"—Nahtanie Yazz—and I never did know his real name. The name "Little Chief" referred to the fact that he was Chief Narbona's grandson, six times removed.

Lucy continued to live with Althbah and Jim, coming to work for me whenever I needed extra help and always doing her share of the work in the hogan and in the cornfields. Little Chief was a fat, sturdy baby, nursed by Lucy through the winter and the following summer. This long period of nursing was for the purpose of carrying the child through the first months of teething and also through the heat of the second summer, a period when many Navaho babies die.

Late in August Lucy announced that she had accepted a position as girls' matron at the Toadlena Boarding School for the following year. I asked, "Do you think you can act as girls' matron and take care of your baby at the same time?" She looked at me sadly and said in a choked voice, "He is not my baby now. I have given him to Althbah." I was astonished. "But you can't give your baby away just like that!" I protested. "That is why I had him," she smiled at bit wanly, "so Althbah could have a child. She was good to me when my mother died and I came here to live. I owe her a great deal, and she would not have lived long without a baby to love and care for." "If Althbah wished to adopt a child," I argued, "there are plenty of orphans in the valley she could have taken." Lucy shook her head. "I told my grandmother that, but she said they would not do, as this baby must be of our own clan." I knew enough about clan laws to know that children can always be claimed by members of their own clan, so there would be no security in adopting a child of another clan.

My mind was slow in comprehending the implications of Lucy's statement. But suddenly I understood that this whole project had been planned by the older members of the family to provide Althbah with a child. And Lucy had been the one who had volunteered to carry out the plan. She had gone to Cortez, 100 miles away, to find a man who would never be known to her family and may never have known her right name, so that he would not be able to come and claim the child in later years. Then she had stayed with Althbah when it was born so that Althbah could have it to love and care for from the very first. As soon as the child did not need her, she was ready to leave it and never again think of it as belonging to her.

I looked at Lucy with something akin to awe as I realized that she had given two years of her life and a child she dearly loved to bring happiness into the life of another woman. A thought came into my mind, "Greater love than this hath no woman than she who purposely bears a child to give to a friend."

12
Silver for a Bride

May's new moon heralded planting time for the Navaho farmers who owned land in both the upper and lower cornfield sections along the Río Tunicha. This area had been leveled and cleared of hummocks many years before the Navahos settled in this valley, as it had been extensively farmed by the Old Ones whose ruined houses dotted the landscape. These acres were divided into plots by irrigation ditches, dams, and terraces as the Navahos built few fences around their cornfields. In March the melting snows on the high Chuska Mountains brought water to the irrigation ditches and the plots of land were flooded. This water contained sediment and humus from the mountain slopes, which fertilized the fields so they could be used for corn year after year without rotation of crops. In March the cornland was flooded to a depth of ten or twelve inches, and this water was allowed to soak into the soil until it completely disappeared, either by absorption or by evaporation. This answered two purposes since the subsoil was first thoroughly soaked and second, all weed seeds, worms, and insect eggs were killed.

By the latter part of April the water had disappeared and the topsoil was dry so the ground could be plowed, and when the new moon of May appeared in the sky, all of the Navaho farmers had their seeds ready to plant. Before the planting began, a Seed-Blessing Ceremony was held in which all took part. A roofless enclosure was erected of poles and brush, large enough to hold all the people who brought their sacks of seeds to participate in this Blessing Rite. A medicine man was engaged to conduct the ceremony and lead the people in the prayer chants which implored the gods for fertility, growth, and fruition. All day before the occasion, farmers came with sacks of the seeds of squash, beans, corn, melons, tobacco, and some brought seeds of herbs and other wild plants. All of these were placed around a fire pit in the center of the floor. That night they were guarded and prayers were chanted from the four directions. The next morning the ceremony began and the seeds were dedicated to the earth, the sun, the gentle winds, the female rains, and the morning mists with rites which used four colors of pollen—white, yellow, blue, and red—and also with other symbols which represented fertility. This ceremony preceded the days of planting and it was thought well to put the seeds into the ground as soon afterward as possible. A span of seven days was allowed for this work. In the latter part of May, when the seeds had sprouted and the first green shoots appeared above the earth, a growing ceremony was held at the time of the full moon.

As the evening approached, all in attendance sat silent waiting for the magic moment when the moon appeared in the east just as the sun was setting in the west. This was the only time in the month when the sun and the moon looked at each other face to face and the only time they exchanged messages. In this hour of silence, it was hoped that the sun and been pleased with the rites they had held in its honor at the Seed-Blessing ceremony, and the moon had been pleased with the prayers at night, then both would agree that all had been done in the proper manner. The sun wore a mask of blue turquoise and was the giver of light and heat, while the moon wore a mask of white shell and was in control of female rain, mist, fog, and dew. Both were too powerful to look at directly and so these masks were used in all ceremonies.

During the seven days of planting, rain in either the day or the night would be considered a blessing, but a hard wind or a sandstorm would be looked upon as an unlucky omen. The first handful of corn in each field was planted in the exact center, with the man pushing the planting-stick deeply enough into the soil to reach the moist subsoil. Then his wife, carrying a basket of seeds, dropped twenty-four kernels of corn into the hole. The second hill was planted at the east, the third at the south, the fourth at the west, and the fifth at the north. All the perfect ears from these hills would be used for ceremonial purposes.

Kee Tuley, who had come to work for us in February, lived with his Aunt and Uncle Gleason in the lower cornfields. When he was eleven years old his mother and father had died and he had been taken to the Riverside Indian Boarding School in California, where he had remained for eight years. Here he had received a good basic training in the three *R*'s and in the carpenter's trade, but little of that would be of use to him in the raising of sheep. His relatives welcomed him home and his aunt now took the place of his mother, but he had been away so long that he was not much help with the family economy. So he had asked Arthur for a job at the post and we were glad to have a lad who could speak English and help with the trade as well as doing the wareroom chores.

Kee was anxious to be married and have a home of his own so as to start in the sheep business. Being an orphan and having been gone so long, he had no inheritance of either sheep or land. Nearly all Navaho young folks who are away at boarding schools have small flocks of sheep and a pony or two awaiting their return, but Kee would need to earn his own. Not long after his return he had met the girl he would like to marry. She was Yahnabah Nez who lived with her parents near Stoney Butte. He had attended a Squaw Dance held in that locality and she had been one of the dancers, so he knew she was not married. She had attended boarding school for about five years but when she was eleven she had suffered an attack of measles which left her so frail the authorities had sent her home. Now, at sixteen, she was plump and healthy.

Kee decided to visit her parents to ask them if she was engaged to someone else or perhaps had some other preference and, taking gifts of coffee and sugar to her mother, he rode across the mesa to visit the home of the girl of his choice. If his parents had been alive they would have made these first advances for him, but his uncle Gleason had given him a young pinto pony and he decided to go and make his own arrangements.

Nathanie and his wife of Toadlena. He gave the oration at the wedding of Kee and Nonabah.

Althbah, who had lost all four of her children.

Silver for a Bride

This was just a formal visit and he was not allowed a moment alone with Yahnabah, but she had noticed him at the dance and had learned that he was a young man looking for a wife. She had already decided that she preferred him over all the older men who had been looking her way, and she would have been greatly disappointed if he had not come to call. Just how she managed to convey this information to him with her parents and other relatives sitting in the hogan, I do not know. But she certainly managed to give him enough encouragement so that he asked his aunt to meet with Yahnabah's mother to see what arrangements could be made to gain her approval of his suit.

After a dignified length of time, Kee's Aunt and Uncle journeyed to Stoney Butte with gifts of calico and corn to extend a formal offer of marriage. The outcome of the visit was quite disappointing to Kee. It seemed that the Nez family could not get along without their daughter, as she had been at home since she was eleven and had learned to care for the sheep, card and spin the wool, weave the rugs, cook, and sew. She was almost as good as her mother at all of these tasks and her leaving would be a great loss to her family. Under these conditions her mother would expect the man who took her away to pay a very large price as he would be getting not only a wife who could support him, but one who owned twenty head of sheep and a small plot of farm land, so all he needed to do would be to build the new hogan. Yahnabah's mother mentioned a "gift" of eight sheep and five ponies. The mother and father were willing for the two young people to be married, as he seemed to be the one that Yahnabah liked best, but he could not take her until he made the required payment.

Again Kee rode to Stoney Butte to tell Yahnabah's parents that he could not make payment in sheep or ponies, but he was working at the trading post and would save his wages to buy silver and turquoise jewelry for her mother and a new, hand-tooled saddle for her father, if Yahnabah would wait for him to earn that amount. It was not possible for Kee to save much of his small wages as the aunt with whom he lived expected him to bring something home in the way of store-groceries when he came home at night, so he was always on the lookout for ways to earn a little extra money. Tourists sometimes asked him to change a tire, or wash a muddy car, and I paid a small amount for the beautiful pieces of petrified wood or rose quartz he sometimes brought to me. One morning he came into the store carrying a prehistoric bowl. It was in the shape of a duck about seven inches long by five inches in width and height. The body was gray with feather markings in black and white. The top was open and there was a hole through the bill, so it had evidently been used for ceremonial purposes. I was delighted to have it as I had never seen one like it.

Kee was quite surprised when I handed him two silver dollars in payment and asked where he had found it. In May, when his uncle was using the planting-stick to make the holes for the seeds, the stick had struck something hard and his uncle had carefully dug the dirt away to find this piece of pottery, so it belonged to his uncle and Kee would give him one of the dollars he had received. There had been no human bones nearby so it was not a Chindee bowl and the uncle had carried it home where it sat around for several months. Kee thought I would like it for my curio shelves, and if I did, he knew where there were several more of various shapes and sizes. He explained something I already knew, that the Old Ones had lived all up and down the valley and had planted the same fields the Navahos were now using. Nearby were ridges of stone made by the fallen walls of the ancient houses, and the Navahos often found pottery while planting or hoeing their fields. The larger pieces were generally broken in the soil and the bits were too small to piece together, but the smaller ones came out whole and these were kept as good luck pieces or to use in ceremonies.

I told him that I would pay him a little something for any good pieces he brought and it was not long until I had four nice bowls and a couple of long-handled ladles to add to my collection, and he had several Mexican silver dollars. These he took to his uncle,

Silver for a Bride

who was a silversmith, and could make the jewelry Yahnabah's mother wanted. I put the pottery on a shelf in the store and several Indians seeing them there asked if I was buying old pottery. When I told them I was, they brought me many pieces they had found in and around the cornfields. There were no two pieces alike and the variety of shapes was surprising. There was a turtle, two frogs, a deer, several bird forms, bowls, water jugs, mugs, pitchers, and ladles both large and small. Most of this had probably been funeral pottery buried in some ancient grave to hold food and water for the departed spirit. During the intervening years, the winds and the rains had eroded the earth away until finally the pottery had drifted down the irrigation ditches to be buried in the soil of the fields. As long as it was separated from the grave or any sign of burial, it could be picked up and even used by the ones who found it. With Kee to guide us, Arthur and I wandered around the higher land bordering the fields, and were amazed to find dozens of mounds that once had been prehistoric stone houses for the farmers, and near each one, the refuse heap or kitchen midden where they had buried their dead. There was plenty of evidence that more than one generation of Pueblo farmers had occupied these homes as, in places, the refuse heaps were higher than the ruined walls. These were not important ruins and represented no great archaeological find, but they were interesting to us and we occasionally spent a Sunday afternoon digging in one of the refuse heaps. We were generally rewarded by finding two or three pieces of pottery and perhaps a stone hammer or a couple of bone awls. There were no Navahos, not even Kee, who would dig in these mounds as they knew they might disturb the skeletal remains of some of the Old Ones who had died so long ago. Then it would become necessary for them to have a Hochonji [Evil-Chasing] Ceremony held to banish the evil spirits that were thought to bring illness or bad luck. As this was sure to be expensive, it was thought best to avoid all contact with the bones of the Old Ones so we dug here and there on pleasant afternoons, finding just enough pottery to keep us interested. Since the Navahos brought us occasional pieces from other ruins to add to my collection, it was beginning to make quite a showing.

One day Kee said to me, "I know where there is an old burial that is different, and it is not Navaho either." I asked where it was and he told me it was near the "Big Black Rock," which was Bennett Peak. The next Sunday we motored to the place he had described and found a sunken place filled with weeds and debris. It seemed like a grave and when Arthur started digging, he found the earth loose and easily removed. Kee refused to help with the digging but watched every shovel of dirt that came out of the pit, sifting it through his fingers and breaking up every hard lump. It was very evident that he was expecting to find something, but we did not guess that it was gold or silver coins until some time later. After four feet of earth had been removed Arthur came to human bones. I had a whisk broom and, climbing into the trench, I carefully brushed the dirt away to disclose a skeleton lying at full length with its head turned to one side. The skull was so paper-thin that it flaked away into the dirt even with the gentlest brushing, but not before we noticed that there was no sign of flattening either in the front or back, and the lower jaw was not especially prominent.

"This is not the skeleton of an Indian," Arthur remarked, as he carefully removed the dirt from around the bones with a garden trowel. "It does not lie doubled in the correct position for an Indian burial," he stated, "and it has no pottery or personal ornament buried with it." "I am sure it was a white man," I replied, "and this burial is certainly too old to be anyone the Navahos would know about." Arthur was digging around the leg bones when he suddenly struck metal. When the dirt was cleared away this proved to be a very cruel type of spur made of copper. He found its mate a few feet away, on the other side of the trench. They were both crusted with alkali and green with age, but a scrape with a knife showed bright copper underneath. This find encouraged us to extend our operations and near the arm bones we found a copper plate about seven inches in diameter, but so encrusted with lime and alkali that the inscription was illegible. After digging and sifting for more than an hour and finding nothing to reward our efforts, we decided there was nothing more and, as the bones were too fragile to be moved, we started refilling the grave with the earth that had been taken out, then looked around for all the stones we could find to place on top. "I think he was a Spaniard," Arthur stated. "I wonder how long ago he came riding into this country and I wonder what caused his death?" "I do not believe he was killed by the Indians," I said. "There were no arrowheads near him and his skull was not crushed. But we will never know. We can only guess that he became separated from some exploring party without water or food." Arthur thought that unlikely and suggested that he might have died from snake bite and said, "It is certain that someone was there to bury him."

Kee seemed disappointed, and when I asked him what he had expected to find, he answered, "The Navahos have known about this grave for years, and when the boys have searched through the sand after a hard wind or rain, they have found pieces of gold and more pieces of silver. I had hoped that this man might have had a sack of silver in his burial." "What did the boys do with the silver they found?" I inquired. "Oh, they took it to a silversmith to have it made into rings," he replied.

Poor Kee! This white man's burial had proved a great disappointment. He had brought us to the grave he dared not open, in hopes that we would find much silver, which he would share and from which he could have jewelry made with which to buy his bride. But Kee was doing quite well without this, as the pottery he had been selling was clear profit.

Some weeks later, a Navaho brought a Spanish-designed iron bit, with iron lacework at the sides and jingling underneath. It was a cruel, jointed bit, broken in two places and rusted into solidity. I still have this relic in my antique collection. Then, when another Navaho brought us an ivory crucifix that had been found near the same spot, and a handful of jet beads that had turned gray because of long contact with the soil, we pictured a wandering padre and his guide riding across uncharted country, following the range of mountains and guided by the volcanic spires that stood like sentinels to point the way north to the San Juan River, about which little was known at that early date.

By harvest time, Kee had earned the required amount to buy the jewelry and the saddle he had promised to give Yahnabah's parents, but there was still a hogan to be built and a team and wagon to be purchased. To earn these would take another year, but now his relatives came to his assistance. Kee paid for the logs that were brought from the mountains but there was no charge for the workers who arrived to build the hogan and the corral for Yahnabah's small flock of sheep. Their new home was built on land she had inherited from her grandmother and was only half a mile from her parents' hogan. There is a strict law among the Navahos against two couples living in the same hogan or doing their cooking over the same fire. And there is another law forbidding a young man to look at the face of his mother-in-law. These two laws were written in the stars when this world was first created. The north star that never moved was said to be the hogan fire, and the constellations of Ursa Major and of Cassiopeia were said to be the married couple who circled this fire but never left it to find some other.

Kee's uncle gave him two farm horses and Arthur ordered him a wagon, to be paid for in installments. Finally the day was set and they chose a Sunday so we could attend. I sent Yahnabah ten yards of silver-colored sateen for a full skirt and turquoise-blue velveteen for her blouse; I also sent black velveteen for her mother's blouse. Kee's uncle, the silversmith, had presented the bride with thirty-six small, handmade silver buttons to trim her blouse, and had also sent her a pair of store shoes. The two new Pendleton shawls for the women cost Kee $34.00, but his father-in-law reciprocated by giving Kee ten sheep. I had not known, before about the flow of gifts that passed back and forth when two clans sought to maintain their prestige in an affair of this kind. There must be no chance for the gossips to criticize either family.

Silver for a Bride

For several weeks Yahnabah had been busy weaving the large rug she would take to the post to exchange for her housekeeping equipment. In the old days, this would have been their bedcover, but now it would buy blankets, a couple of thick quilts, coffeepot, cooking skillets, pans, bucket, tableware, broom, towels, and everything she needed with which to start housekeeping, as well as a goodly supply of groceries. It was traditional for the bride to furnish the new home her husband had built for her. She had carried out another tradition by weaving a beautiful saddle blanket, patterned in red, gray, black, and white, with long red tassels on two corners. This she would present to her husband as soon as the ceremony was ended and while the guests were still assembled so that she could enjoy their approval.

When it became certain that the wedding was about to take place as scheduled, Kee came to me and diffidently asked if the white people would consider a Navaho wedding legal. He had been away at school so long he had begun to doubt the legality of the old Navaho customs. I was then so new on the Reservation that I could give him no answer, but told him I would write to the attorney of the Bureau of Indian Affairs and find out. My inquiry received a prompt answer and part of it read: "A marriage ceremony performed according to the laws and customs of any people of any tribe, nationality or religious sect, living within the borders of the United States, shall be considered legal in every respect." Kee was glad to hear this ultimatum, but was not so happy when I said that the missionaries might consider it a pagan rite. Then I suggested that some day soon, he and Yahnabah could go to the mission and have a short ceremony in which they would receive the missionary's blessing; then all would be satisfied.

When the wedding day arrived, we were late in getting started and so we missed the early morning rites when the hogan was blessed and the prayers for long life, happiness, and fertility had been sung over the young couple. There were the rites and prayers to banish all evil influences that might cause them trouble. Then they returned to her mother's hogan where the main part of the ceremony would take place. We arrived at midmorning and entered the hogan to find the young couple sitting with their backs to the west wall and dozens of friends and members of the two clans crowded into the room, which luckily was quite large. Of course Yahnabah's mother was nowhere to be seen as this family still adhered to the taboo that the bridegroom must never look his mother-in-law in the face on penalty of blindness. But we knew that she was in the nearby cookhouse where she could direct family procedure and observe all who came or went.

We had interrupted the harangue of one of Yahnabah's uncles, Nathanie of Toadlena, who had been appointed by her parents to deliver the wedding sermon. In other words, he was to expound the law as to the conduct and responsibilities of a married couple. The old chief was an orator of some renown and greatly enjoyed his assignment. After about an hour of instructions directed at the young couple, he turned his attention to the other young people in the room and to their parents. I have no idea what halted this flow of oratory but suddenly he ceased talking and sat down near the bride's father. I wondered what a young, white couple would have done if subjected to this frank and uninhibited harangue regarding their connubial duties and given in the presence of friends and relatives. But it was accepted since it was standard procedure and one of the main events of the day. Kee and Yahnabah both sat quietly with hands folded in their laps and eyes fixed intently on their hands. If I had not known they were enjoying all of this attention, I would have been sorry for them. But this was a great day in their lives and they were anxious to have everything take place according to the best traditions. The longer the speeches, the greater the crowd, the more numerous the gifts, the more important they would feel, for well they knew that every guest present would recount each detail of the occasion to any and every listener for weeks to come. The bride's dress, the groom's generosity to the mother, the family's wealth, and the wedding feast would furnish topics of conversation in many hogans during the long winter evenings.

After a period of respectful silence, a messenger was sent to the cookhouse to tell them that the speech was finished and it was time to bring the water and the mush. A younger sister came into the hogan carrying a large wedding basket filled with corn mush, the corn meal used for making this having been ground by this sister using a cornstone and a metate. Following her came another girl with a bowl of water and a gourd dipper.

Now the bride's father sprinkled a line of white pollen on top of the mush from east to west and then another from south to north. After this he placed lines of yellow pollen parallel to the white lines. White was for the groom and yellow was for the bride. Then he mixed the two colors of pollens and drew a circle around the edge of the bowl to indicate long life for both the bride and the groom. When the medicine man had finished blessing the mush and the water, both the basket of mush and the bowl of water were placed directly in front of the young couple. Kee, using his forefinger and thumb, took a large pinch of mush from the center of the basket and Yahnabah's hand followed his in taking mush from the same place. This was repeated in taking pinches of mush from the south, the west, the north, and lastly from the east. The symbolism of this meant that she would follow his lead in all things. Then the basket was handed to her relatives who helped themselves to generous pinches, and then passed it to the guests, so it was sampled by everyone in the hogan and finally came back to the medicine man who ate the last fragments.

While the basket was being passed around, Yanabah picked up the ladle and dipped it into the bowl of water to pour over the hands of the groom, then he did the same for her, indicating that they were willing to assist each other in all endeavors. There were no towels for drying their hands but a small amount of white corn meal was sifted over Kee's hands and yellow corn meal over Yahnabah's.

The empty mush basket, the water bowl, and the ladle were taken out by the two girls who had brought them. Then Kee and Yahnabah gathered up armloads of gifts that had been brought to the hogan, and went to the home that awaited them. The medicine man in charge of the ceremony went with them, carrying the whirling-stick with which to start the first fire in the new house. With cliff rose cotton and pine splinters handy, the medicine man squatted by the central fire pit, deftly twirling the fire arrow and chanting hogan blessing songs. As soon as a spark caught in the tinder, he handed it to Yahnabah to place under the wood in the fire pit, for this was her house and this was her fire, and the wood must not fail to burn. Then he left the young couple and returned to the crowd to participate in the feast that would last throughout the remainder of the day, until sunset sent all guests hurrying to their homes.

13
Hosteen Beaal, E S P

THE HOMESTEAD of Hosteen Beaal was not located near our trading post and he did not sell his wool or lambs at our store, so we were on the Reservation several years before making his acquaintance. One sunny afternoon in September, I decided to attend a Squaw Dance that was being held in the valley below Sheep Springs near a large Navaho pond. In former years this had been the ceremony in which the Navaho women welcomed home a victorious war party and its purpose was to heal the injured, honor the victors, and allay the power of any enemy ghosts that might have followed their trail. Now this ceremony had become a harvest festival and a "girl-meets-boy" affair, although most of the ancient trappings and ritual had been retained. There was still the display of enemy scalps on the end of a wand, and there were rites to appease the ghosts of slain enemies. But much of the time nowadays was spent in feasting, horse racing, gambling, gossiping, trading, and in the public announcements of marriages, births, and deaths.

As I watched the colorful assembly of women and girls dressed in beautiful velvet blouses, full, sateen skirts, and brightly-patterned shawls with their men-folk in just as bright shirts and blankets, I thought it the gayest pageant I had ever seen. Whole families had arrived in covered wagons drawn by fat ponies, which were generally driven by the women or by an aged grandfather, as the men preferred arriving on horseback with their high-cantled saddles studded with silver, and with the red and blue yarn tassels of their saddle blankets almost reaching the pony's knees. This was an occasion when every Navaho family displayed its wealth of silver and turquoise. Men wore wide belts of silver conchas, wide, silver bracelets set with turquoise, and necklaces of white shell, round silver beads, coral, and turquoise. Some even wore silver hoops in their ears. Nearly all of the women had dozens of silver buttons on their blouses, on their shoes and on their handmade hair ornaments. Sometimes all of the family wealth was worn by a marriageable daughter who would be taking part in the evening dances.

One of the riders, on a very large roan horse, who attracted my notice because of his age and his garb of a medicine man, was halted at the center of the dance arena. When I asked about him I was told that he was Hosteen Beaal from Chaco Canyon and that he was master of ceremonies for this three-day Squaw Dance. "He is a very important Navaho," I was told. "He used to be one of the leading war chiefs and he knows all the prayers and rites of the War Chant. He is also an Eagle Chanter and is the only Navaho left who can conduct an Eagle-Catching Ceremony." The Navahos revere the wisdom of their older people and as he stood in the stirrups to address the assemblage all noise and bustle ceased as all turned to face him and listen to his words. His speech was an exposition of Navaho traditions and rules of conduct, lawful pursuits, and responsibilities. Then he recited admonitions to young people and to the parents of growing children, which lasted more than an hour. When he finally completed his harangue, he dismounted and a boy led his horse away as he entered the ceremonial lodge. It was nearing noon and I rode my pony back to the post, but would return for the evening dance, which began at moonrise.

It was the following spring in 1920 before I heard the name of Hosteen Beaal again and learned that he was now living with his son, Beaal Tso, in the lower cornfields. It was Esther Williams, the girl who was my housemaid that summer and who also was a great help in caring for Lynette then eight months old, who spoke of him.

Esther had graduated from the Shiprock Boarding School after previously attending the Fruitland Mission School. In the fall she was planning to enroll for nurse's training at the Ganada Mission Hospital, but this summer she was spending with her parents, Dudley and Ahson Williams, in the upper cornfields. When I asked her to work for me, she accepted gladly as there was little room for her in her parents' hogan, while at the post she would have her own room and still be able to visit her parents frequently, and could become better acquainted with her other relatives. Esther was a large, competent girl, well-trained for housework and, best of all, accustomed to the care of babies and small children. She took over full responsibility for the housework and I could spend my time with the baby, or assist in the store, or even go for short rides on my pony, which was my favorite form of amusement. She was not daunted by the emergencies that frequently arise in the care of small children, and she could kill a black widow spider, a centipede, or a scorpion without a moment's hesitation. One day, as Lynette was playing in her playpen, she happened to loosen one of the babypins that fastened the back of her white dress and I walked near just in time to see her pop the pin into her mouth. I was horrified. "Esther! Oh, Esther," I screamed. "The baby has swallowed a pin." Esther was working in the kitchen, but it did not take her two seconds to reach the playpen, grasp Lynette by the ankles, hold her upside down and give her a smart thump on the back. As the pin flew out of Lynette's mouth Esther caught it, righted the baby, and plumped her down on the blankets, then handed me the pin saying, "Better get rid of this. Babypins are the invention of the devil." I can assure you that all babypins, gold or otherwise, were dumped through the hole of the seat in the outhouse.

Esther's Navaho name was Illibah Dijolei and her father's was Hosteen Dijolei, a name that meant "round, like a bead." When he was eight years old his parents were afraid to keep him on the Reservation on account of Ute raids, which at that time were encouraged by the government, so he had been sent to an Indian boarding school at Grand Junction, Colorado, where he had remained eight years. On his return he had lived with an uncle who was a medicine man of some renown among the Navahos. He was a chanter of the Male Shooting Ceremony, which had formerly been used to bless the hunters who went east to hunt buffalo and other game animals.

The hunting of buffalo, antelope, and deer had ended with the coming of white hunters with guns, but the ceremonies continued and were now aimed at the shooting and killing of such ailments as rheumatism, arthritis, and all other muscular illnesses the human body may experience. This Shooting Chant had come to be regarded as one of the most powerful rites of healing known to the Navahos and, as Dudley was an apt pupil, he was soon able to earn a very good living as a medicine man. He married a pretty girl from the clan of Bitter Water and bought a cornfield in the upper valley where he built his hogan. Esther was the first child born to this couple and I believe that she was always the favorite, although there were six more children. The last was a boy twelve years younger than Esther and already selected as the one who would follow his father's profession and become a medicine man.

One morning when Billy Yazzi started to water our three riding horses, he found the bars down and the horses gone. When Lynette was born, Arthur had bought a Hupmobile, but its use was limited to the main graded roads and also to dry weather. For transportation over the Reservation along uncharted roads or trails, we kept three horses. There was Bay Billy, who was my mount, Roanie who was Arthur's, both being cow ponies from Colorado, while Dusty was a smaller Navaho pony of indeterminate coloring and ancestry. Our favorite recreation was horseback riding, which took the place of movies, clubs, parties, and all the other social amenities of city life. Six miles east of us there was a queer sunken valley known as the "Badlands." It was possibly the bed of an ancient lake, as the floor was of hard, blue clay and sounded hollow when we walked across it. Along its sides we found a layer of petrified oyster shells, a huge dinosaur tooth twelve inches in diameter, black shark's teeth still sharp and shiny and, after a hard windstorm I discovered the rounded back of a petrified turtle, which was fully two feet across. We also found the stump of a petrified tree that seemed to have the buds of large flowers bursting through the bark, and there was a different kind lying flat in the shale with its crown of fernleaves clearly printed in the stone. There was a chunk of ivory too heavy to carry home and some large petrified bird eggs, which we took home for paperweights. We named this place the "Valley of Bones" and wished some museum would send an exploration party to see what petrified relics they could find. A little beyond and below this was Black Canyon, named from the petrified trees it contained, the fragments of which were as black and shiny as obsidian. It seemed that there was something new to find in any direction we cared to ride.

Our horses sometimes grazed in the flats south of the post during the day, but were always rounded up and penned in the corral at night. Billy followed their tracks to the highway and decided that they were being ridden or driven to the north, but could trail them no further as several horses had passed, obliterating their tracks. They were not in the cornfields where they might have gone if the bars had been carelessly left open, and they were not at Black Rock Spring. We dispatched a boy to Warm Springs eight miles north of us on the main highway and, when he failed to find any trace of them, we decided they had been stolen. As they were in good condition, they would not need to halt for grazing, and there would be no trail as any horse thief would be wise enough to cover their tracks by driving them ahead of several other horses. So by this time they would be well away from our district where they were apt to be recognized. We were at a loss as to what should be done until Esther said, "Why don't you ask Hosteen Beaal to find them?" "What makes you think he could find three horses he has never seen?" I asked in return. "And besides, he lives fifty miles from here." "Oh, no! He doesn't," she replied. "He is now living with his son in the lower cornfields. He has decided that he is growing too old to conduct ceremonies so he is teaching the prayers and rites to two of his sons." Esther visited her parents and friends in the valley often and was well aware of all that was going on.

I had heard that certain older men and women of the Navaho tribe were mediums and could go into trances that enabled them to find lost or misplaced articles, but I had thought it to be some sort of act or trick to impress their friends and relatives. Not wishing to hurt her feelings, I said, "Perhaps he could point out the direction in which they were taken, but they have gone so far by this time they will be out of his vision." "He can see everything anywhere." Esther was certain. "He has the Eagle Eye and his spirit goes higher than an eagle can fly, so he sees everything. He sings the Eagle Chant, which commands the eagles to tell him what they have seen far and wide. One day, when I was younger and was herding sheep on the east mesa, I saw a man riding along at the base of the cliff. It was Hosteen Beaal and when he saw an eagle in the sky, he walked out a little way and held out his arms. He was calling the eagle down." "Did he have a gun?" I questioned. "No, no gun," she stated. "It was the power in his eyes, and in a few minutes the eagle was hopping at his feet like a tame crow. I hid in the bushes until he was gone for no one should see such a powerful magic." She was telling me a story she believed to be true, but which I could not credit, but neither could I rationalize it with anything she might have seen. "Well," I conceded, "if he thinks he can find out from the eagles where our horses have gone, there is no harm in having him try." I did not actually believe he could find the animals but my curiosity was aroused and I was anxious to witness a Navaho trance rite. I asked Billy Yazzi and Kee Tso to ride to the lower cornfield, take an extra pony with them, and bring Hosteen Beaal to the trading post.

When the three returned and had tied the ponies to the hitchrail, I went out the store door to greet them. Arthur went with me although he thought I was spending money "on a lot of foolishness." I still suspected he was just as curious as I. Hosteen Beaal, crippled with arthritis and nearly blind with cataracts, still retained a sharp mind and a gentle dignity. Several Indians explained to him the loss of our three horses and our efforts to locate them. Then they asked if he would be willing to use his powers in our behalf,

Lucy lived with Althbah and her husband Jim, whose home, on which Jim is shown working, was the nicest one in the cornfields.

Lucy and her baby, Nahtanie Yazz ("Little Chief"), at the time she gave him to Althbah.

saying that we would be willing to pay him if the horses were found. He did not seem much interested in the pay, but his son volunteered the information that he really needed a new shirt, if that would not be asking too much. Arthur assured him it would not be more than he could pay.

We asked him what he needed for his trance rite. "Did he need a fire? Did he need a dark room? Did he need to be left all alone?" The answer to all of these questions was, "No, not anything like that." It seemed that all he would need was a blanket full of clean arroyo sand to spread on the ground in a flat place. Three of the younger men soon brought a couple of blankets filled with clean sand and smoothed it out over a circular space not more than four feet in diameter. There was a fair-sized audience by this time as word had spread of the trance rite that was to be held, and it seemed to be as much of a mystery to them as it was to us.

Squatting in the center of the mat of sand, Hosteen Beaal opened his medicine bag and put a pinch of sacred pollen in his mouth, marked his forehead, his chin, and his eyes, and then he tossed some over the top of his head and shoulders down to his hands and feet. Soon his head shook, then his hands and feet, and then his whole body. Suddenly the shaking stopped and the chant ceased. He stretched out one hand slowly until the forefinger touched the sand in front of him. There was an occasional sound from his lips as the finger traced lines and trails in the soft sand in front and to one side of him.

I'll admit to a chilly feeling along my spine, in spite of the fact that the sun was shining brightly and the air was warm. After a time his hand stopped moving and he shook himself and gave a long sigh, as a person would who was waking from a deep sleep. When his eyes were open, one of his sons asked, "What did you see? What did your spirit tell you?" Slowly and with some effort, as though his thoughts were scattered, the old man spoke: "Two men came on horseback. One horse was black and the other gray. They threw the corral bars on the ground and drove the horses out and headed them north. They did not want the small one but it followed and they did not drive it back. They drove them to Mesa Springs, thirty miles to the north, and let them feed most of the next day. When they rode on the next afternoon, they left the small horse behind and you will find it still grazing with some Navaho horses near the Springs. They drove the two larger horses another fifteen miles to a Yeibichai Ceremony being held near Shiprock. They have entered the horses in the races and they seem to be winning. That is all I have to tell."

Arthur looked at me and laughed, "Well, of course that's where they are," he said. "The Navaho boys are always after me to let them race those horses! I should have guessed where they were myself! There was no magic in finding them, just a matter of good common sense." But Hosteen Beaal received his shirt, which I felt was well-earned, and all of the crowd were given cigarettes. Personally, I felt that we had witnessed something quite unusual, but Arthur's matter-of-fact view point prevented me from taking it seriously. It could be simply the wisdom of an old man who had learned to analyze the actions of his own people.

"Will you send Kee to Shiprock after the horses?" I asked Arthur when the Indians had left. "No!" Arthur replied. "Let them alone; the boys will bring them home when the races are over. They are being taken care of and for once in their lives, they are earning their hay and oats."

I did not forget the incident and a couple of months later when a valuable saddle and three Pendleton shawls were stolen from our shipment of trade goods that was on a freight wagon coming from Gallup, my first thought was to call Hosteen Beaal. Arthur was skeptical and remarked, "Oh, no! Not again!" and when I nodded, he said, "Those things were stolen in the Tohatchi Flats; he could not possibly guess it right this time!" However, Esther and I were insistent that he best not waste any time or the goods we had lost would have changed hands too many times to be found. Again the old Hosteen came to the post and the trance rite was repeated in the same manner, and again he gave us an accurate description of the thief and the stealing of the saddle and the other goods.

"It was night," he told us. "The freighter had left Gallup in the morning and, after crossing the mountains, was preparing to camp near Tohatchi Creek. He unhitched and hobbled the four horses, built a small fire, and ate his evening meal. Then, taking a bottle from his coat pocket, he sat by the fire until the bottle was empty, after which he wrapped his blanket around him and crawled under the wagon to fall asleep immediately. The thief, who had been following and watching him for some time, soon rode up to the back of the wagon, untied the flaps, and climbed inside. Quietly loosening the ropes, he slid a large saddle and a bale of Pendleton shawls out of the back opening. Then he found a sheep-lined jacket and several cartons of cigarettes to which he helped himself. Then, sliding to the ground and carefully closing and tying the canvas flaps, he donned the jacket, changed saddles, folded the shawls over the saddle, and filled all the jacket pockets with cigarettes. Then he rode toward the east. Anyone seeing him ride away would not know that he was carrying stolen goods unless they noticed the small saddle on the pony's rump. He turned his horse to follow a trail that led across the valley to the high mesa country to the southeast. The next day he stopped at Coyote Canyon Trading Post and pawned the large saddle and also two of the shawls for a small amount of money, as he did not want anyone to see them in his possession. With the money in his pocket, he rode away toward Crown Point Indian School and trading center. You will find your saddle and the two robes at that canyon post." This ended Beaal's story, but it had been so accurate we could follow it all the way and the next morning Arthur drove to the Coyote Canyon store to talk to Mr. Grey, the trader at that place. Sure enough, the stolen merchandise was there and the trader had suspected that they were stolen goods. After Arthur had paid the price on the pawn tickets, he loaded the blankets and the saddle into his car and came home. The jacket and other things were never recovered.

After this successful solution of a major theft, Arthur was not so skeptical of Beaal's abilities to trace lost articles, but he still insisted there must be some logical explanation. As for me, I was completely convinced that he really did possess what is now termed ESP, which I had termed extraordinary spiritual power long before I had read of extrasensory perception. He was willing to use this for the benefit of anyone who asked his help. I asked Esther how he and the other Indians explained this, and she said, "Everything that happens leaves its picture in the air. So he goes to sleep and sends his spirit out of his body to find that picture. When it returns, he knows all about what has happened." I did not have a better explanation, so I accepted hers.

During the remainder of that year we consulted Hosteen Beaal about many things both large and small, so the word soon spread that he was our protector. He was really a powerful deterrent to crime in our valley and theft was almost non-existent in our section. Once or twice we used his reputation as a threat to expose theft, and the articles were returned at once. When my camera was stolen from the car, I spread the word that we would have a trance rite the next afternoon. When I went into the store the next morning, I left the kitchen door unlocked. Before noon the camera was lying on the kitchen table. Again, when Arthur's leather jacket was taken from the car, we circulated the report that we would get Hosteen Beaal, and before the day was over, the jacket was found on the back porch. No one cared to have him point his finger at them and say, "There is the thief."

Hosteen Beaal could accomplish more than tracing stolen merchandise or missing livestock; he could also locate individuals who were wanted for crimes or for family emergencies. When the school principal asked us if we knew where Nonabah's father could be found, as she was very ill in the school hospital, Arthur answered, "We will find him!" Hosteen Beaal told us that we would find him working at the sheep-dip not far from Teec-nos-pos and Arthur picked him up there and took him to Shiprock that same afternoon. When Etsitty's little boy ran away from school and was lost on the mountain, Beaal told his father which trail to follow and the child was safe at home before midnight.

In the late fall we had a much more urgent reason for seeking the old man's assistance. The Two Grey Hills Trading Post was being run by a young couple named Roy and Ina Nissen, with a younger brother as helper. In September, lambs were being sold and the men were gone so much of the time that Ina asked a friend to stay with her while she ran the post. One late afternoon, when the store was locked for the night and the two women were preparing their evening meal, there was a knock on the door. Ina opened the door and asked the Indian, who was standing on the steps, what he wanted. He answered that he would like to buy half a bale of hay for his horse. She closed the door and went back into the house to get her sweater and the keys to the barn. Remembering that their pet bear had not been fed that night, she picked up a pan of bread and milk she had fixed for his supper. The bear was in a high-fenced pen near the barn and there was a small opening near the ground where she could slip the pan under the fence. She stooped over to push this pan through the opening and remembered nothing more until she awoke in the hospital in Farmington.

An hour later the truck driven by her husband came up to the barn and its headlights illuminated her body lying near the bear's pen. He and his brother ran to her and tried to rouse her, but failed to do so. It seemed that the back of her head was crushed and there was blood everywhere. They carried her into the house, washed the blood away as best they could, and covered the wound with cotton and bandages. Placing a cot in the back of the truck, they took her to the hospital in Farmington. "The bear has turned savage and has attacked her," they said. But how could he do so when he was still in his pen? They could not tell. The doctor at the hospital was surprised that she had lived to get there. "Her skull is fractured in two places and the vertebrae in her neck are injured. But this was not done by a bear as there are no scratches or claw marks. This injury was made by a club or some heavy instrument."

When, a day or so later, we heard of this statement by the doctor, we decided to ask Hosteen Beaal to tell us what he could about the affair. If there was a killer in our valley who would attack a white woman, none of us were safe until he was captured. There was no hesitation about sending for him this time, and our messengers were soon back with the old Hathile. After the same ritual and a much longer trance than usual, he gave our interpreter an exact account of all that had happened.

It seemed that a young Navaho had been in jail several years for beating his wife to death in a drunken rage. When he was released he harbored a deep hatred for all white people and was anxious to be avenged for the years he had spent in prison. He had worked a few months in the Navaho coal mine near Gallup where he had earned money to buy a saddle, bridle, and other things he needed. Then he had stolen a horse and had ridden over the mountains and down into our valley. At the Toadlena Trading Post there were so many people that he did not care to stop, and it was evening when he came to the Two Grey Hills Post. The car was gone and he supposed that Mrs. Nissen was alone so he called her out on the pretext of buying hay, and had hit her over the head with a whippletree that was lying near the barn. He had not intended to hit so hard, but when she fell and did not move, he thought he had killed her. Going to the house, he was surprised to see someone sitting by the table knitting. Not knowing how many other people might be in the house, he gave up the idea of robbing the store, mounted his horse and rode south along the foot of the mountains.

He hid in a clump of bushes during the day, as he was afraid someone might be on his trail, but rode on as soon as it was dark. Before morning, he came to Mexican Springs Trading Post where he discovered there was no one at home. He opened the barn door and helped himself to hay and oats, then he chopped out a window frame in the store, went in, and outfitted himself with all new clothing. He also took a Pendleton robe, a large sack of groceries, and a supply of cigarettes. After loading these things on his horse, he set fire to the store. (This part of the telling was not known to us at the time but it all proved to be true.) Leaving the burning building, he rode south through the mountains to an abandoned hogan some distance north of Gallup, and that was where he was now hiding.

We asked Hosteen twice if Mrs. Nissen would live, as the doctors had given her husband little hope. His answer both times was, "Yes! After a long time she will be well again." And this pronouncement again proved to be true. We sent word to the Navaho Indian Agency describing the location of the criminal's hide-out and several Navaho policemen were sent to surround the area. He surrendered without causing trouble, was taken to court where the verdict was "Insanity," and was sent to a U.S. institution for mental patients.

After this Hosteen Beaal's reputation spread across our side of the Reservation and he had so many requests to find lost articles and animals that he was troubled. "I can not do all of this," he complained, "My spirit grows weary and the vision becomes dim. I will go back to my home beyond Pueblo Bonito where there are not so many people." But before he went, he was called upon to hold three important trances, one of which netted him the reward money offered by the government for information leading to the arrest of two killers.

On one of the roads leading out of Gallup, there was a small trading post run by a man who called himself Jack Jones. This store was not on the Reservation and therefore not subject to federal regulations. However, there was a federal law against selling liquor to the Indians that applied to his place of business just the same as to other trading posts. In spite of this law a few Indian traders and many boot-leggers carried on a thriving liquor trade along the edges of the Reservation, as it was quick, easy money. Jones's store contained the usual assortment of trade goods, but back of the store in a wareroom excavated in the rocks, he kept a keg or two of whisky and any Indian with cash could buy a bottle.

One morning as a couple of freighters were driving past, they noticed that the store door was swinging open and banging in the wind. They went inside to investigate, and found the trader's body wrapped in a blanket under a store counter and his head under the kitchen stove. One of the men stayed at the place and the other rode one of their horses back to Gallup to inform the sheriff. The officers who investigated this case could find plenty of clues as there were bloody handprints, footprints, and spatters all over the place, mingled with broken bottles, overturned furniture and even the blood-smeared meat cleaver with which the deed had been committed still lying on the kitchen floor. It was easy to see what had happened and to guess why it had happened, but there was no way of telling who the killers might be. A few days later a reward of $500 was offered for any information that would lead to the capture of the criminals.

We were sure that Hosteen Beaal could find them and Arthur asked the sheriff to commission him to try. "I doubt if he can do anything with this case," the sheriff replied. "But we have done all we can, and there will be no harm in hearing what the old man has to say." He seemed to think it would be a waste of time, but also he was curious to witness a trance rite. So we arranged a date when the officials could come. Hosteen Beaal came with no more ostentation than previously and the trance rite was held as usual with his son, Beaal Begay, acting as interpreter. After the old man had wakened from his trance, he gave his son the following tale.

It had started in a barroom in Gallup, where two Navaho Indians were trying to buy liquor and, when the clerks had refused to sell to them, they had become truculent so the clerks had shoved them out the back door. Here a bootlegger had furtively sold them two bottles of something that certainly deserved the name of firewater. Mounting their horses they had ridden out of town, drinking as they went, and had emptied the bottles by the time they reached the Jones's trading post. They were crazy for more liquor and knew that this trader generally had some to sell. Entering the store, they demanded whisky but Jack Jones knew they had been drinking and were dangerous, so he told them that he was all sold out.

The two Indians did not believe this and thought there must be some hidden either in the store or in the living quarters, so they decided to search for it. The foremost Indian was behind the counter when he saw Jones pick up his gun and, reaching for the first weapon he could find, he grabbed the meat cleaver from its hook and swung such a powerful blow that the trader's head was completely severed from his body and sailed through the air and through the open door into the kitchen. Then the two proceeded to search every nook and cranny but they did not find the hidden store of liquor.

By the time their search was over, the two were somewhat sobered and were frightened by the deed they had committed. They rolled the head under the kitchen stove where it would be out of sight and, wrapping the body in a blanket, they hid it under the counter. Helping themselves to new articles of clothing and a supply of groceries, they mounted their horses and rode off toward the west. Avoiding Fort Defiance they continued through the mountains to the Chinle Valley where their relatives lived. That was where the officers would find them. Hosteen Beaal could never mention names but he could describe individuals. "One of these men has a scar on his left cheek," he stated. "The other is short and lame in his left hip." In four days the Gallup officers had located the two killers and Beaal received a check for $100. I wondered what became of the rest of the reward money, but perhaps he was lucky to get any of it.

Before he left our valley, Beaal traced a Mexican thief who had been stealing sheep from several Navaho families, and he also located the hiding place of about $3,000 worth of turquoise and silver jewelry that had been stolen from our pawncase. As far as we were concerned, this was the most important revelation he ever made. Arthur, the two girls, and I were in California for a three-week vacation when we received a telegram saying that our trading post had been robbed of all the cash on hand and also all of the pawned jewelry that had belonged to our Navaho customers.

Navaho Neighbors

We hastened home to discover that the thief had escaped with about $400 in cash and more than $3,000 worth of turquoise, coral, and silver jewelry, leaving no trace of his identity. The Navahos whose jewelry had been stolen were very much upset as much of this pawn had been handed down to the present owners through several generations.

After a couple of days of futile inquiry, we sent for Hosteen Beaal to see what he could tell us about it. His son brought him to the post and spread the usual mat of sand. By this time he was almost totally blind and so crippled that he could walk only a few steps, so there was no possibility of his having seen any of the events he described to us. He remained in the trance a longer period than usual and made a great many tracings in the sand in front, and also to one side of where he sat, while we, with a number of Navahos, and even a group of tourists whose car had happened to be passing, stood at a respectful distance and waited for whatever he might reveal. After he awoke, his son interpreted his words and it was like the description of a silent movie.

When Paul Brink, our store manager, had locked the store for the night, put gas in his car, and started on the road to the Toadlena Indian School, a youth had been watching him and had followed a short distance to be sure that he did not turn back. Then the youth had ridden to the back of the store wareroom where a wide plank door, barred inside with a wagon tongue, admitted boxes and bales of freight. Using a long thin-bladed knife, the young Navaho had pried the wagon tongue from the slots which held it, pushing at the same time so that it fell down to the floor. He then went through the wareroom into the store and helped himself to everything he could carry away. First he had hammered open the pawncase and filled two gunny-sacks with silver and turquoise beads, bracelets, belts, bridle ornaments, and other valuables. These he tied behind the saddle and, returning to the store, broke open the cash register, dumped the silver coins into a paper sack and then made rolls of the paper money, which he stuffed into the pockets of his pants and his jacket. Closing the store door and tying down the latch, he mounted his horse and rode away just as a hard gust of wind and dust whipped through the alley.

Up to this point I was wondering if the medium was not using telepathy to read someone's mind but his next recital proved that this could not be true, as the thief himself never knew that it had happened. He said, "The wind was blowing quite hard and, as the youth swung himself into the saddle, a roll of bills fell out of his pocket and blew along the ground until it dropped over the bank into the arroyo. Take me down there and I will find it." The men carried him to the arroyo where he dug around in the sand until he had located $85, which the thief had lost. Then Hosteen said, "Take me to Rock Mesa and I will point out the cave where the thief has hidden the sacks of pawn." Horses were quickly available and many accompanied him to Rock Mesa where they found the two sacks of stolen jewelry in a deep, narrow cleft in the rocks. Hosteen Beaal did not name the youth, but said that he lived in a hogan near Black Dike Springs. There was only one youth of that age and general description living near the Springs and, when questioned, he admitted the robbery. He returned all the money except $75, which he had spent or given away. The superintendent of the Shiprock Agency asked Arthur if he intended to have the youth indicted for robbery, but Arthur said: "No! He is tubercular and he would not live long if he was sent to prison. All the important things have been returned and I think he has had a good scare."

So the superintendent took him to jail in Shiprock and put him to work on the school farm until he had repaid us the full extent of our loss, and then kept him at work until he had paid a government fine. He had good food and the work was not hard, so he was in better health when he returned than he had been for a long time.

After this, Hosteen Beaal decided to return to Pueblo Bonito in order to teach another son the myths and prayers of the Eagle Chant. We were sorry to have him leave as we had depended on him to solve many annoying problems. Later, I discovered an elderly Navaho woman whose husband had been a medium and when he died she found she could practice his art. I never called on her to solve any major losses, but she did locate a lost coat and a few minor articles.

By the time Hosteen Beaal was 95, he was completely blind and did not try to walk at all. He was cared for by the families of his four sons, two of whom were medicine men. He died at the age of 104 and his mind was clear to the very last. Even in these helpless years he was greatly respected and somewhat feared because of having attained such great spiritual powers. He had been what might be thought of as a Navaho Mahatma Ghandi.

14
Mountain Bear Hunt

THIS IS THE STORY of several members of Klah's family and clan relatives who lived in the Tunicha Valley. This was the family that had accepted us into their clan and were concerned about our welfare. It was Klah who held the Blessing Rites over my two babies and it was Klah's sister who came to sit by their cribs when I was ill. She was anxious to take the place of a grandmother to them, for in the average Navaho household, it is the grandmother who watches over the babies to guard them from such dangers as crawling into the open fires, or being bitten by some poisonous insect. It was also Klah's family who came to us for assistance when they were unable to solve their own economic problems in their own way.

There were five hogans on Klah's homestead, four or five corrals, and two or three sheds which were roofed shelters with pole-and-brush sides. At the time of which I am writing, his sister with her youngest daughter, Daisy, and three granddaughters, Lucy, Caroline, and Evelyn, occupied the largest hogan. These three younger girls were the children of her eldest daughter who had died during the flu epidemic, and whom Klah had immediately brought to his home where he and his sister could care for them. Klah's cabin stood at a little distance from the others and was a square room with a large fireplace in one corner, a wide stone chimney, stone walls, pole beams in the ceiling, and a plank door that could be closed and locked when he was away. Here he kept his valuables—his medicine bundles, ceremonial blankets, baskets, buckskin robes, furs, prayer-plumes, and trunks filled with masks, dance kilts, rattles, and sacks of plant pollens. From the ceiling-poles hung large bundles of reeds, yucca spikes, and herbs of various kinds. This cabin was where he slept when he was at home, and it was where he made preparations for the ceremonies he was called upon to conduct, but all of his meals were served, and all the cooking was done in his sister's hogan. Klah's mother's hogan was a small log structure located near the largest sheep corral where she could hear any unusual noise made by the dogs or the sheep during the night. Just outside her door there hung the iron blade of an old plow and beside it lay a metal fire poker which she could use as a gong to summon the family at any time of day or night. Two of Klah's sister's girls had married brothers; Hanesbah had wed Sam Manuelito, and Althbah had married his younger brother, Jim Manuelito. The two young couples had built their hogans not far from Klah's so all of their sheep could be herded in one flock and the younger men could oversee the irrigating and the farm work together.

One morning Jim Manuelito came to the store in a state of great excitement. He reported to Arthur that one of their best sheep dogs and two or three lambs had been killed in the night and another lamb had been carried away. Arthur immediately went with him to view the scene of the depredation and reported that some animal had jumped over the fence, killed the nearest dog, injured a number of sheep, and then made off with one of the smaller lambs. The tracks inside the corral had been obliterated by the milling sheep and the hard clay outside held no tracks but in a sandy hollow at a little distance there were the unmistakable tracks of some large animal, blurred by the weight he had been dragging along the ground. They thought it must have been a bear, although these animals seldom strayed this far from the safety of the brushy canyons on the mountainside or the deep caves among the rimrocks, and if they did wander this far from their usual haunts, they were seldom known to bother the sheep. "If a coyote had jumped into the corral," Jim remarked, "he would have killed at least a dozen sheep, so it must have been a bear." Several Navaho boys spent

Mountain Bear Hunt

the day hunting for tracks and along the side of arroyo they found a trail of bear tracks that led toward the mountains. When the men examined these tracks, they agreed that this bear was traveling rapidly and was probably safe in a canyon by this time and would not turn back. But the older Navahos said, "He will come again." They predicted that "once a bear has tasted mutton, he is always a killer." They thought the only thing to do was to form a hunting party, follow his trail, and shoot the animal before he was too well hidden in the mountains.

Arthur agreed to help, so preparations for a hunt were made. Two guns were borrowed from neighboring traders, Arthur cleaned and oiled his 30-30, sent to town for a supply of cartridges, and set up targets for practice shooting. Under ordinary circumstances, the Navahos do not hunt or kill bear of any description, nor do they ever use its flesh for food. One Navaho woman explained to me that bears were thought to have been human not too long ago, and these were supposed to be the ancestors of the Navaho people. She also remarked, "They are still human under their fur coats. Have you ever seen a mother bear nursing her babies?" That was why I was surprised when Sam and Jim asked for guns and volunteered to join the hunt.

The next Sunday the day dawned bright and warm and the leaves of the aspens gleamed yellow along the mountainsides. It was much too pleasant out of doors for us to remain at home, so I asked permission to take a picnic lunch and accompany the hunting party to the mountains. The only road possible for cars, was the one that led over Cottonwood Pass, and the late summer rains had left that in poor condition, but we would go as far as we could. I loaded the family car with blankets, lunch box, thermos of drinking water, coffeepot, frying pan, and camera. With the two girls, Lucy, the two dogs, Mutt and Jeff, and me inside, it was a well-loaded car. However, the load was more bulk than weight, which was just as well, considering the steep grades we proposed to climb. We would follow the pickup driven by Arthur and would be accompanied by Kee, Sam, Jim, and one of their younger brothers. They had taken the truck as they thought it would be needed to bring home the dead bear.

After leaving the highway we climbed to the top of first mesa, which we followed for ten miles, when there was another steep climb up the side of a second mesa whose flat top stretched for five more miles to the foot of the mountains. Here the tree-clad slopes presented one steep breath-taking climb after another as we wound our way slowly upward. The two engines boiled in the thin air, and we stopped after each hard pull to allow them to cool. Finally we came to a bench of mountainside that was covered with low mountain oak, aspen, and ghostly white birch. At this time of year, the bear population lived along this bench to fatten on the acorns, nuts, rose hips, and whatever fat grubs and pupa they could find under the bark of fallen logs. So here the men parked their truck by the side of the road and made preparations to search the thickets on foot. I decided to drive further until I came to the bench of tall pines at the foot of the rimrocks.

So again our car toiled upward for perhaps another mile, until we came to an open glade dotted with majestic pines that towered eighty feet in the air and were several hundred years old. It was an ideal camping spot as the ground was covered with soft pine needles interspersed with odd-shaped, black rocks of volcanic origin. At one side was a canyon perhaps fifteen feet deep, down which tumbled an ice-cold rill of sparkling water. I was glad to stop the car with its bumper parked against a mammoth pine, as the slope here could be quite deceptive, and then I rested on the pine needles. Soon I suggested that we build a fireplace, and I started digging away the needles, leaves, and sticks, while the girls gathered the rocks.

There was no hurry as it would be quite some time before the men would arrive at this place and we could have our noon picnic. When the fireplace was finished, we walked around looking for moss agate, quartz, or other interesting stones, while Mutt and Jeff sniffed in every hole and at the foot of every tree that might

Hosteen Beaal, Eagle Chanter and medium.

A Navaho grave, marked by three poles, a broken shovel, and a ruined saddle.

harbor a squirrel. The mountain jays screamed at us from branches just over our heads and sent the dogs into frenzied spasms of barking. Some time had passed when, from below us, we heard the bang of a rifle. The echoes from the rimrocks had barely died away when he heard two more from the same direction.

"Sounds as though they have shot the bear," I remarked to the girls. "We had better go back to the car, take out the lunch box, and start the fire." While the girls were gathering sticks and pine knots for the fire, I decided to take the canvas camp bucket down to the creek and fill it with water. There was a narrow path winding down the side of the canyon, and I had just dipped my bucket into the stream when I heard something below me around a curve in the bank, splashing its way upstream. A few yards below me, the creek made a sharp bend, and rocky sides were almost sheer, so I could not see what was approaching, but I heard a couple of impatient "woofs" and lost no time scrambling up the path the way I had come. I paused at the edge long enough to glance back into the canyon and was just in time to see the head of a cub bear as it appeared around the bend. I waited a moment and another cub appeared close behind the first. I could hear the mother behind them emitting an occasional "woof" as if telling the cubs to hurry.

Running to the car, I called the girls and the two dogs to hustle inside; then we closed the doors and fastened the side curtains. If the bear came toward us, I would toot the horn and start the engine, which noise would possibly frighten it away. In the meantime we sat as quietly as possible, listening to the sounds from the creek, while our brave dogs cringed at our feet, this being the first time they had ever caught the scent of a live bear. We could all hear the harsh breathing and an occasional squeal from a cub nipped by its mother for being too slow. As they came to the place where I had dipped the water, there was a loud angry "woof," for the old bear knew we were not far away. But it did not change its direction or its purpose, which was to get its cubs as far away from men with guns as possible. I was not as frightened as I might have been if there were grizzlies in these mountains. The black and brown bear of this section were not especially fierce and usually avoided human habitations and contact whenever possible.

We waited in the car until the last splash and the last "woof" had faded in the air. Then we opened the doors and took out the blankets to spread on the ground, the matches to light the fire, and the boxes of food. I think we moved about as quietly as mice for we were still a bit breathless thinking of what might have happened. A large, blazing fire soon revived our spirits and we waited for it to burn down to a bed of glowing coals and hot ashes. Then the large, black coffeepot filled with water was placed on one side of the fire and several ears of corn were buried under the ashes. When I heard the men approaching, I spread the steaks on the iron grill that stood a few inches above the coals. They had left the truck some distance below and had walked up the last slope carrying their guns just in case the bear should be sighted in the underbrush.

As they leaned the guns against a tree, I asked, "Did you kill a bear?" I thought they might have one in the truck. Arthur replied that they had seen one in the thickest part of the oak grove, and each man had taken a shot at it, but no one had hit it. After the first shot it had quietly disappeared around a high rock. Although they ran through the brush in the direction it had gone and had tried to follow its trail, they had not been able to come up with it. They decided the country was too rugged for anyone to trail bears, so they drove the truck part way up the trail and then walked up the last slope to find where we were camped.

I looked at the girls and shook my head, for I had not intended telling the men about the bears we had seen until I was sure the three bears had time to reach their sanctuary in the cliffs. But the girls were too excited to refrain from telling all about it. "We came nearer to getting a bear than you did," Lynette declared. "Only there were three bears, not just one." "Or perhaps a bear came nearer getting us," I added. The men were excited and we had to show them just where the bears were when I saw them and where I had stood. "Which way did they go?" Arthur asked. "Oh! that-a-way, I guess. I did not watch them go, as I was inside the car," I told them, but I waved my hand toward the north although the canyon climbed directly west. My sympathies were all with the fleeing mother bear and her cubs.

"Do you think we could overtake them now?" Arthur wanted to know. "Not in a thousand years, the way they were traveling," I replied. "They are over the mountains and into Arizona by this time, besides the steaks are about ready to eat." The hunters were hot and tired from scrambling through the thick brush and were glad to bathe their faces in the cold water of the creek, and then rest under the pines while the food was cooking. At this 8,000 foot altitude, the air was thin and cold, but sweet with the scent of the majestic pine and fir trees that stood like patriarchs of some long-forgotten age.

Soon the steaks were broiled a deep brown, for Navahos do not eat meat that is not well done; the corn was taken from the hot ashes, the coffee was ready, and plates and cups were passed around. Buttered bread accompanied the steak, while cookies and bananas followed. No one was in a hurry, so it was midafternoon when the two cars started down the mountain.

It was a rather downcast group of hunters who disbanded at the post to face the jokes and laughter of those who had gathered to see the bear they were supposed to have brought home with them. But Arthur cheered the group by saying there would be no more sheep killed in our valley, as the bear was much too frightened to ever come back. "She is probably running yet!" he assured the men. But Sam and Jim were not too sure about this. They asked to keep the two borrowed guns for a week or two, so as to be prepared for any emergencies.

However, that night passed without a warning clang from Grandma Klah's gong and everyone drew a breath of relief thinking that now all danger had passed. But the following night the sheep were again thrown into a noisy turmoil. The sound of the gong rang through the night air! The horses squealed, and the dogs barked! In the darkest hours before the coming of dawn, men grabbed their guns and ran on bare feet to kill the killer. They were too late! Two sheep lay dead in the corral and one lamb was missing. In the morning Arthur again visited the scene of the disaster to examine the tracks.

Tracks there were in plenty but there was not one bear track among them. These tracks, both inside and outside the corral, were made by a wolf or a very large coyote. Coyotes were seldom this brave or this large, and the timber wolves had mostly disappeared, migrating to the mountains of Colorado or Utah when the deer and the antelope had vanished from the mesas and highlands of New Mexico. Still it might be possible that a wolf had strayed south from the La Plata Mountains and was now making his home in this particular valley. The Navaho sheep dogs could never make a stand against this vicious animal, and so it was decided that two men would stand guard throughout the night. The one who shot the wolf could keep its pelt as a trophy. Arthur was anxious to add a wolf pelt to his other hunting trophies and offered to be one of the guards on this first night, with Sam as the other.

When darkness fell, Arthur, with his gun and blanket, climbed to the roof of the wagon shed, from which height he had a clear view of the sheep corral. Sam, with his gun and blanket, lay flat in the bottom of a wagon that had been stationed a little distance from the opposite side of the corral. They remained at their posts until dawn, but there was no disturbance at any of the corrals or sheds that night. However a neighboring sheep owner, who lived several miles down the valley, reported hearing his sheep bleating and his dogs barking in the night, but the disturbance had quieted by the time he got there. His sheep dogs were two large collies and one police dog, so he decided the intruder had been frightened away. When Arthur and Sam heard this they decided to keep guard the next night also, as they were sure there would be a return raid soon, and they wished to be ready for it.

Arthur said that he dozed off frequently, but his uncomfortable position kept him from sleeping soundly. It was after midnight when he heard the sheep moving uneasily in the corral and an old goat snorted as if alarmed at something nearby. One of the sheep dogs that always slept in the corral with the sheep growled low in its throat but quieted instantly as if afraid to bark. Arthur's eyes had become somewhat accustomed to the starlit night and he was able to discern moving objects. Now he put his gun to his shoulder, pointed it toward the corral, and waited silently. He had watched only a few moments when he saw a dark shape slink from behind some bushes and move toward the corral fence. He knew this was the beast for which they had been waiting, so now he took careful aim and fired. A second afterward there was another shot from the wagon where Sam had been hidden, and a dark shape leaped high in the air with a wild yelp, then fell back to the ground where it lay motionless.

Arthur held his gun ready for a second shot but when the animal did not move, he knew it was dead. Both men carried flashlights, which lighted Arthur's descent from the shed and Sam's leap from the wagon, then both turned their lights on the dead animal and both exclaimed at the same time, "A DOG!" There could be no doubt about its being a dog, but what a dog it was, or rather what a dog it might have been if it had been cared for and given good treatment. The massive head, the long legs, the wide chest, and the unusual length of body told of mixed breeds not often found in sheep country. He may have been a mixture of mastiff, bloodhound, and police dog as he had some characteristics of all of these. His hide was stretched tight over his ribs and spine, his great head hung on a thin neck, and his hipbones seemed about to pierce their covering. This was starvation, not of a few days or a week or two, but the slow, relentless starvation of many months, perhaps years. Where he had come from was hard to guess. It may have been from some distant ranch from which hunger had forced him to leave to hunt for a living. Or he may have jumped from some truck that was passing through this country months ago, and had little to eat in a long time. He looked more like a watchdog than a killer of sheep, but hunger such as he must have experienced could change the nature of any animal. The other members of the family had been awakened by the shots, and, dressing hastily, they now stood around eying the dead dog and exclaiming over its size. Someone had brought a lighted lantern and the eyes of the sheep looked like blinking, yellow stars in its glow. A Navaho dog came trotting along to sniff and growl at its fallen enemy, and then slink away into the darkness. Finally the curiosity of the women and children waned and they drifted back to their hogans. Two Navaho men tied a rope around the hind legs of the dead animal to drag it over a little rise of land and leave it behind some bushes where it would remain a day or two as "Exhibit A" for visitors to wonder about. Arthur started his car and drove home. When I met him at the door his only remark was, "It was not a bear or a wolf. It was just a darn hungry dog!"

15
Coyote, Chindee-Man

THE NAVAHO'S widely-accepted belief in witchcraft, spells, hexes, and other forms of black magic was the foremost topic of discussion among the employees of the Fort Defiance Indian School when I arrived there on August 9, 1912. In June of that year, I had accepted an appointment from the Indian Office in Washington, D.C., as teacher of primary grades at this boarding school on the Navaho Reservation. I had taught, the previous year, the same grades in an Indian day school at Keshena in the Menominee Indian Reservation in northern Wisconsin, but had been troubled by a persistent cough during the latter part of the winter and thought a dry climate might be better for me, so now I found myself a member of the Fort Defiance teaching staff.

Peter Paquette, the superintendent, with John Walker and Mark Dooley, his office staff, were away when I arrived at Fort Defiance as there had been a murder committed, which they were obliged to investigate. There was an agency Ford for their use on trips to Gallup or to places along the graded roads, but it could never negotiate the trails leading to the Chinle mountainside where the trouble had taken place. Their conveyance had been a light spring-wagon pulled by a team of sturdy farm horses so, as this was a slow method of travel, they had taken a canvas tent and provisions for six days. They had been gone five days when I arrived and the next afternoon they drove into the school compound and stopped in front of the morgue, as they had brought the victim's body wrapped in the canvas tent.

The morgue was a low, stone building with adobe roof and floors that had been the laundry building for the soldiers who had been stationed here some years before the school had been established. It had been condemned for any use except storage and occasionally as a morgue when a corpse must be held overnight for an autopsy. The Navaho school children and their visiting parents would not walk past it day or night, but made the long circle around the plaza to reach the other side.

That evening when all employees were gathered in the dining room, the three men were the targets of many questions, which they answered to the best of their knowledge. It seems that the victim had been a medicine man who had long been suspected of using black magic to harm his enemies. The Navahos acknowledged this to be a powerful vocation and greatly feared anyone they believed capable of its practice, and they had outlawed its use many years ago. The last avowed practitioner of this magic cult had been roped and dragged to death behind four wild horses. There was not supposed to be anyone left who could teach the rites, the evil incantations, or the other things that would be needed to make the poison brews. But there was still an uneasy suspicion that some medicine men had ways of gaining this knowledge from spiders, crickets, scorpions, owls, or bats. It was thought that they could converse with the coyotes and buzzards and could command the spirits of the dead.

No one ever admitted to any such knowledge or to having these extraordinary powers as to do so was almost sure to prove fatal. Even to create the suspicion of having used black magic was dangerous as was demonstrated in this case of the medicine man from Chinle. He knew the ceremony of the Hochonji Rites [devil-expelling], but it was said that he could change it to a "devil-calling" ceremony, and anyway, he always charged too much for his rites. Still he was often asked to hold sings over people who had bad luck or thought they were being harmed by evil influences, and he grew rich with the sheep and ponies he received in payment. The more animals he owned, the more pasture he then pre-empted, until his neighbors on the north and the south resented his encroachment on their grazing grounds. Finally there were open quarrels, and some of his sheep were driven over a cliff. Then to avenge this act, he poisoned one of their pools so that a few sheep died and a child sheepherder became very ill. The medicine man was then charged with mixing poisons and using black magic. In any Navaho community, a clan war is a very serious affair and may result in two or three deaths. When the mother of the sick child died, her husband took matters into his own hands. Asking his brother to go with him, he went to the medicine man's hogan, called him to the door, and then, as the old man turned to flee, he split his head open with the ax he was carrying. He did not consider that he had committed a crime; this was just something he had to do in retribution for the death of his wife and to rid the neighborhood of an evil resident.

When Superintendent Paquette sent two policemen to bring the murderer to the Fort Defiance Agency, he came willingly, seeming confident that he would be set free as soon as he could explain the matter to the authorities. But this was a major crime committed on the Reservation, and these Indians were wards of the government, so the authorities at Fort Defiance Agency had little to say about it. This case must be tried before a federal judge and an impartial jury, with a lawyer for the defendant and a prosecuting attorney—not to mention two interpreters, one to explain what was being said to the defendant and the other to translate the answers given by the Navaho. This was probably the first witchcraft trial since the days of those in Salem.

It was probably one of the strangest murder trials on record, as the two defendants freely admitted approaching the medicine man's hogan carrying an ax, with full intent to kill the victim. Their only defense was that he was a sorcerer who was doing much harm in the community and especially to them, and the only way to stop him was to kill him. They also said that they had been appointed to do it and if they had refused, two other Navahos would have been appointed to do the killing. They said that it was a law among the Navahos that anyone practicing black magic must die.

The defending attorney in arguing their case brought out the fact that no later than the seventeenth century white people had believed in witchcraft, and many people had been tortured and put to death by burning at the stake. He quoted one of the judges of the Court of the Queen's Bench in saying that witchcraft was one of the crimes recognized by the common law of the realm, and was punishable by death. He spoke of Cotton Mather, a clergyman in the 1600's who had written on witchcraft and possessions and whose teachings and denunciations had helped to secure the executions of nineteen persons, mostly girls and women. He argued that all primitive peoples have dealt with the evils of black magic as best they knew how, and what good could come of punishing men for following a tribal law. He presented such a strong defense that the sympathy of the audience was all for the two Navahos.

The prosecuting attorney argued that a murder had been committed by premeditation and the perpetrators must be punished to the fullest extent of the law, no matter what justification or extenuating circumstances there might be. If these two were allowed to go free after taking the law into their own hands, the result would be a break down of all law and order on the entire Reservation. Every Navaho who had an enemy or a grudge against his neighbor would feel free to erase him from the earth, and never expect to be punished for the deed. It was a convincing argument and resulted in a hung jury. So the case was recessed for six months, then delayed for another period of time until, without another trial, the two men were paroled to the superintendent of the Fort Defiance Agency who was charged to guarantee that they commit no more murders.

During my stay at Fort Defiance, I heard of no more trouble over black magic, but one of my pupils was a slim boy of twelve who suffered from epilepsy and would occasionally fall to the floor, twisting and jerking in convulsions. The other children were afraid of him and would run screaming that he was a Chindee, or that someone had bewitched him with the evil eye. For days afterward, they would refuse to play with him or to sit next to him in the schoolroom. They treated fainting spells the same way, and when the patient recovered they would call him "dead-one-come-to-life-again." Children can be cruel little monsters at times.

After these experiences at Fort Defiance, I was not surprised to find the belief in black magic one of the dominant forces in the lives of the Navaho families living around the Newcomb Trading Post. The religion of these Indians might be called spiritism, as every created object or element was credited with possession of spiritual powers, whether that object was animate or inanimate. Father Sky and Mother Earth were the first in power; then came the sun, the moon, the stars, and the four winds. The lightning, thunder, hail, rain, and snow held equal importance, and then came the oceans, rivers, mountains, and deserts whose spirits could be friendly if approached correctly, but could be very destructive if offended. Even day, night, morning, and evening were included in the pantheon of immortals. Solitary objects such as the sun, the moon, fire, water, and wind were granted both good and evil spirits so they were capable of beneficial acts, but also of great destruction when occasion arose.

In the beginning there was supposed to be two divisions of spiritual force, one of them beneficial and the other destructive. Then, as each being or object was created, it was endowed with spiritual life. There were four good spirits implanted and then one that was evil, so that good ruled the world but was ever plagued and frustrated by evil. This rule of four to one applied to all creation. There were four sacred mountains that stood guard at the four corners of the Navaho world; then in the center stood Coyote Mountain, the home of many evil spirits. There were four rivers that watered the land and flowed to the ocean and there was one that sank into the earth and was lost in dark caverns. This rule also applied to trees and plants so that where there were four that could be used for food or healing purpose, there was one that was poisonous and dangerous to touch. This same rule held good for all birds, animals, insects, reptiles, and human beings. There was an old prophecy that when this balance became upset, and evil spirits became more numerous, life on this earth would cease—first the human race, then the animals, birds, insects, plants, and lastly the inhabitants of the oceans would disappear and the earth would sleep until spiritual life was reborn.

In the religious education of any Navaho child there were as many "Thou shalt not's" as there were in the old Mosaic laws of the Jews, or the more intricate and severe laws of the Medes and Persians. The penalty that would follow the breaking of these laws was generally death, or a lesser infraction might result in paralysis, blindness, or mental derangement, all caused by the good spirit's being overcome by an evil spirit. Needless to say, the majority of the inhabitants of the Navaho Reservation were conservative law-abiding citizens and the medicine men were much in demand to ward away the evil effects of unexpected contacts with violent or angry forces or elements. This might have been a flood of muddy water, a tornado, lightning, or a destructive fire, or possibly a kick from a horse that caused a broken bone, or it could be the bite of a poisonous insect or snake.

Among the Navahos, there seems to be a universal fear of handling or even looking at the body of a person who died before old age arrived, especially if this person died in an accident or of a high fever. These were considered to be signs that evil spirits were already in possession of the sick person and might harm anyone who ventured near. But there was no fear or hesitancy in handling or preparing the body of a very old person for burial, and none in the burial of a baby. The old person had walked to the end of his trail of life and had reached the Rainbow Trail of the spirit, which he was anxious to follow. And also his body was so old and weak that no evil spirit would care to enter it, and the body of a baby was of no use whatever to evil spirits, so no harm would come from this handling either. There was an old saying, that when twelve old persons died, one directly after the other, the Earth would rise and shake herself from east to west, then from north to south, causing great destruction. It was said that this had happened eight times and would occur four times more before the end.

Spirit matter cannot die, so when death released the spirit from the body it was said to take a form similar to the one it had on earth and start its journey to the north. It must walk on this earth for four nights and during this period an older relative must stay near the place of burial to chant the prayers that guide it on its way. On the fifth night its earthly journey is over and it travels the Rainbow Trail to the Land of the Spirit People, so earthly prayers are not needed. But there were always some who died and had no one to say the correct prayers and they became lost and failed to find the crossing to the Rainbow Trail. These spirits returned to look for their old bodies, and if these had received the traditional burial, they entered the graves and caused no more trouble. But these graves must never be disturbed or the angry spirits would come forth to distribute more ills than were ever released from Pandora's fabled box.

If the bodies had not been buried, but had been lost in deep water or disintegrated above ground, the spirits sought shelter in the dead bodies of insects, birds, toads, moths, or crickets, coming alive at night to cast evil spells on anyone they might meet. Some wandered the earth with no definite form to become the voices that were carried on the winds that moaned through the trees and whistled down the canyons. Others found homes in old skeletons that had been uncovered by erosion and lay near the surface of the ground. For this reason it was almost impossible to hire a Navaho to dig in the prehistoric ruins for pottery or other relics, as they were almost sure to uncover human bones.

After Arthur and I had acquired a small collection of prehistoric pottery and stone implements, we sent some that were nearly duplicates to those we kept to different colleges and museums. The curator of a museum in Cleveland wrote to ask if we could send him a number of pieces typical of our section and he would also like a complete prehistoric skeleton if one could be found. Arthur's brother Earle, was staying with us at the time, and he undertook to fill the order. After a couple of days spent in digging around several ruins, Earle had collected a box of bones consisting of two skulls and one almost complete skeleton. The curator had sent a check to cover the labor and the cost of expressage, so I put the bones into a carton and placed the box on the front porch near my shelves of pottery. It would take very expert packing, wrapping, and boxing, as these things were as fragile as Spode china, especially the skulls, which would be completely ruined if crushed.

When Earle had left, Arthur and I decided to go to town one Saturday evening and not to return until Sunday afternoon, so we left Billy Yazzi in charge of the cow, horses, and chickens and as guard around the place, although the house and the store were locked and barred. We had placed an army cot on the north end of the long front porch which was three-fourths enclosed. We had given him a couple of army blankets and he was supposed to spend the night on this porch while we were away. When we returned Sunday evening, we found that Billy had taken his blankets to the hay barn and had slept on a pile of loose hay. I asked him why he had left the porch where it would have been much easier to keep watch on the store, and this is what he said: "What is in that box by the pottery shelves?" he wanted to know. "I think there are Chindees in that box! Along about dark I unroll my blanket on that cot on the porch and lie down to sleep with Jeff under the cot. Then about midnight Jeff begins to growl and backs deeper into the corner, so I sit up in the blankets and look around good to see what might be the trouble. Then I hear a noise that might be a groan over by the pottery shelves and there is a little red light under the cover of that cardboard box, and then Jeff growls some more and I think someone has left a flashlight burning in that box and I had better go and turn it off. But my scalp was prickling and I saw the lid of the box start to tip upward and pretty soon the red eyes of one Chindee face was looking straight at me and then pretty soon there was another Chindee looking at me over the edge of the box. They both had white smoke coming out of their noses and were making low moaning sounds. The outside door was at my end of the porch and so I grabbed my blankets, opened the door, and called Jeff out, then slammed the door and we both ran to the barn. That porch is a Chindee place and I think there must be dead men's bones in that box."

I assured him that the box did not belong to us, but to Arthur's brother, Earle, and that it was leaving for a long journey to a museum as soon as the stage arrived the next day. We could not afford to let our house or store get the reputation of being haunted by Chindees. This was the word that Navahos applied to all apparitions or unexplainable manifestations much as we mean when we say ghosts. Some of these Chindees were considered harmless as they were the good spirits who had returned to this earth accidently and now occupied the bodies of moths, millers, fireflies, lightning beetles, and other harmless insects. But others were evil and took the forms of crickets, rats, mice, bats, owls, weasels, badgers, and coyotes. The most feared and the most talked about of all of these were the coyotes, for they were supposed to have the power of appearing as men when they wished and then they could act as evil magicians to turn men into animals simply by touching them.

Rock Mesa was a bare height of rocky land, too extensive to be called a butte, but unlike most mesas on our side of the mountain, it stood high and alone some miles from the nearest highlands. Two canyons with many splits and clefts led into its sandstone depth and all around there were many cracks and crevices of all shapes and sizes. For generations this Rock Mesa had been a mausoleum for the Navahos of this section, and many crevices held burial over burial. As the Navahos do not believe in digging holes in Mother Earth, and as these rocky walls were protection against the badgers and coyotes, this rock formation had made a convenient cemetery. When traveling in the daytime, most Navahos gave this Mesa a wide berth and at night they did not venture near.

John Klah tells about trailing a couple of lost horses that had strayed to the foot of this mesa where the grass was green and high, as no sheep were ever brought to graze along its sides. It was just after sunset when he saw a Navaho on horseback riding toward him, but still some distance away. He stopped his horse to wait until the rider approached near enough to ask if he had seen the lost horses. The horse and rider disappeared in a little gully and did not come in sight again. John Klah thought they had changed their direction, so he rode along the side of the mesa toward the spot where they had disappeared. When he reached the gully there was no horse or rider to be seen. The hoofmarks went up to the solid rock and disappeared, with no other horse tracks anywhere around. Just then he happened to look up toward the point of the mesa and there sat a coyote watching him and it seemed that it was laughing. He knew then that the rider had been a Coyote-Man from some burial, and he turned his horse to ride away as fast as he could go. But every time he turned to look back along his trail, he could see two red eyes following him until he crossed the bridge, and then it was gone. He was sure he had fallen under the spell of the Coyote-Man and that some bad luck would come to him or some of his family. Then, when he fell off a wagonload of cornstalks and broke his ankle, he had no doubt that it was the result of his meeting with the Chindee.

A Navaho girl who worked for me one summer told the following story: It seems that her aunt and uncle lived near the foot of the mountain where there was a small spring of clear, cold water that was enough for their own needs, but could not be shared with anyone else, as they were obliged to dip it dry every evening for their sheep. Then it would take all night for it to fill again to furnish water for the household the next day. On the other side of a low ridge there was another family who lived by a similar spring but it went dry, and then they wished to share the water from the uncle's spring. When they were told that there was not enough water for both families and knew they must move to another part of the mountain, the man was very angry and threatened the uncle and aunt in all sorts of ways. He thought he could frighten them away so he could have the spring for his own family and livestock, but they did not scare easily and he was obliged to move.

One evening when it was quite dark, the aunt heard something

A well-built hogan belonging to Dudley Williams and his family. The large bake oven in the foreground was used for roasting corn in quantities.

These Navahos are in a relaxed mood, as they are shown gathering for the feast.

scratching and rattling outside the door and, when she opened it there stood the largest coyote she had ever seen. It was standing on its four feet, but as she stepped back, it stood up on two feet to remove its mask, and she thought it was a man. Then it threw something at her that hit her on the cheek and then her neck, after which the caller turned and ran away on all four feet. She closed the door and looked around on the floor to see what had hit her and the thing she found was the black, withered finger of a dead hand. She and her daughter dared not touch it, but picked it up with two sticks, carried it out, and buried it in the ash heap. The next morning they built a big fire over it as that was the thing that would kill its evil spirit. But soon the aunt's head began to swell and that side of her face turned purple and then black, her tongue was so swollen she could not talk, and finally her throat closed, and she choked to death.

There was another tale of witchcraft which came to me from an older woman who had learned the Blessing Chant from her husband, then, when he died, she took his masks and medicine bundles and became a medicine woman. She was sometimes called upon to hold her rites over people who had come into contact with a Chindee or a coyote. One of these cases was a girl who lived on the mountain where there were many low-branched piñon trees and much juniper brush. Every evening when she brought the sheep home from grazing, she could hear something walking in the brush beside the trail and just a little way behind her. When she stopped to look for it there was nothing to be seen, but when she continued walking the steps were not far behind. She told her parents about it and her father said that he would watch by the side of the path.

The next evening it happened again and just as she was passing some thick bushes something fell over her head and shoulders, but whoever had thrown the coyote pelt disappeared in the bushes when she screamed. Her father came running and took her home, but the girl was so bewitched (frightened) that she forgot how to talk and could only whimper and howl like a coyote. The medicine woman was called and sang the Blessing Chant and also the "Restoring to Health Chant" over her and, after five days and five nights of chanted prayers, the girl recovered. But the family was afraid it might happen again so they moved away from the mountains and went to live in the lower cornfields.

There is really no end to the Chindee stories that might be told, and these are the tales that are related around the hogan fires on a long winter night when the wind spirits are whispering outside the door and whirling the smoke around the ceiling. The Navaho children sit near their mothers and shiver with anticipation of hearing about gruesome deeds and strange happenings, just as white children shiver over "Jack the Giant-Killer" or "Hansel and Gretel." A storyteller must be able to produce chills and thrills in any language.

The Coyote-Man who starts robbing graves is really taking his life in his hands, as the penalty for robbing graves is death. Many wealthy Navahos are buried with a goodly amount of wealth in the form of silver and turquoise belts, bracelets, beads, and rings. This belonged to the owner when he was alive and his friends and relatives have been well acquainted with all the jewelry that was buried with him and would recognize it instantly if they ever saw it again. One summer a prominent man in our valley died and was buried with much wealth included in his wrappings. All of his jewelry was redeemed from our pawncase and much of it was placed on his body. Two horses were killed not far from his grave and their saddles were chopped into bits and left lying near them. His wife had brought a blanket to sell and had asked for silver dollars, so I knew his burial would contain money as well as jewelry.

Some weeks later, two Navaho Indians from Arizona came into the store and started asking questions about the dead man. They wanted to know how rich he had been and who the relatives were who had charge of his burial. They received little information from the Navahos who were in the store at the time. They had come across the mountain to our valley to attend a Yeibichai Ceremony, and had heard that Hosteen Tso was dead. They had brought whisky with them to sell to the Indians at the dance, and perhaps they thought that someone would become drunk enough to tell them the location of the burial and how much wealth there was in it. I was later told that they had sold their liquor the first night and were gone the next day.

The next Yeibichai to be held took place near the little town of Cuba in the Jemez Mountains and, as Klah was the officiating medicine man, many of our Indians attended. When they returned there was a hasty council meeting held, as several of those who went had seen the buried man's concha-belt, his turquoise bracelets, and his strings of beads hanging in the trader's pawncase. They were fairly sure who the culprits were but they did not know where to find them. Four young men who were of the same clan as the deceased were suddenly missing from our valley, but no one spoke of them or questioned as to where they might have gone. They returned two weeks later, but still nothing was ever said as to where they had been or what their mission was or if it had been successful. Perhaps some of the Navahos knew but they would never admit to this knowledge, and we made no inquiries.

16

An Autumn Feast

THERE WAS NOT MUCH TRADE in the store during the last week of August in 1925 as the Navaho families who had returned from a three-month sojourn on the tree-clad slopes of the Chuska Mountains were busy re-establishing themselves in their homes near the cornfields. Their log or stone hogans had been battered by summer rains and dust storms, the pole shelters and sheds were devoid of siding and thatch, while the long poles of the corrals had been used to make fencing for the fields. Both men and women joined in the tasks of digging short trenches in which to mix the adobe clay with crushed tumbleweed for a binder, which produced the adobe plaster to be used on the roofs and sides of their hogans. Poles must be brought from the mountains for new sheds and corrals, but these sheds would not be thatched with anything but a layer of sunflower stalks until the corn had been harvested. Then the cornstalks would be tied in bundles and piled high on the shed roofs where they would be available for the sheep and horses when snow or ice covered the pasture lands.

There had been no frosts as yet and it was not time to harvest the corn, beans, squash, or pumpkins, but the melons were ripening and the corn was in the milk so the Navahos were living on the produce from their fields and meat was seldom on their menu. It would take three or four weeks to rebuild their homes and corrals, burn the tumbleweed, and tamp the hard adobe floors on which to flail their beans. These floors would be fenced to bar the entrance of livestock and would later be used as a place to spread the unhusked ears of corn to dry in the autumn sun. Some of the Navaho men had gone back to the mountains with their teams and

An Autumn Feast

wagons to secure their winter supply of firewood and, when their own needs were supplied, they would sell the next loads to us. We had need of much wood during the winter and the long, windy months of spring as our store was heated by a large, round oak heater that burned both wood and coal. The house had a kitchen range and four fireplaces, all of which burned both wood and coal. We were indeed fortunate in having a resin type of coal exposed in the high bank of a nearby arroyo, as Navaho men are not miners and generally refuse to delve in Mother Earth. But this ledge protruded from the side of the bank so the Navaho wagons could drive almost under it while the men carved off large slabs with which to fill the wagon bed. It might be supposed that this coal would be so weathered and slacked by the rains that it would produce little heat, but this was not the case. It was a hard coal that might be termed semianthracite, thoroughly streaked with mineral resin that could be lighted with a single match, and then the resin boiled and bubbled like pitch. We had the haulers cut this into "logs" about eighteen inches in length, so that two of these in any of our fireplaces would burn slowly all night without leaving clinkers or much in the way of ashes. But we generally burned piñon in the evenings to make a cheerful blaze.

I was in the kitchen one afternoon waiting to take a batch of bread from the oven when Lynette, who was seven, came running from the back yard onto the porch. "Bring the key, mamma," she called. "There is a wagon loaded with coal outside the gate and they want to unload it in the coal shed." The large gate was between the garage and the wool barn and we kept it locked to keep wandering stock and other intruders out of our yard. I picked up the keys and walked across the yard to our gate. It was a huge affair of two-by-fours and woven-wire fencing, hung on heavy iron hinges and fastened with a strong chain and padlock. I unlocked the gate and pulled it toward the side of the garage to admit the wagonload of coal. This was paid for according to the number of slabs and chunks that were tiered in the shed and I stayed to make the count. Chee Todue and his wife, Dora, were on the wagon seat as it drove into the yard, and while Chee was unloading the coal, I visited with Dora. She spoke English well and had been matron at a Navaho day school in Arizona at the same time that Chee had been caretaker at the same school, but both had been homesick for their own relatives and had returned to build a home east of the cornfields. Now their three children were attending the Navaho's Toadlena Boarding School where they could be visited frequently.

I counted the slabs as they were unloaded and then gave Chee a slip of paper stating the number, which he could take to the store and exchange for the goods he desired. At this time of year they were not buying much in the way of groceries except sugar and coffee so most of the credit slip went for warm clothing for the coming winter. There was a new shawl for Dora, a heavy shirt for Chee, and shoes for both. This came to more than the amount on the slip, so Dora took from her wrist a heavy, silver bracelet set with two large turquoise stones and handed it to Arthur to place in the pawn case, where it was tagged with her name as security for the amount still due.

While I was talking with Dora, she told me that Chee and several other Navaho men of our section were planning on holding a rabbit hunt the first Sunday in September and she asked if we would care to watch the hunt and attend the barbecue afterwards. There were rabbit hunts held every year and ordinarily the hunters needed all the game they killed as food for their families, but this year there were many jack rabbits and many cottontails. During the past winter, the coyotes had become so numerous that numbers of Navaho sheep had been killed. As coyotes are among the animals the Navahos do not kill, the government had allowed professional hunters to operate on the Reservation and had offered a bounty for every coyote scalp they brought to the Indian agency. With fewer coyotes to bother them, the rabbits thrived and became numerous in all the valleys; in fact there were so many that they were a pest in the cornfields.

The Navahos decided to kill as many as they could and have a community barbecue according to ancient tradition. In the past

An Autumn Feast

ages this hunt was held on foot and the only weapon carried was a rabbit stick. It was a ceremonial affair that officially opened the hunting season for the hunters of the tribe. After the rabbit hunt, organized parties of hunters roamed over the mesas and mountains looking for deer, elk, and an occasional mountain sheep. In the valleys and plains were many bands of antelope and the hunters sought to bring home enough meat to last the tribe through the winter and the following spring. The meat would be cut into strips and dried in the smoke of cedar fires, the tallow would be melted and stored in tightly-woven reed baskets that could be hung from the ceiling, while the pelts were tanned for garments, shoes, robes, and other useful articles. Even the sinew found a use as bowstring or thread, and the blood was mixed with clay to make a hard cement for the floor.

During the many years that the Navaho depended largely on the flesh of wild game for their food supply there were strict laws governing the time and manner in which hunting could take place and game could be killed. Some early lawmaker had realized the danger of destroying the animals they depended upon for their existence, and had established a number of laws to guard against this possibility. Game animals were not to be killed during mating season, and does were not to be hunted while carrying young. In late winter and in early spring the meat was not supposed to be good to eat, as the deer, elk, and sheep had been living on tree twigs and bark, which gave the meat a bitter taste. Then too, their fat was gone and Navahos care little for lean meat. They have a saying which is like our wishing someone good luck. It is: "May you always have fat meat to eat."

The chief or the councilmen who created these laws knew there must be some method of impressing them on the minds of the people and especially on the minds of the hunters of future generations. They believed that all laws are written in the stars, so they chose one set of stars to be the hunters' constellation, and in this there were eight that formed a slender cluster of stars just under Canis Major, which resembled two jack rabbit tracks, one closely following the other. The Navahos know them as *"Gah-a-tay"* or "Rabbit Tracks" and, as they are not always in the same position, their movements during the changing seasons determined the periods when hunting would be allowed. This always came in the fall when the deer were fat and the fawns were large enough to live on grass and other foliage. There was also another set of stars called the "Horns," which seems brighter in the fall and marks the open-hunting season on mountain sheep.

Among the several constellations which the Navahos watch anxiously in the autumn is one they have named Hosteen Tsee-kai. These stars outline an old man with his feet ajar and his hands on his knees. He is also known as the "Grandfather of the Harvest," who stands in this stooped position in order to carry a large load of autumn harvest. According to Hosteen Klah, the stars which form this group are a rectangle of six that form his body, hands, and feet; one above this is for his head, two over the one are for his head plumes, and another is for the igniter that keeps his face lighted. This set of stars is located in our constellation of Corvus. Hosteen Tsee-kai appears in the eastern sky in autumn and the Navahos study its appearance. Then they believe that if the stars appear full and bright there will be a plenteous harvest of well-ripened crops and the weather will be fair for the harvest. If the stars are faint and flickering, it indicates that the harvest will be poor and there will be little food for the winter and spring months.

At the present time, there were no game animals in the Chuska Mountains and the Navahos depended on sheep and goats for their supply of meat, but still the old laws were more or less followed by most of the tribe, and when organizing this rabbit hunt they all agreed to follow the old procedure with the exception of using horses instead of hunting on foot. We had heard this sport mentioned during previous autumns, but we had never taken time to watch one or to learn the details of the hunt.

Now I accepted Dora's invitation with pleasure and began asking questions about the ceremonial laws that would govern the event. It seems that anyone could join the hunt who desired to do so, providing they owned a horse and could throw a rabbit stick. This stick was a curved club about two feet long, hardened in the ashes, sharpened along one edge, and blunt and round on the other. It was balanced so that if it missed its mark, it would circle back, somewhat like a boomerang. Guns, bows and arrows, and even slingshots were not allowed on this day, as the hunt must follow the old pattern and the first rabbit that had ever been killed for food had been dispatched with a curved stick.

The first Sunday of September dawned bright and warm and was a perfect day for outdoor activities. The Newcomb family was up early to do the chores and be ready to accompany Chee and Dora when they came by. It was not long until they were there, Dora driving the team and wagon and Chee riding his fastest pony. Arthur did not wish to leave the store alone and our clerk had borrowed a horse and joined the hunters, so Arthur stayed in the store while Priscilla and I rode in the wagon with Dora and her sister.

As I was filling a thermos with drinking water and fixing a snack for Priscilla, who was two years old, Lynette came whirling into the house in a dither of excitement. "Oh, mama," she cried, "Chee says I can ride with the hunters. He says he will take care of me if I will not get in the way." "Goodness, no! You are much too small, and you could not keep up with them anyway," I answered, as I visualized a bevy of hunters striking out across the brush-covered flats. "Oh, yes I can," she argued. "My horse is faster than any of the Navaho ponies and I will stay behind Chee." Lynette's riding pony was an elderly mare of a strawberry roan color, which had been given her by a horse trader the summer before. This horse dealer had stayed with us a couple of weeks while he was buying surplus horses from the Navahos. He had brought this mare from Mancos, Colorado, where he had purchased several head, but she was too old to be of any sales value, so he had given her to Lynette. He had said, "She is old but she is part Arabian and as gentle as they come. Her teeth are about worn out, but if you will feed her bran mash she is good for several more years."

Lynette was delighted to have a horse of her own and fed her sugar and cookies until Ginger followed her around the yard like a faithful dog. When Lynette asked her Dad's permission to ride in the hunt, he replied that he did not see any harm in her doing so as long as the hunters were not using guns, so I grudgingly gave my consent also. But neither of us had any idea of what this ride would be like, or the ditches, bushes, and other hurdles the horses would be expected to jump.

A couple of miles south of the trading post, there was a flat meadow about a mile in diameter that had evidently been an old lake bed, which held moisture when the land around it was hard and dry. It was overgrown with all sorts of vegetation such as sagebrush, rabbit brush, bunch grass, tumbleweed and cacti making a perfect cover for quail, sage hens, and rabbits. This piece of brushland was chosen as the hunting arena, and I was sure they could not have found one that presented a more unpleasant prospect for an early morning canter. Between the brush there were intertwining ditches and gullies that made even walking through it hazardous. But I was not worried about Lynette riding across it until I arrived on the scene, and then it was much too late to stop her.

I was carrying Priscilla in my arms and I rode on the wagon seat beside Dora, who managed the team as competently as any man. We stopped on the point of a low mesa where it was possible to overlook the valley below, and it was not until then that I was aware of the manner in which the hunt was to be conducted. Between thirty and forty mounted Navahos, each carrying two rabbit sticks, rode out to surround the brushland and stationed themselves in a circle with their horses not more than forty feet apart. From where we sat there seemed to be a continuous ring of riders outlining an area of dense brush about half a mile in diameter. I moved my field glasses from one horse to another until I came to Chee's rangy black, closely followed by Lynette on Ginger, and I realized that she was the only girl in the circle although there were several boys of different ages. These boys, who followed their fathers in the hunt, were there for the purpose of retrieving the

An Autumn Feast

stunned rabbits and the rabbit sticks so their fathers would not be delayed.

When the circle was completed a gun was fired and the horses started moving, slowly at first, and then faster and faster, like a gigantic merry-go-round, but without the smoothness. Wherever there were bushes or ditches the horses leaped high and kept going but, like the merry-go-round, there was a shrill monotonous chant. Every rider in the circle was yelling something that sounded like "*Wah-hah-a-a-hoo-hoo*," partly to keep his horse moving at a fast clip, and partly to frighten the jack rabbits from the bushes. In the ancient days, when the men ran on foot, this same cry probably rang across the valley and, as it came loud and strong from our side of the arena and diminished to echoes as the distance increased, I could almost believe I was living in a bygone age. The horses made little difference in the general effect. Here were Stone Age men hot in pursuit of the game which was their livelihood, using one of the most primitive weapons ever devised by a human being, and with but one idea, which was to kill and kill. The chant drifted up to us like the ululation of a pack of timber wolves, and I wondered if my child was taking part in the chorus.

The hunters wore trousers tucked into tall, red deer-hide moccasins, and headbands to bind their hair, which was generally worn long. Only a few wore shirts as they needed freedom for their arms in throwing the sticks. They had not been riding long when numbers of jack rabbits made great leaps in endeavoring to break through the circle to gain safety on the mesa, but few escaped the throwing sticks. Others attempted to cross the circle only to be met by hunters on the other side. Many of these jacks were as large as small lambs and would often leap as high as five feet into the air. As soon as a hunter made a kill and stopped to pick up his game and retrieve his rabbit stick, another rode along to take his place and so the circle of riders grew smaller and smaller, forcing the rabbits to a common center where dozens were killed. Only a few cottontail rabbits were killed in this manner as they hide in their burrows or under any convenient rock or thornbush when frightened. But jack rabbits leap high into the air to locate the direction of the pursuit, and then trust to their powerful hind legs to carry them away from danger.

I had been keeping fairly close watch on Chee and Lynette, which now was not difficult, as there were frequent stops when he dismounted to pick up a rabbit or to retrieve his stick. I looked across the circle to watch a couple of riders who were chasing a rabbit that had broken out of the ring of riders, and when I looked back, there was no sign of Ginger or Lynette. Then I saw Ginger scrambling out of a ditch with Lynette close behind, and Chee stopping to help her climb back into the saddle. I could almost hear him saying, "Are you hurt?" But evidently she was not, as she continued her ride. The horse had stumbled when crossing a ditch and Lynette had been thrown over its head into a clump of bushes but, as far as I could tell from a distance, she had not been hurt and had decided to stay in the hunt. However, when they came to our side of the valley, she left the circle and rode up to the wagon. There were three rabbits tied to her saddle which Chee had asked her to carry as they were proving a hindrance to his movements. Lynette held up a bloody arm where a stub of the bush had torn the skin and jabbed into the muscle. I had no first-aid kit with me, so we turned the team around and headed for home although the hunt would not be over the until the sun reached the zenith.

Shortly after noon the men would bring their game to the place selected for the barbecue and leave the number needed for the feast. Each hunter was sure to bag four or five large jack rabbits, and a few would bring in one or two cottontails. About three dozen of these would be left for the women to dress and cook in the barbecue pit. The greater number would be taken to the hunters' homes and would provide meat for several days, not a scrap of which would be wasted.

I bathed Lynette's arm with carbolic soap and treated it with iodine, a treatment that hurt worse than the original injury, but we were a long way from a doctor and it did not pay to take chances.

An Autumn Feast

After our noon meal, I took the girls in the car and drove to the barbecue grounds as I wished to learn how the women would prepare the food for the many people who would be there later in the day. I especially wished to know how the rabbits would be seasoned for the roasting. The roasting pits had been dug early that morning in hard clay ground, which would not crumble when hot, and fires had been kept burning in them for several hours to form deep layers of hot ashes. Nearly three dozen rabbits had been dressed and lay in a long pile on a piece of white muslin. Near the second roasting pit were mounds of unhusked corn ears, perhaps twice the number of the rabbits. The husks had been knotted at the ends and the ears then dipped in water and now they were ready to be buried in the hot ashes.

I watched as a Navaho farmer drove his wagon into the circle of activity and unloaded thirty-five or forty watermelons not far from the pits. During the forenoon hours the women who had remained at home had been busy at the adobe, outdoor ovens, mixing and baking the round, hard loaves of oven bread which would serve not only as bread, but also as plates and saucers. Near the dressed rabbits a number of women were mixing corn mush with herbs, spices, salt, and sage, then dividing it into the small, long rolls with which the rabbits would be stuffed before they were tied with strips of cornhusks. When each rabbit was stuffed, it was salted and then rubbed generously with a mixture of powdered herbs, which included sage, wild mustard, peppergrass, mint, and one or two others whose taste I did not recognize. After this, each rabbit was dipped in corn meal, sprinkled with a little water, and then wrapped in the green leaves of both melons and corn. Dora explained that these leaves had sweet juices and their steam as they baked would give the meat a pleasant flavor. As each wrapped rabbit was tied securely with strands of cornhusks and the women had completed their part of the job, the men raked the burning sticks and the hot coals out of the pits so only soft ashes remained. If hot coals or burning sticks were left, they would burn through the wrappings and the meat would be charred. It was the men who placed the rabbits and the corn in the pits of soft ashes and then raked a thick layer over them. On top of the ashes the men placed a five or six inch layer of green corn and melon leaves and this was supposed to create enough moisture to keep the meat from becoming hard and dry. Over this there was a three or four inch layer of earth, and then a long, bright fire was built on top of that. The men in charge of the corn pit had carried out the same method of procedure with the ears of corn. There was nothing more to be done except keep these small fires burning for the next two or three hours. The women helpers began to depart, and I was helping the girls into the car when Dora called to say, "Come back when the sun is 'so high,' " and she pointed to the western sky some little distance above the horizon. "We'll be back," I shouted. "I wouldn't miss it for the world!"

At four-thirty Arthur locked the store as Kee, our store handy man, and Glenna had been gone for some time now, and there was little likelihood of customers visiting the store while the feast was in progress. We took enamel pie-plates, cups, spoons, and forks along with salt, butter, and milk for the girls, and drove to the barbecue grounds. Our appearance on the scene seemed to be the awaited signal for opening the pits and starting to serve the food. As I looked around I thought every man, woman, and child in our valley must be present and accounted for with no one left at home to watch the sheep. Some were helping uncover the rabbits and the corn, others were setting out the cups into which to pour the coffee, and others were cutting the melons into quarters, but the majority were just milling about waiting for the food to be served. Now the women who had charge of the bread broke each loaf into large crusty chunks and handed one to each person as they passed by. This would serve as a plate to hold perhaps an eighth of a rabbit, as several men with long, forked sticks lifted the rabbits out of the pit and peeled off the charred wrappings. The hot corn was placed on a canvas where all could help themselves and do their own husking. Then, as the crowd became seated in family groups, the women served them steaming cups of coffee.

An Autumn Feast

Chee came to the car, where we were sitting on the running-board awaiting our turns, with a whole cottontail rabbit held on two, double-pronged sticks and laid it on some papers I had spread on the hood of the car. Then Dora came with corn, chunks of bread, and coffee. We were glad to unwrap the corn and the rabbit ourselves, as the air had become quite dusty around the fireplaces owing to the many people walking back and forth along the sides of the pits. Soon the serving ended and all were seated in groups to enjoy the feast in leisurely fashion. There was much laughter and rude banter as to the capacity of certain members of the crowd, the fat people taking the jokes in good humor while trying to turn the remarks to include those who were tall and thin. An older man, who had been one of the first to be served and was a senior councilman, now arose and started an oration about the unsatisfactory actions of the younger generation, while the women gathered in groups to repeat the latest gossip. It seemed to me that, if my memory had not failed me, I could draw a close parallel with other banquets I had attended at other places, among other people.

Slowly the sun sank toward the tops of the western mountains as men and boys went back for second and sometimes a third helping. There was plenty of food for everyone to eat his fill, but all must finish before the sun had set or the food might not agree with them. The Navahos do not hold their banquets at night. In fact there is little food eaten during the hours of darkness unless it is inside the hogan or the ceremonial grounds, as night is the time when evil spirits are abroad. Only witches and wizards mix and brew their potions at night. So now a few hurried to take the last ears of corn and to share the last rabbit. As for the melons, they had long since disappeared.

So the feast ended with expressions of satisfaction and much praise for the women who had prepared the food. As we joined in praising the banquet, and the cooks who had prepared it, we were glad there had been an exceptional number of rabbits that year, and certainly it had been the best roasted corn I had ever tasted. As for the rabbit, it might have been loin of gazelle such as Esau brought his aged father, or it might have been breast of turtle-dove from the gardens of Hesperides for all we could tell, as it was like no food we had ever tasted. It may have been a primitive feast, cooked in a primitive manner, but the food was delicious beyond comparison or expectation.

17
Reservation Gold

IT IS SAID that every mountain range, colorful canyon, or high mesa in the Southwest carries some legend of a lost gold mine, and the mountains, canyons, and flat-topped promontories of the Navaho Reservation are no exception. In the years when Fort Defiance was staffed with soldiers, many of these men turned to prospecting as an interesting and sometimes profitable diversion from routine duties. The mountainous regions of Arizona and New Mexico surrounding the Fort had never been visited by white men and the Indians did no mining. In the Navaho religion there was a strong taboo against digging into the breast of Mother Earth and against the removal of any of her treasures. Several soldiers were killed by the Apaches and the Navahos before they were aware of this taboo. These deaths did little to deter other soldiers and adventurers from searching the canyon walls and the quartz outcroppings of mountain cliffs for signs of the yellow metal. With such intensive search, it was inevitable that a few strikes were made and the lucky prospectors were able to display a few gold nuggets, gold dust, or samples of gold-flecked ore. However, no claims were recorded and no mines were operated openly, although some say that a few fortunes were made by smuggling gold out in sacks of corn. When the soldiers were marched away, the locations of these strikes were not disclosed to friend or foe, as their discoverers expected to return and reap wealth. Perhaps a few did come back, but none were known to carry away any large amounts of gold.

During the first years of our stay at the Newcomb Trading Post, there was no state or U.S. law against prospectors searching the Navaho country for minerals or oil. Nor was there a law against paleontologists' carrying away wonderful specimens of dinosaur bones, petrified trees, and clamshells, or to prevent pothunters from digging in prehistoric ruins. These people who came to our valley for only a short stay boarded with us, so we were informed of their interests and the treasures they found. In the wind-eroded canyons and in the old lake beds were fossils from many different ages, so the searchers were amply rewarded. But there was one man who spent his time and his money in vain, and he was a man who had come in search of gold.

When weather and roads permitted, the mail stage came from the south on Tuesdays and returned from the north on Saturdays. The mail contract read that "the mail carrier shall make the trip from Gallup to Farmington and back again, once each week, delivering mail to authorized stations along this route." The day and hour of its start or arrival to or from any particular place was left to circumstances and the driver's personal convenience or, more accurately speaking, to his ability and luck in keeping his truck in running condition. A great deal also depended on the weather and the roads. His truck, in which he carried passengers, mail, and freight, had originally been a high-wheeled Pierce-Arrow sedan, but its own maker would never recognize it in its present incarnation. First it had been stripped to its bare bones, wheels, and engine. Then, behind the long stem of the steering wheel, a high spring seat from a farm wagon had been installed, which would hold two persons comfortably and three persons uncomfortably. A canopy or hood of brown canvas sheltered the driver and the passengers unless the wind blew, in which case the canvas was stretched over the load in the back to tie it in.

The body of this truck was a double-decked wagon box sitting slim and deep between the high wheels and chained to the frame at the four corners. The gearshift and the brakes were located on the running board outside the body of the car and were operated by the driver inserting a broom handle in the proper slot and then pushing this lever either forward or back and holding it in place by sheer will power, while the car resisted with jerks and groans.

Reservation Gold

My one ride in this remarkable vehicle was a trip of sixty-miles to Gallup, made half a century ago, and the memory of the thrills and vicissitudes of that journey can still send cold chills playing tag up and down my spine. The road or trail from Gallup to Farmington as it was marked on the map of New Mexico, was a series of straight lines that traveled north to the San Juan River and then east to Florieta Mesa. In reality it was anything except straight, consisting entirely of curves, dips, arroyos, and steep mountain grades, never predictable and seldom twice in the same place. After a sandstorm it might circle one way and after a hard rain it would be sure to circle another; therefore road conditions had much to do with the time of day the mail might reach our post. If sand dunes drifted across the road, the driver would circle toward the mountains to find higher ground, and if the side of an arroyo scaled off, taking the road with it, he would walk until he found another crossing that had been made by Indian wagons. The criterion of a successful trip was not time or speed, but the feat of finally arriving at the desired destination with the correct number of mailbags, boxes, bales, baggage, and passengers.

During the dry seasons of spring and fall the mail route passed directly in front of our store, but in the rainy seasons it swung closer to the mountains and missed us by seven or eight miles. During the weeks when the weather was clear, the arrival of the mail truck was the event of the week, and I generally prepared a midday meal for the driver, with food to spare just in case there was a passenger who had failed to bring a lunch. This Tuesday morning in early May was "Mail Day," and so I had made the usual preparations. By 12:30 P.M., I began wondering how long the lamb roast, browned potatoes, onions, and gravy would stay hot, when one of the Navahos outside the store door reported a cloud of dust approaching from the south. The Navahos were first to hurry through the open door, with Arthur and me not far behind, as together we watched the arrival of the stage. Clashing gears and squealing brakes quieted suddenly and the driver's voice boomed a cheerful greeting. I hustled back to my kitchen to reheat the coffee and to dish the food, while our private mailbag, boxes, and parcels were unloaded. Then I called the men to dinner. There was only one passenger, whom Arthur had already invited to share our meal, and he had been glad to accept.

He was a small, brown man, dressed in brown shirt, tan dungarees, tan boots, a high-crowned, felt hat with a braided horsehair band, and he carried a brown leather jacket. During the course of the dinner, we learned that his name was Juan Gomez, that his occupation was mining, and that he had come from Trinidad, Colorado, in search of a lost gold mine. He asked permission to stay at our post for a few days, assuring us that he would be no trouble to us as he had brought his own bedroll and could pay for his meals and accommodations. He said he would be away most of the day following the trails that had become dim on the map he was carrying. Arthur told him that the bunkhouse was free to visitors, and also his meals whenever he found it convenient to join us. An hour later, with much manipulation of broomstick gearshift and blaring of klaxon horn, the Pierce-Arrow was on its dusty way toward Farmington, but now there was a Navaho Indian perched on the high seat beside the driver.

That evening when the store was closed and the kerosene lamps were lighted, Gomez brought out his precious map and spread it on the table for us to see. He told us that this map had been given his father, Feliz Gomez, who had been a guide under Colonel Dodge and had wandered all over the northern and western parts of New Mexico with a group of surveyors who were mapping the mountains, mesas, and landmark-rocks to establish trade routes along which good drinking water might be found.

The elder Gomez had taken this trip as it gave him an opportunity to prospect for gold and silver along the eastern slopes and in the many canyons of the Chuska Mountains. He had found several places where there was float gold in the gravel of creek beds, but it was in such small quantities that he did not think it worth his time following the lead. However, in a creek not far from Black

Wall he had found coarse grains of gold and, not far from this place, he had found a pocket from which he had panned more than a dozen small gold nuggets. He could not stay to explore further as his survey party was moving to another location, but he had made a map and had planned to return someday and gather wealth from his discovery. When this dream faded, he had given the map to his son and told him many details to enable him to follow the directions on the map.

The younger Gomez had been a boy at the time and had no funds with which to venture forth on a prospecting expedition, but he had followed his father's vocation and had worked in silver mines in Silverton, Colorado, in Leadville, and finally in Old Mexico. He had married and raised a family, so that it was many years before he had the money and freedom to quit his job and start on this quest for gold.

The design he laid on our table was part picture and part map, drawn on coarse, brown wrapping paper, faded tan in spots and cracked along the creases. All of the markings were made in blue ink with the exception of one red cross. Two sketches of large rocks standing alone in the valley were the most noticeable markers, and these were so well drawn that we instantly recognized them as Bennett Peak and Ford Butte, two enormous rock spires located about eight miles north of the post. From each of these a straight, dotted line angled southeast by south to meet at the red cross, where a narrow outcrop of rock had been sketched. For a little distance there was a crooked line that curved to the south. Near the rocks was written the word *"agua"* and along the curved line was the word *"bianca."* We concluded that the red cross must indicate one of the springs along Black Dike. But there were several springs along this rock wall and the map gave us no clue as to which it might be until Juan pointed out that the water from the spring flowed southeast. We knew of only one spring whose waters flowed in that direction and that was one of the largest springs in the valley with a creek that emptied into a pond, which was the watering place of several herds of ponies, cattle, and sheep. To us then the map certainly indicated that Feliz Gomez had found gold in the boiling sands of Bennett Peak Spring.

Early the next morning, before opening the store, we loaded Juan and all of his equipment into the car and drove the seven miles to the spring. An abandoned government house with roof, walls, and floor intact stood a short distance from the pond, and Juan decided to make this his headquarters while exploring the location. The windows were gone and the doors were minus locks and hinges, so Juan nailed roofing paper over the windows of the kitchen and made strap hinges for the doors, which he barred at night with two-by-fours from the porch. In this room he stored his bedroll and other equipment and it looked safe enough, but he was still afraid of the Navahos as his father had told him they were unfriendly to miners. We assured him that anyone or anything residing in that particular house need have little fear of being disturbed by the Navaho Indians. We also told him that the vandalism the house had suffered had been committed by truckers and campers and not by Indians. They might try to stop him from digging near their spring, but not one of them would approach the house either day or night.

The Indian agency had built this house for the district farm and stock supervisor and his family. There had been a barn just below it, which sheltered three horses, a wagon, and a goodly supply of hay and grain. One stormy night a lightning bolt hit the barn and ignited the hay. The flames spread so rapidly through the hay that it was impossible to save the horses. Then the stockman and his family were caught in the flu epidemic and one of the children died before they could get it to the Shiprock hospital. Although the child was buried in the Shiprock cemetery, the Navahos still called the house a Chindee hogan where evil spirits dwelt. Shortly after this happened, some Navaho child spread the rumor that as she was watering her sheep at the pond a hard wind started to blow, and ashes from the barn came up in a cloud that looked just like a horse, and she heard the shrieks and groans of the dying horses. Such tellings spread rapidly in Navaho country and so even on the sunniest of days, this place was given wide berth by passing Indians.

Days and weeks lengthened into months as Juan hacked and shoveled his way deeper and deeper into the igneous rock. Little fairy caverns lined with sparkling white, rose, and gray crystalized deposit came into view, and some of this formation contained streaks and dots of yellow. It was exciting to watch him now, and we drove to the spring frequently to speculate with him as to the number of rich pockets he might find deeper in the rock. He showed us a glass jar containing yellow flakes and we often wondered if he had discovered many nuggets. If he had, he never mentioned them to us. It was hard, slow work crushing the rock and putting it through the acid solution he had brought with him, but the yellow flakes in the pint fruit jar were gradually creeping toward the top.

Then one day in late July when we had driven to his camp to deliver his weekly supply of groceries, we found him dressed in his best clothes, and with his equipment neatly packed and strapped. He had exhausted his funds, he explained, and would now go home and cash his findings. He would buy a car, he stated, and next summer he would return with more equipment so that he could collect the gold twice as fast. He showed us the fruit jar, which was now a little more than half-full of bright yellow flakes and powder. We passed this from hand to hand, testing its weight with some surprise. But we really thought it was a small return for three months of such grueling labor. Juan rode with us to the post, stored his mining equipment in our wareroom and, that afternoon we watched him mount the high seat of the mail truck and ride away toward the south. He never returned.

The next summer on a warm Sunday afternoon almost a year from the time Juan had left his mine, Arthur and I decided to motor across the valley to find some unexplored butte or rock on which to picnic and look for ruins. About six miles from our place we saw a low-crested hill with a short arm of black volcanic dike extending to the east, which we had not visited and which looked interesting. Driving to the base of the hill, we left the car, took our baskets of food and scrambled to the top. As I was spreading our lunchcloth on a fairly flat rock, I saw a number of shards of prehistoric pottery scattered among the smaller stones. I turned to Arthur with the remark, "If prehistoric people lived here years ago, there must have been water somewhere near." After lunch I walked to the eastern rim of the rocky crest and looked straight down to the sand at the foot of the cliff. There I discovered a path of wet sand that headed under the rock with its length winding away to a deep arroyo. Along its edge grew luxuriant rabbit brush, sage, saltbushes, and other native shrubs.

"There's a spring under this rock," I announced excitedly, for it was a rare occurrence to find water in this semidesert country. Quickly we packed the remnants of our lunch, carried the baskets to the car, and unstrapped the shovel which was always tied to the front bumper. We did not move the car, but hurrying around the hill, we approached the face of the cliff. Under a jagged ledge of slanting rock there was a high-arched cave half-filled with wind-blown sand. In the center of the sand was a turbid pool of water and everywhere were the hoofprints of sheep and goats.

Not too many years ago this had been a boiling spring with a creek flowing southeast and emptying into an arroyo, which it had helped form. We walked around the pool on wet, hard-packed sand and examined the walls of the cave. Long, grooved scars, such as might have been made by a miner's pick, were plainly apparent on both sides and the back. This cave had certainly been enlarged by human hands using metal instruments. These marks could not have been made by primitive men using stone tools. Arthur decided to dig near the southern wall where the sand was nearly dry, and when his pit was about two feet deep, his shovel struck metal. When the covering of sand was removed we found the broken blade of a hand-shovel such as miners carry in their packs. We looked at each other with the same thought in our minds: "Could Juan have missed his father's location by a mere four miles?" Then

Arthur voiced another thought. "It could be that Juan did not wish us to know where he was working, and the other place was just a blind."

There was no way of knowing how old those scars were. They might have been made one year ago or it might have been fifty. Arthur enlarged the trench and finally uncovered the handle of the shovel but that was all, and it told us nothing more than we already knew. He finally gave up in disgust saying, "Any little old mound in an ancient ruin would tell us more about the people who lived there, than this does."

Some weeks later a car stopped at the post and a man who gave his name as Alfredo Gonzales handed Arthur a note which read: "DEAR SIR: Please give my boxes and duffle to the bearer of the note, and I wish to thank you for your kindness while I was on the reservation. I have not been able to get a prospector's license so I will not be coming back. My yellow flakes were not gold, they were iron pyrites. Yours truly, JUAN GOMEZ." We looked at each other in blank astonishment and a good bit of disappointment, as we had hoped he had found gold.

There has been no further attempt to locate the lost mine, but two questions come into my mind whenever I think of Juan Gomez and his treasure map. The first is why would a man who had been a miner all of his life spend three hard solitary months collecting fool's gold? The other is that if there were iron pyrites in that glass jar, why did I need to use both hands in lifting it from the table? I do not expect these questions will ever be answered, and I do not expect there will be a gold rush to our part of the Reservation. But Alfredo Gonzales did answer one I asked of him: "Did Juan Gomez buy a car when he returned to his home?" "Oh, sure," he replied. "He has a very nice car now."

The U.S. government passed a law barring all prospecting on the Navaho Indian Reservation, and so Juan was the only prospector we ever knew, but we heard many stories of the days when the soldiers roamed the mountains and scrambled through the canyons in eager search for the yellow metal. A few old men and women could still remember those days and could be bribed into relating the events that took place at that time. Most of these tales were garbled and incomplete, but I have one from a very old Navaho who has now given his herds and his flocks to his children and has taken time to ponder and relive the days of his youth, and to tabulate his memories in something like correct sequence. Here is the story.

On the sunny side of a squat, gray, adobe hogan in the Valley of Hidden Waters, old Hosteen Tsechai sits alone. His blanket sags from his bent shoulders as his clawlike fingers fumble at their unending task of rolling cornhusk cigarettes. A halo of thin, scraggly locks as white as winter snow, half-hidden by a headband that once was blue, frame the wrinkled, sun-blackened face of this ancient Navaho. Withered lips fail to hide the few yellowed fanglike teeth remaining in his shrunken gums to twist his countenance into a mask of savagery as he puffs at his handmade cigarette and gazes with age-dimmed eyes at the distant mountain peaks. As the sun sinks slowly down the blue bowl of the cloudless, western sky, the red rocks of a certain canyon wall gleam in its rays like a bloody gash on the mountainside. Then the filmed eyes grow strangely bright and the thin lips draw together in a stern line of silence as memory pictures another day of golden sunset when the red rocks cascaded like a torrent of blood.

In his thoughts he is carried back to a bright October morning more than eighty years before, when the two white men came riding into the Valley of Hidden Waters. Soldiers they were, wearing uniforms and carrying knapsacks, canteens, and army rifles. They had stayed in the cornfield settlement only long enough to trade their horses and saddles for axes, picks, shovels, two burros, and provisions to last several weeks. Then they had loaded the burros and disappeared up the winding arroyo that led to Red Canyon.

No one knew why they had deserted the army post at Fort Defiance and had come to live in Navaho country, but many eyes watched the strangers and carefully noted their movements. First there had been the building of the crude, log cabin on the mountainside near the brink of Red Canyon. Then the white men had proceeded to make a low dam of stones, brush, and earth in the canyon bed to form a small pond with a rock spillway. Always in the evenings the two sat outside the cabin door studying a sheet of paper that looked old and yellow in the fading light.

When the dam was completed, the watchers saw the two strangers wander up and down the canyon with pick and hammer, tapping at rocks, digging into shale, exploring caves and crevices as if in search of something they knew must be there. Then one day their wanderings ceased and both men worked at one slanting crevice with picks, shovels, and an occasional shallow blast of gunpowder. The larger pieces of rock they pounded into bits, and then rock and sand were carried to the spillway and washed in a crude, wooden cradle. The Navaho watchers knew then that the two white men had found the place for which they were searching, and that the lure which had brought them to Navaho country was gold.

"Let them dig and gather their gold," the headmen of the tribe decided. "They are deserters from the army and dare not go back to their own people." So the winter months slipped away with the miners working the mine and buying provisions from the Indians. With spring came planting of the fields, irrigating, and shearing the sheep, so the Indians were too busy with their own labors to watch the white men. By midsummer the crevice where the miners worked had become a cave of fair proportions. They had been careful to make but a small opening at the entrance, which they sought to conceal from curious eyes by a pile of jumbled rock and brush. But the trails and the cave were never concealed from Navaho eyes.

When the soft blue haze of autumn shadowed the mountains and the summer birds had gone, the canvas sacks hidden in the hollow log that was part of the cabin wall, were as heavy as one man could easily lift. "We have been here a year now," one white man said to the other. "Let us pack our gold on the burros and leave before the coming of winter." "I had been thinking of that," the other replied. "We can travel north to the San Juan River and then turn east to find the main mountain trail well above Taos. No one will know us in that country and we have plenty of gold to pay our way." So the two bought no provisions from the Navahos to store for the winter; and they hunted no game on the mountainsides, but spent their time hurriedly digging more gold to take with them on the long journey.

"These men are about to leave with their gold," the Navaho watchers told the headmen. "They are packing their sacks and supplies for moving." Then the headman of the valley called a council meeting to bring together all the Navahos living on the eastern and northern side of the mountains. This council would decide the fate of the two white men who, for the past year, had lived near them and been their friends. There was a large gathering as Navahos came from near and far. Campfires blazed high at night and the sound of the war drums reached the white men as they sat in the doorway of their cabin. "The Indians are holding a harvest pow-wow," they remarked, little dreaming that their own fate was hanging in the balance. Then they studied an old war map and marked the trail they expected to follow until they reached the railroad at Abilene.

Three days of talk at the council meeting, in which every man who wished to express an opinion was given time and careful consideration, brought forth a unanimous decision—the two white men must never leave Navaho country either with or without the gold. No word of this discovery of free gold in the Canyon of Red Rocks must ever be allowed to reach the ears of white men! No samples of ore or of sand that glistened should ever be allowed to leave the canyon if the Navahos wished to preserve the ownership of their ancestral lands and maintain their peaceful manner of life. The older members of the tribe had knowledge of the stampedes caused by the discovery of gold or silver, which they de-

Reservation Gold

scribed at length. At the close of the last speech everyone knew that the two white men must be destroyed.

This was a problem. Who could be asked to do the deed, and in what manner should it be done? There was no Navaho who had a right to kill the two men, as the miners had harmed no one and had paid fairly for all provisions they had purchased. The only Navaho taboo these men had broken was the one forbidding the despoiling of Mother Earth with pick, shovel, and gunpowder, and then robbing her of the hidden treasure. Since Mother Earth had been the one who had been wronged, then it must be Mother Earth who administered retribution.

Well above the miners' cave a shelf of rock supporting tons of soil and loose rock jutted out from the face of the canyon wall. It was as solid as the mountain itself, but if it could be weakened, any heavy rain would cause it to fall and the avalanche that followed would practically fill the canyon. No trace of the mine would ever be found. Night after night the Navahos worked to widen cracks in the ledge and chip away the rock foundation. Small progress was made but the Navahos are a patient people and they all took turns.

If the miners had been content to load their burros and leave in early fall, they might have been allowed to go. But greed was their undoing. There was one flask of powder remaining and they decided to set off one more blast deep in the ore-bearing vein in the hope of securing rich and easy gains. Lighting the fuse, they retreated to a crevice near the entrance. The blast was greater than usual and they felt the earth tremble. As they scrambled to escape through the doorway rubble, the ledge above them broke loose and cascaded into the canyon, taking the two men with it. The avalanche that followed cut a scar on the mountainside that will remain through the ages.

Mother Earth had again hidden her treasure and, after the passing of eighty years, no one knew its hiding place except an old, old Navaho who once was a boy of nine herding sheep on a mountain slope opposite a jutting, red cliff, which suddenly, with a sound as of distant thunder, crumbled and poured a red avalanche into the canyon's depths. Now he sits alone on the sunny side of a gray adobe hogan in the Valley of Hidden Waters, dreaming of days and scenes that have long been buried under an avalanche of years.

Epilogue

SEVERAL YEARS passed pleasantly and then came the disaster that all traders dread—fire. The following is an item published in the Albuquerque *Journal*:

> In 1936, May 9th, fire completely destroyed the trading post owned and operated by Mr. Arthur J. Newcomb on the main highway sixty-five miles north of Gallup. Fanned by a stiff south wind, the whole compound consisting of the Newcomb home, the trading post, the manager's house, the camp cottages, and the garage were soon ablaze. Believed to have been started by faulty wiring, the fire was first seen by a passing motorist who notified Mr. Newcomb that the house roof was on fire. Mrs. Newcomb and the two girls were in Albuquerque where the girls attended school. One of the loveliest collections of prehistoric pottery in the Southwest, collected by Mrs. Newcomb over a long period of years, was completely destroyed as was her collection of more than 400 pressed specimens of herbs and medicinal plants used by the Navajo Medicine men. Also lost was a collection of old time ceremonial baskets and hundreds of films of Navajo people and scenes. Mr. Newcomb is planning to rebuild.

Searchers who sifted through the ashes found a few, small pieces of undamaged pottery, and a lump of melted silver. They also discovered the melted glass that had been my set of Heisey's engraved glassware, a whiter lump that had been my grandmother's milk glass cake stand, and a fluted glass berry bowl, which had held six individual berry dishes.

There was a small amount of insurance and so there is now a new trading post just in front of the place where the old one had stood. In fact some of the stones from the old walls were used in constructing the new building. The Newcomb family is no longer there, but the Navahos still trade wool, pelts, and rugs for groceries and clothing, while gasoline and candy bars are still sold to the tourists, and the Navahos still call it the Newcomb Trading Post.

Index

Allemigo, Ahson: 99
Allemigo, Rosalie: 98f.
Aloysious, Martin: 119f.
American Museum of Natural History, N.Y.: 126
Anat-sazi (Ancient Ones): *see under* Pueblo Indians
Apache Indians: 13, 111, 215
Arizona: 13, 18, 57, 124, 185, 200, 215
Artifacts: 126ff., 153f., 155–56
Aztec, N.M.: 110; Pueblo ruins at, 127

Badlands (valley), N.M.: description of, 164–65
Barbecues: 26, 141, 204, 210–14
Bay Billy (horse): 164
Beaal, Clyde: 138
Beaal, Ena: 140
Beaal, Eskay: 140–41
Beaal, Hosteen: 161f., 165, 173; Trance Rite, 167; locates stolen horses, 167–68; locates stolen goods, 168–69; ESP, 170; locates individuals, 170–71; Nissen affair, 172–73; Jack Jones affair, 174–75; locates jewelry, 175, 176–77; last days of, 177–78
Beautiful Mountain, N.M.: 28, 30ff., 33
Beautiful Mountain Uprising: *see* Navaho Revolt of 1913
Begay, Ahson: 64f., 72f., 77f.
Begay, Ahsonchee: 72ff., 74f.; attacked by steer, 77–78
Begay, Beaal: 174
Begay, Etsitty: 58
Begay, Hosteen: 64f., 74, 78; accident, 67–68; Hochonji Chant for, 70–72
Begay, Jolie: 64f., 77f.
Bennett Peak, N.M.: 154, 219
Bennett Peak Spring, N.M.: 220

Bets and betting: 25f., 102f.; *see also* gambling
Bicenti, Louise: 95
Bichai (Navaho sheepowner): 57
Bi-joshii (Navaho medicine man): 28ff., 31, 33f.
Bitter Water: 164
Black Canyon, N.M.: 165
Black Dike, N.M.: 219
Black Dike Springs, N.M.: 177
Black magic: *see* magic, black
Black Rock Spring, N.M.: 93, 165
Black Wall, N.M.: 218
Blankets, Navaho: 19, 78, 87, 104; saddle blankets, 15, 42, 79ff., 90ff., 157, 161
Bloomfield, George: 80
Blue Mesa, N.M.: 8, 16, 40, 75
Blue Mesa Trading Post, Blue Mesa, N.M.: 9, 20, 27; history of, 19–20; improvements to, 22; description of, 23–24; additions to, 35–36; location of, 75–76; *see also* Newcomb Trading Post
Bosque Redondo, N.M.: 14, 18f., 28, 34, 88
Boston, Mass.: visitors from, 36–37
Brink, Rev. L. P.: 95ff., 141
Brink, Paul: 176
"Builder, The": 66
Burial mounds: 117, 126ff., 129, 153; Spanish grave, 154–55
Burial pit: 125
Burials, Navaho: 95f., 126f., 200; cemetery, 197

Canyon of Red Rocks: *see* Red Canyon
Captain Toms Wash (arroyo), N.M.: 9

Caroline (granddaughter of Hosteen Klah's sister): 179
Carrizo Creek: 84
Carrizo Mountains, Ariz.: 81
Carrizo Valley: 85
Ceremonies and rites: 100f.; Yeibichais (nine-day Fire Dances), 15, 26, 37f., 39–40, 168, 200f.; healing rites, 45–46, 48–49, 52, 68; Blackening Rite, 69; Thunder Stick Rite, 69; Blessing Rite, 72; Seed-Blessing Ceremony, 148–49; Growing Ceremony, 149; Eagle-Catching Ceremony, 162; Male Shooting Ceremony, 164; Trance Rite, 166–68, 170, 173f.
Chaco Canyon, N.M.: 126, 162
Chants: 45, 101, 102; Yeibichai (nine-day), 26; Knife (healing), 44, 51; Rain, 54; Hochonji (devil chasing), 68–72, 153, 190; House Blessing, 73; Blessing, 114, 199; War, 162; Eagle, 166, 177; Restoring to Health, 199–200
Chicken-pull (sport): 135–36
China Springs, N.M.: 32
Chindees: 68, 109, 117–18, 144, 152, 192, 195ff.; coyote-man, 197ff., 200; *see also* witchcraft
Chinle, Ariz.: 47, 52, 189f.
Chinle Valley, Ariz.: 44, 175
Chuska Mountains: 27, 39, 54, 57f., 64, 75, 148, 202, 206, 218
Clans: 9f., 50, 56, 59f., 62, 95, 114, 124, 146, 156, 158, 179, 191, 201
Clothing, Navaho: *see* dress, Navaho
Colorado: 13, 35, 164, 186
Colorado River: 124
Constellations: 205–206
Corn, planting of: 149–50
Cortez, Colo.: 144, 146
Cottonwood Pass, N.M.: *see* Washington Pass, N.M.
Coyote Canyon Trading Post, N.M.: 169
Crowpoint, N.M.: 100
Cuba, N.M.: 201

Daisy (daughter of Hosteen Klah's sister): 145, 179
Davies, Ed: trading post of, 80
Day, Charles: 4

Day, Sam: 4
Debbah (Navaho girl): 53f., 56, 61, 63
Day, Christine (Mrs. Charles Day): 3f.
Denver, Colo.: 38
Diseases: 103, 143; influenza epidemic (1918–19), 93ff., 149, 220; measles epidemic, 143, 150
Divorces, Navaho: 10–12
Dodge, Chee: 57
Dodge, Col. Grenville Millen: 218
Dooley, Mark: 189
Dress, Navaho: 5, 14, 46, 161–62
Durango, Colo.: 30, 38, 40, 94
Dust storm: description of, 82–87
Dusty (horse): 164

"Earth-Baby": 24
East Mesa, N.M.: 129
Eau Claire, Wis.: 8
Escon, Ethnahbah: 55f., 59
Escon, Hosteen: shooting of, 55–63
Etsitty (Navaho man): 170
Evelyn (granddaughter of Hosteen Klah's sister): 179

Farmington, N.M.: 35, 79, 144, 171, 216ff.
Fire Dances: *see under* ceremonies and rites
Florieta Mesa, N.M.: 217
Ford Butte, N.M.: 219
Fort Bliss, Tex.: 32
Fort Defiance, Ariz.: 3, 6, 19, 36, 56, 97, 175, 189, 192f., 215, 224; description of, 4
Fort Defiance Navaho Indian Agency, Fort Defiance, Ariz.: 3, 191f.; description of, 6; morgue, 189–90
Fort Robinson, Neb.: 32
Fort Sumner, N.M.: 12f., 19
Fort Wingate, N.M.: 19
Foutz, Mr. (of Tocito Trading Post): 91
Fox Indians: 8
Fruitland, N.M.: 20, 85

Gallup, N.M.: 3f., 20, 22, 32ff., 35, 40, 79, 128, 139f., 168f., 172ff., 216f., 229
Galusha, J. R.: 31f.
Gambling: 100, 161; *see also* bets and betting

232

Index

Game (animals): 8, 28, 124, 164, 186, 204–205; Navaho laws governing, 205–206
Games, Navaho: 25, 134; moccasin ("hide the ball") dice game, 100, 101-104; guess the number (dice game), 101
Ganado, Ariz.: 110
Ganado Mission Hospital, Ganado, Ariz.: 163
Gila River: 124
Ginger (horse): 207–208, 210
Gleason, Aunt (of Kee Tuley): 150f.
Gleason, Uncle (of Kee Tuley): 150ff., 156
Goats: *see* sheep and goats
Gold and gold mines: 215f., 218ff., 221, 223, 225f.
Goldsmith, Mr. (of Sheep Springs Trading Post): 80
Gomez, Feliz: 218–19, 220
Gomez, Juan: 218; search for gold, 219–23
Gonzales, Alfredo: 223
Good Shepherd Mission, Ariz.: 5, 97
Gorman, Mr. (soldier): 19
Grand Junction, Colo.: 163
Grandmothers, Navaho: 80, 179
Grayhair, Grandfather: 98, 105
Grayhair, Grandma: 98, 105
Grey, Mr. (of Coyote Canyon Trading Post): 169
Gus (bull snake): 120–22

Hathile, Hosteen: 73
Hatot'cli-yazzi (eldest son of Bi-joshii): 29f.
Haystacks, The, Ariz.: 4
Hochee, Ahson: gives shelter to the Newcombs, 87ff., 90
Hochee, Grandma: 87ff., 90
Hochee, Hosteen: 87f.
Hochonji (devil-chasing) Chant: *see under* chants
Hogans: 15; description of, 13, 87–88; construction of, 66–68, 72; taboos concerning, 64, 68, 123, 220–21; *see also* homes, summer (Navaho)
Homes, summer (Navaho): 64–65, 80
Hopi Indians: 15, 18

Horse races: 25f., 161
Hudspeth, A. H.: 31
Hunt, Leigh: 38
Hyde brothers: 126

Influenza epidemic: *see under* diseases

Jemez Mountains, N.M.: 201
Jewelry, Navaho: 25, 27, 53, 91, 136, 151, 153, 155f., 162, 200f., 204; theft of, 175ff.
Jim, Grandma: 137, 142
John (clerk at Newcomb Trading Post): 45f.
Johnson, Burger: 38, 40
Jones, Jack: 173ff.
Jones's Trading Post, N.M.: 173f.

Kasus, Juan: 26
Keams, Mr. (soldier): 19
Kee (Navaho handyman): 139f., 182, 212
Keedah (handyman at Newcomb Trading Post): 103, 110
Keeyani (Navaho sheepowner): 57
Keshena, Wis.: 189
Kirtland, N.M.: 10
Klah, Grandmother: 180, 185
Klah, Hosteen: 26, 45, 54, 94ff., 97f., 144, 201, 206; description of, 43; sister of, 93, 95, 98, 114, 179; guards Newcomb family, 114–16; belief concerning snakes, 118; cabin of, 179–80; family of, 179–80
Klah, John: experience with Chindee (coyote-man): 197–98
Klizhin (Navaho man): 98
Klizhin, Nell: 98f.

La Plata Mountains: 186
Leadville, Colo.: 219
Little Chief (Nahtanie Yazz): 145
Lodges, medicine: 15, 39, 44f., 47, 51, 66, 70f.; description of, 46
Long Beach, Cal.: 104, 142
Long Mustache: *see* Nez, B'Dougal
"Long walk": 12, 88
Lookaround, Jerome: 8
Lucy (granddaughter of Hosteen Klah's sister): 133f., 136ff., 142ff., 145f., 179, 181

233

Lukachukai Mountain, Ariz.: trading post at, 30

Magic, black: 189, 191 ff.; death of medicine man, 190–91; *see also* witchcraft
Mail truck: 216–17
Mancos, Colo.: 207
Manning & Maple Wholesale Company, Gallup, N.M.: 8, 37, 80
Manuelito, Althbah: 95, 136f., 142ff., 145f., 180
Manuelito, Hanesbah: 180
Manuelito, Jim: 136f., 142ff., 145, 180ff., 185
Manuelito, Sam: 180ff., 185ff.
Manuelito, Zonnie: 137, 142; death and burial of, 143–44
Marriage ceremony: *see under* Nez, Yahnabah
Matthews, Dr. Washington: 15, 16 & n.
Measles: *see under* diseases
Menominee Indian Reservation, Wis.: 189
Menominee Indians: 8
Mesa Springs, N.M.: 168
Mesa Verde, Colo.: 127f.; pottery, 127
Mexican Springs Trading Post, Mexican Springs, N.M.: 172
Morieto, Dorcas: 100
Morris, Earl: 126f.

Nah-cloie, Hathile (Laughing Chanter): 16
Nalyeinezgonnie (the Enemy Slayer): 70
Narbona, Chief: 145
Naschiti Trading Post, Naschiti, N.M.: 80
Nathanie (of Toadlena, N.M.): 158
Navaho Indian Reservation: 5, 8, 14ff., 18f., 21, 24, 26f., 32f., 37, 43, 45, 50, 54, 57, 60, 74f., 91, 93ff., 98, 100, 105, 110f., 116f., 133, 137f., 142f., 157, 161, 163, 173, 189, 191f., 194, 204, 215, 223; Northern division, 25; drought on, 54, 56, 124f., 138; harvest time on, 73–74; grazing privileges on, 75
Navaho Indians: arrival in Arizona and New Mexico, 124–25
Navaho Revolt of 1913: 27–34

Navajo Council: 10
Nelson, Charles: 20
Nelson, Richard: 38
Newcomb, N.M.: 76, 105, 138, 140
Newcomb, Arthur J.: 22ff., 27, 35, 37, 40, 45ff., 48ff., 51, 53ff., 56, 59ff., 62f., 76, 78, 94f., 99, 102ff., 110f., 114, 116, 118, 125, 147, 130f., 134, 136f., 139ff., 143, 150, 153ff., 156, 164, 166, 168ff., 175, 177, 180f., 184ff., 187f., 195ff., 204, 207, 212, 217f., 221ff., 229; purchases Blue Mesa Trading Post, 8–9, 20; collects saddle blankets, 79ff., 82ff., 85ff., 88ff., 91f.; mother of, 105f., 142; acquires Gus, 119–22; removes snake from hogan, 122–23
Newcomb, Earle: 22, 122, 195ff.
Newcomb, Lynette: 80, 88ff., 91, 105f., 109f., 112f., 115, 142, 162ff., 184, 203, 229; journey during dust storm, 81, 83ff., 87; on rabbit hunt, 207f., 210
Newcomb, Priscilla: 207f., 229
Newcomb Trading Post, Newcomb, N.M.:. 20, 49f., 50, 53, 79, 92, 97, 123, 126, 161, 165, 193, 208, 215; additions to, 37; trade room of, 108; fire at, 127, 141, 229; robbery of, 175–76; rebuilt, 229–30; *see also* Blue Mesa Trading Post
New Mexico: 13, 19, 31, 57, 124, 126, 138, 186, 215, 217f.
Nez, Ahson: 42, 44
Nez, B'Dougal (Long Mustache): 55ff., 58ff., 62f.
Nez, Betty: 98f.
Nez, Yahnabah (Mrs. Kee Tuley): 150f., 156; marriage of, 156–60
Nissen, Ina: attack on, 171–73
Nissen, Roy: 171
Noel's Sa-nos-tee Trading Post, Sa-nos-tee, N.M.: 32f.
Nonabah (Navaho girl): 170
Nordenskjöld party: 126
Northern Navaho Indian Agency, Shiprock, N.M.: *see* Shiprock Agency

Oliver, John L.: 19

Papago Indians: 98
Paquette, Peter: 189, 191

Index

Pelts: 53, 77f., 87, 108–109, 138, 140, 205, 230
Pennoyer, Lady: 37ff.
Pennoyer, Lord: 37f.
Phoenix, Ariz.: 137
Phoenix Indian Agency, Phoenix, Ariz.: 97
Picnic, school: 134–35
Pima Indians: 98
Pope, Judge William H.: 31, 34
Pottery, Prehistoric (Pueblo): 75, 126, 129ff., 152–54, 155, 195, 222; children's toys, 127f.; Newcomb collection, 128, 229
Property rights: 10, 54–55, 64
Prospectors: 215, 223, 224–27
Pueblo Bonito, N.M.: 173, 177
Pueblo Indians: 13, 15, 18, 88n., 124; Anat-sazi (Ancient Ones), 75, 117f., 129, 148, 152f.
Pueblo villages: 15, 18
Purdy, Delia: 138, 140f., 144

Ranchers: 74
Religion, Navaho: 15–16, 193–95, 215
Rabbit hunt: 204–10
Red Rock Trading Post, Red Rock, Ariz.: 81, 90; description of, 85
Ria Giega Valley, N.M.: 57
Ria Giega Wash, N.M.: 56f.
Río Chaco, N.M.: 57f.
Río Chaco Valley, N.M.: 10, 58, 129, 131
Río Grande: 14f., 18
Rites: *see* ceremonies and rites
Roads: 3–4, 22, 32, 35f., 40, 79, 81ff., 106, 139, 164, 181, 216f.
Roanie (horse): 164
Rock Mesa, N.M.: 95, 144, 177, 197
Rugs, Navaho: 12, 21, 24, 27, 78ff., 87, 91, 100, 157, 230
Ruins, prehistoric (Pueblo): 117f., 125, 153f., 195, 221; description of ruined house, 129–31; diggings in, 126–27, 216

Sabin, Clara: 5
Sabin, Lew: 5
Saddle blankets: *see under* blankets, Navaho
St. Michaels Mission, Ariz.: 6
Sand painting: 70, 72

San Juan River: 19f., 81, 95, 124, 156, 217, 226
San Juan River Valley: 76
Santa Fe, N.M.: 31, 34
Schools, Indian: 9, 13, 15, 35, 93f.; at Ft. Defiance, 3, 6–8, 56, 189; St. Michaels Mission School, 5, 33; at Shiprock, 25, 59, 81, 162; Newcomb day school, 40, 105, 133–34; at Santa Fe, 54; at Toadlena, 79, 141f., 146, 176, 204; at Phoenix, 98; at Crown Point, 100, 169; Ganado Mission School, 110; at Riverside, Cal., 150; Fruitland Mission School, 162; at Grand Junction, 163
Schools, public: Newcomb, N.M., 138, 140
Scott, Brig. Gen. Hugh L.: 32ff.
Sheep and goats: 21, 54f., 206; varieties of, 5, 18–19, 21; wreck of stock truck, 139–40
Sheep Springs, N.M.: 95, 161
Sheep Springs Trading Post, Sheep Springs, N.M.: 80
Shelton, William T.: 25, 27, 29ff., 32f.
Sherman, Lauretta: 105f.
Sherman, Tom: 105
Shiprock, N.M.: 29, 56f., 63, 105f., 145, 168, 170, 177
Shiprock Agency, Shiprock, N.M.: 25f., 30f., 35, 51, 59, 81, 177, 220
Shiprock All-Indian Fair, Shiprock, N.M.: 24–27
Ship Rock Peak, N.M.: 9, 81
Shorty, Nethie: 102, 104
Silversmiths: 12, 53, 153
Silverton, Colo.: 219
Snakes: attitude of Navaho Indians toward, 117f.
Squaw Dance: 150, 161–62
Stallings, Mr. (of Red Rock Trading Post): 81, 90f.
Stallings family: 85
Stoney Butte, N.M.: 150f.
Sulphur Springs, N.M.: 78, 82
Sunflower Lake, N.M.: 129
Sweat house: 69; description of, 44
Sweden, Crown Prince of (1923): 128

Table Mesa, N.M.: 40

Taboos: 45, 64f., 136, 140, 153, 156, 158, 181, 197, 203f., 213, 215, 227
Tall Man: 10
Taos, N.M.: 226
Taylor children (from Sheep Springs Trading Post): 138
Teec-nos-pos, N.M.: 170
Thapaha, Betsy: 94f.
Thapaha, Laura (Mrs. Tom Sherman): 100, 102ff.; family of, 93–94, 95–97; at Phoenix boarding school, 97ff.; birth of twins, 105–107
Thapaha, Naltsos: 93ff., 96
Thapaha, Stanley: 93, 96f.
Thapaha, Stephen: 93, 96f.
Thoreau, N.M.: 139
Toadlena, N.M.: 79, 99, 141f.
Toadlena Trading Post, Toadlena, N.M.: 172
Tocito Trading Post, Tocito, N.M.: 91
Todue, Chee: 203f., 207f., 210, 213
Todue, Dora: 203f., 206ff., 211ff.
Tohatchi, N.M.: 26, 60, 94f.
Tohatchi Creek, N.M.: 169
Tohatchi Flats, N.M.: 32, 168
Towaoc, N.M.: 26
Traders and trading posts: 5f., 8, 14f., 16–17, 19, 32, 34, 37, 60, 68, 80f., 93, 110, 126, 173, 181, 229; trade goods, 5, 17, 19f., 22, 91, 110, 138, 168, 173; description of, 20–22
Trance Rite: see under ceremonies and rites
Tribal laws: 12, 50
Trinidad, Colo.: 218
Tsas, Hosteen (Wide Man): 11
Tsechai, Hosteen: story of gold prospectors, 224–28
Tso, Beaal: 162
Tso, Bi-wan: 26
Tso, Dinnao: 60, 63
Tso, Hosteen: burial of, 200f.
Tso, Kee: 166, 168
Tsonsala Mountain, Ariz.: 57
Tsosie, Kee: 3f.
Tuley, Kee: 152ff., 155; courtship of, 150–51; marriage of, 156–60
Tunicha Arroyo, N.M.: 19, 76
Tunicha Creek, N.M.: 58, 148
Tunicha Mountains, N.M.: 28, 74
Tunicha Valley, N.M.: 179
Turquoise: 25, 38, 69, 71, 128, 162
Two Grey Hills, N.M.: 54, 59, 64, 125
Two Grey Hills Trading Post, Two Grey Hills, N.M.: 171f.
Tzee-Zhin, Hathilie: 69

Utah: 35, 186
Ute Indians: 26, 111, 163

Valley of Hidden Waters, N.M.: 224, 228

Wagon races: 25–26
Wagons, Indian: 14
Walker, Mr. (soldier): 19
Walker, John: 189
Warm Springs, N.M.: 165
Washington, D.C.: 13, 27, 29, 32f., 37, 46, 57, 75
Washington Pass, N.M.: 33 & n., 64, 181
Water rights: see property rights
Watermelons: culture of, 26
Weber, Father (of St. Michaels, Ariz.): 33f.
Whitedeer, John: 8
Williams, Ahson: 163
Williams, Dudley (Hosteen Dijolei): 163–64
Williams, Esther (Illibah Dijolei): 110, 162–63, 164ff., 168, 170
Wisconsin: 8, 66, 122, 138, 144
Wisconsin Rapids, Wis.: 8
Witchcraft: 189; trial, 191–92; tales of, 198–200; see also magic, black
Women, Navaho: 9–10, 11, 18, 25f., 40, 53, 79f., 89, 161
Wool: 10, 18ff., 21, 53ff., 161, 230

Yazzi, Billy: 43f., 82, 92, 164ff.; medicine ceremony for, 45–52; experience with Chindee, 196–97
Yazzi, Nebbah: 50ff.
Yeibichais: see under ceremonies and rites

Zuñi Indians: 15, 18

The text for *Navaho Neighbors* has been set on the Linotype in 11-point Old Style No. 7, an exceptionally legible modernized face based upon a cutting by the Bruce Foundry in the early 1870's. The paper on which the book is printed bears the University of Oklahoma Press watermark and has an effective life of at least three hundred years.

Augsburg College
George Sverdrup Library
Minneapolis, Minnesota 55404